SOE's Ultimate Deception

Operation PERIWIG

Fredric Boyce

SUTTON PUBLISHING

First published in the United Kingdom in 2005 by
Sutton Publishing Limited · Phoenix Mill
Thrupp · Stroud · Gloucestershire · GL5 2BU

British Library Cataloguing in Publication Data
A catalogue record for this book is available from the British Library.

ISBN 0-7509-4027-1

Typeset in 10.5/15pt Photina MT.
Typesetting and origination by
Sutton Publishing Limited.
Printed and bound in England by
J.H. Haynes & Co. Ltd, Sparkford.

C40604257/

SOE's

Ultimate Deception

CONTENTS

ACKNOWLEDGEMENTS

The idea for writing this book came from a seed planted by the late Professor Douglas Everett during our co-authorship of *SOE: The Scientific Secrets*. Professor Everett was a member of SOE's scientific team and became involved in a technical aspect of Operation Periwig. Another former SOE member who enthusiastically answered my questions about the operation was Angus Fyffe, whom I thank most warmly.

I must record my sincere thanks to Rex Aldridge, who gladly undertook to read, pass judgement upon and suggest improvements to the three chapters on the German opposition to Nazism. Any mistakes which remain are, of course, entirely my responsibility.

Major R.G. Woolsey, the Secretary of Ganton Golf Club near Scarborough, went to considerable trouble to locate the photograph of Ronald Thornley, who had been their captain in 1954. His efforts are very much appreciated.

The National Archives, formerly the Public Record Office, were their usual efficient selves and arranged for the release of a few personal files that hadn't quite reached that stage.

Similarly, the Imperial War Museum Photographic Archive was most helpful in my search for suitable images for inclusion in this book.

I would also like to record my thanks to the Special Forces Club, Denis Rigden, Joachim Fest, Hull Daily Mail Publications Ltd and especially to Uta Freifrau von Aretin, who readily provided the photograph of her father, Henning von Tresckow.

Fredric Boyce

ABBREVIATIONS

ADC	Aide-de-camp
AEF	Archangel Expeditionary Force
'C'	Symbol of the Head of the SIS
CB	Companion of the Bath
CD	Symbol of the Head of SOE
CGT	Confédération Générale du Travail (General Confederation of Labour)
C-in-C	Commander in Chief
CIGS	Chief of Imperial General Staff
COSSAC	Chief of Staff to the Supreme Allied Commander
CSDIC	Combined Services Detailed Interrogation Centre (MI19)
DCIGS	Deputy Chief of Imperial General Staff
DKE	Deutscher Kleinempfänger (German People's Radio)
DMI	Director of Military Intelligence
DPW	Director of Political Warfare
EMFFI	Etat-Major des Forces Françaises à l'Intérieur (General Staff of the French Home Forces)
GAF	German Air Force
GCCS	Government Code and Cipher School
GCHQ	Government Communications Headquarters
GHQ	General Headquarters
GOC	General Officer Commanding
GRU	Glavno Razvedyvatelno Upravlenie (Soviet Military Intelligence)
GS(R)	General Staff (Research)
IFTU	International Federation of Trade Unions
ISK	Internationaler Sozialisticher Kampfbund (International Socialist political group)
ITF	International Transport Workers Federation
KCB	Knight Commander of the Bath
KCMG	Knight Commander of the Order of St Michael and St George
MEW	Ministry of Economic Warfare

MI(R)	Military Intelligence Research
MI5	The Security Service
MI6	Secret Intelligence Service (also known as the SIS)
MI9	Military Intelligence organisation dealing with escape routes out of German-occupied territories
MI19	Military Intelligence organisation gathering information from enemy prisoners of war
MoI	Ministry of Information
NSDAP	National Socialist German Workers' Party (Nazi Party)
OKH	Oberkommando des Heeres (the German Army High Command, as it was known after 1935)
OKW	Oberkommando der Wehrmacht (the Wehrmacht High Command, as it was known after February 1938)
OSS	Office of Strategic Services
OWI	Office of War Information
PID	Political Intelligence Department
PoW	Prisoner of war
PRO	The Public Record Office (now the National Archives)
PWD	Psychological Warfare Division
PWE	Political Warfare Executive
RA	Royal Artillery
RE	Royal Engineers
RN	Royal Navy
RNVR	Royal Naval Volunteer Reserve
RSHA	Reichssicherheitshauptamt (Imperial security headquarters, Berlin)
SA	Sturmabteilung (lit. 'assault detachment')
SAS	Special Air Service
SCAEF	Supreme Commander Allied Expeditionary Force
SD	Sicherheitsdienst (German security service)
SFHQ	Special Forces Headquarters
SHAEF	Supreme Headquarters Allied Expeditionary Force
SIME	Security and Intelligence Middle East
SIS	Secret Intelligence Service (also known as MI6)
SOE	Special Operations Executive
SO(M)	Special Operations (Mediterranean)
SPD	Social Democratic Party

SS	Schutzstaffel (Hitler's private protection army)
STS	Special Training School
TNA	The National Archives (formerly the Public Record Office)
USAAF	United States Army Air Force
VCSS	Vice-Chief of the Secret Service
W/T	Wireless Telegraphy

INTRODUCTION

In 1998 a book of some considerable length was published that lifted the lid in a most readable way on some of the inner workings of the Second World War clandestine organisation, the Special Operations Executive (SOE). Its author was the organisation's 21-year-old codemaster, later to turn playwright, Leo Marks.

Some said publication of *Between Silk and Cyanide*[1] had been postponed until 'the authorities' were happy that its revelations did not endanger national security or at least cause them embarrassment. But it was a fact that its release onto the world's bookshelves coincided with a long-awaited relaxation of the firm grip that had kept many of the historical records of SOE from public scrutiny for over half a century.

The release of the documents at the Public Record Office (PRO), now the National Archives (TNA), gave rise to several television documentaries, but, as is often the way with such programmes that are made to fit into a tight time-frame and to appeal to a wide audience, in some cases they raised as many questions as they answered.

One of the eighty-one chapters in Marks's book dealt with a, until then, virtually unheard-of deception operation carried out jointly by SOE and that other shadowy organisation, the Political Warfare Executive (PWE). The chapter on Operation Periwig detailed Marks's involvement with the preparation of codes designed specifically to deceive the Germans – which presupposed that they would have to capture them under convincingly authentic circumstances. The proposed method of infiltrating the codes into the hands of the German security services has been a source of speculation, confirmation and denial. What cannot be denied is that Operation Periwig was a highly imaginative, if not bizarre, response to the exhortation of the Allied Supreme Commander, Eisenhower, to all forces to redouble their efforts to break the German will to resist. It was a deception plan that, had the war continued for another nine months and the severe restrictions placed upon SOE's activities been lifted, might well have achieved some success.

The sheer audacity in the conception of Operation Periwig demands that its background, problems, actions and results be looked at from the viewpoint of the twenty-first century and with what written and anecdotal evidence remains.

Chapter 1

A Potted History of Deception

In the Western world deception has negative connotations, but it is nevertheless practised to some degree in every field of human endeavour and in many areas of animal behaviour. In its simplest form it is a straightforward lie or, in the animal world, a piece of cunning camouflage. Deception seems to have become an essential requirement for the survival of the species, and as the species evolves and becomes increasingly more sophisticated in its needs, so the means it uses to deceive potential predators or competitors becomes more and more complex.

One of the earliest things a baby learns is to gain attention by crying. Even if all its basic needs have been fulfilled, it will know that by crying as though it is uncomfortable or hungry it can attract its parents' attention and some cosseting it would not otherwise receive. Although there is nothing wrong with the child, it deceives its parents into thinking there is. As the child gets older, so the methods it uses to persuade people to do its will become more involved. And this process continues to various degrees throughout life. The child may not become a fraudster, but the inherent ability to deceive seems to be a function of intelligence, a faculty that fortunately brings with it an appreciation of social responsibility. Sometimes petty thieves may get away with the crudest and most blatant of deceptions to gain entry to a house for burglary; relationships may break down through one party deceiving the other; and politicians may attempt to cover their unpopular actions by acts of deceit.

In the animal world the mink and the ptarmigan have evolved to change their appearance between summer and winter and so deceive their hunters or those they hunt by blending into the background. There is no better example of this than the chameleon, which changes its colour to suit whatever surface it happens to be on. But, it may be argued, deception – real deception –

requires more than an instinct developed over millennia. It requires an active use of the brain for a specific purpose related to the present time.

Man has fought man literally for his survival since the earliest times, and as these conflicts have grown in size and intensity, so the means used has become more complex and the tactics more imaginative. Every great battle has its examples of achieving the element of surprise and of feinting tactics to lure the enemy into a disadvantageous position.

According to *Design for Military Operations: The British Military Doctrine*, surprise is a principle of war that should be directed primarily at the mind of an enemy commander rather than at his force. The aim should be to paralyse the commander's will. Surprise can be achieved by a variety of methods; the most important must surely be deception. In battle it is not sufficient for a commander to merely avoid error: he must deliberately cause his enemy to make mistakes, and deception has precisely that aim. Deception has been a skill practised by the great generals in history, although for many it has also been their downfall.

The first requirement of the successful deceiving commander is an understanding of his opposite number's character. If he has a reputation for rashness, impetuosity, excessive audacity or, indeed, personal ambition, he may be easily exploited by a deception plan. If the deceiver can find out his opponent's prejudices, he is at an advantage, because there is a fair chance that whatever in the proposed plan does not fit with those prejudices will be ignored. The plan should therefore be based on what the enemy commander himself not only believes but hopes for. The military works with doctrines and organisational patterns as well as the psychological patterns of their individual members, and this forms the basis for deception. It also means that reliable intelligence about the enemy is essential.

Over the years deception in warfare has been viewed variously. In the first century AD it was commonplace among, yet not publicly endorsed by, the Romans. In the early Middle Ages, when most battles were hand-to-hand affairs with few opportunities for deception, the Western creed of chivalry considered such acts contemptible. In the Middle East, however, the Byzantines regarded deception as an essential part of warfare and took pride in their skill at it. In the late fifteenth century the ad hoc armies of the medieval period gave way to mercenaries and warfare as a profession based on discipline and training. Musketeers supplanted pikemen; firepower formed a higher proportion of armies than cavalry. By the beginning of the eighteenth century most countries had standing armies led by professional officers to whom deception in warfare was a normal path to victory.

More recently the Marxist-Leninist system had no qualms about using deception. They regarded it as a convenient and, indeed, legitimate technique to use in peace or war. In the culture of the West, however, it was often regarded as somewhat immoral. It has been said that for many years it ran counter to Americans' concept of military honour, and it was used by them only sparingly in the Second World War. The British, on the other hand, despite their reputation for 'fair play' have shown themselves to be remarkably skilled in deception, and by the end of the Second World War were past masters in the art.[1]

In the world of deception innovative minds seek to spin intricate webs of information in an unstable and hostile environment. This work is carried out at great risk but also with the potential for greater gain. Deception in war is the art of misleading the enemy into doing something, or not doing something, so that his tactical or strategic position will be weakened. Two common types of military operation help to define this concept – deceptive and cover operations.

A deceptive operation includes all the signs of a genuine attack. It sets the enemy thinking that pretended hostile activities are real ones. It creates in the enemy a false sense of danger in one area, causing him to reinforce his defences there, and consequently to weaken them in another area where the genuine assault is due.

Cover is a type of deception that leads the enemy to believe that genuine hostile activities are a harmless feint. It induces a false sense of security by disguising the preparations for a real attack so that the enemy will be taken by surprise when it does come.

The use of animated dummy figures is an example of a simple deceptive operation, while a rumour campaign suggesting that troops embarking for the tropics are really bound for the Arctic is a simple cover operation. The scale of deception plans can range from small and simple to huge and complex.

Every deception operation must be founded on sound, reliable intelligence. The intelligence process may be seen as a simple cycle: direction, where the commander must tell his intelligence staff what he needs to know; collection of the information by overt or covert means; processing of the information gathered into usable intelligence and its distribution to those who need to know it; constant re-evaluation and updating of the information; and the effects of changes on the intelligence being disseminated.

From the viewpoint of a deceiving commander the crucial parts of an enemy's intelligence-gathering cycle are the collection and processing stages, for here lie the opportunities for planting false information aimed at the credibility of their sources and agencies. Knowledge of what he is seeking during processing will greatly assist the deceiving commander in planting the apparently genuine but false information.

Any commander embarking upon a deception operation should bear in mind the following principles. He should aim his plans at the mind of the opposing commander. He should understand how that man's mind works and avoid the temptation of providing him with what he thinks the opposition would like to hear. He should never forget that he is trying to make the enemy act in a manner to assist his own plans. The commander's coordination and control should be centralised to ensure deception staff are in easy communication with him. Security is of the utmost importance to success. The genuine operation must of course be secure, and the deception plan must be equally so. The very existence of a deception plan should be divulged strictly on a 'need to know' basis. 'Windfall' inputs of unsolicited information should be avoided unless their security is guaranteed by exceptionally good disguising. If the genuine deception plan is discovered, the security measures must be such as to ensure the deceiving commander's real intentions remain secret, perhaps by leaving several interpretations open for the enemy's consideration. The sources of information used in the deception must be as near 'genuine' as possible. It should also be borne in mind that the credibility of information will be increased if it is confirmed from several sources. The enemy commander must be led to believe that he has obtained the information by accident or his own efforts. Preparation and timing are of course crucial: a deception commander must have sufficient time to develop his concepts. Finally, the facility to obtain or estimate feedback from the target is invaluable in allowing a degree of flexibility to be employed.

In the perfect deception operation, pieces of information are allowed to reach the enemy in such a way as to convince him that he has discovered them by accident or by the alertness of his agents. If he works out the connection between these items of 'fact' himself he is far more likely to believe that the deception is the truth. The variety and scale of the pieces of information that can be offered to the enemy are enormous: dummy installations and military equipment, skilfully composed rumours for circulation at home and overseas, the dropping of propaganda leaflets on the enemy, fictitious radio traffic between imaginary military units, deliberate indiscretions by friendly diplomats in neutral countries casually let drop at dinner parties, and the most skilful use of enemy agents under their captors' control to leak fragments of information to their former 'masters'. This latter practice proved vital to the success of many of the Allied deception plans in the Second World War.

The use of spies, or more precisely double agents, in deception operations as opposed to straightforward information-gathering is a powerful tool. The ordinary spy is exemplified in history by the postmaster at Versailles, who, in the war of 1701, was in the pay of Prince Eugène of Savoy-Carignan and opened letters from the French court to their generals, sending copies to the Prince. An example of an unwilling double agent is provided by the secretary of England's King William of Orange, who was persuaded by François, duc de Luxembourg to keep him informed of everything. When the King discovered the treachery he forced the secretary to send misleading information to Luxembourg, resulting in the French being caught by surprise at Steinkirke in 1692.[2]

It was not until the twentieth century that the use of double agents had their greatest impact on the outcome of operations in warfare. The organisation of this kind of deception had its origins in the Middle East in the desperate days of late 1940 when, in normal military operations against the Italians and Germans, it was found advantageous to make use of captured men who had expressed a willingness to work for the Allies in spreading deliberately misleading information. Where these men had been caught undertaking espionage for the enemy, their 'turning' to work for the other side was assisted by the waiving of the one penalty that any spy could expect.

The techniques for using these double agents in support of deception plans, as distinct from the more usual work they had been caught doing, were developed by a specialist unit formed by the C-in-C Middle East, Gen Wavell, and known as 'A' Force. Under Lt Col Dudley Clarke this unit was set up specifically to devise and conduct deception operations. It is claimed that all other deception devices and arrangements later used so successfully by both British and American forces sprang from these origins.

The physical presentation of false information may often be seen as being ambiguous, particularly where items that the deceivers would like the enemy to know are of the kind not normally committed to written communications. Electronic deception by radio also has its limitations: considerable physical resources are required, and the compilation of a suitable transmission requires much skill to maintain authenticity. Then, of course, one has the uncertainty over whether the enemy will be able to receive the message or, indeed, whether he is even listening. Double agents, on the other hand, have the accuracy, speed and certainty for use in deception operations over relatively long periods and at considerable range. If they are backed up by both electronic and physical deception methods, then, if the enemy breaks through the security around the operation, he will find confirmation of the story he has uncovered.

The use of double agents in the Second World War occurred simultaneously in Egypt and Britain but was managed completely separately in the two countries. In Cairo, Security and Intelligence Middle East (SIME) had been set up to combine all matters of security and intelligence in the Middle East theatre of war and involved officers of both MI5 and MI6 working closely together. Intelligence jobs that could not find an obvious allocation, especially if they contained an element of unorthodoxy, tended to finish up at SIME. In London, turned agents were dealt with by Section B1a of MI5 under Lt Col T.A. Robertson.

Dudley Clarke in Cairo worked out and laid down some strict principles for the use of double agents: the contacts of an agent used for passing deception information should be entirely imaginary, as should be his own espionage activities; a deception agent must not be allowed access to the outside world, irrespective of his own allegiances; and no deception links should ever be used for intelligence purposes other than deception. Should this occur for any reason, then the link should cease to be used for deception. According to Jon Latimer in *Deception in War*,[3] sometimes these principles were not followed in London – with almost disastrous consequences.

For the classic example of military deception we must go back to Greek mythology and Homer's twenty-four books of the *Iliad*. The war between the Greeks and the Trojans began when Paris, a Trojan prince who had grown up as a shepherd, eloped (with Aphrodite's connivance) with Helen, wife of Menelaus, King of Sparta. Menelaus was not best pleased and formed an alliance with other Greeks to besiege the great city of Troy. The city was well fortified and the siege continued for ten years.

After so long the Greeks formed a cunning plan. They built a huge wooden horse, left it on the beach ostensibly as an offering to Athena, the Greek goddess of wisdom, and withdrew out of sight, giving the Trojans the distinct impression they had given up the decade-long siege. The Trojans were naturally curious about this enormous equine monument, but Cassandra, a Trojan princess who had learned the art of prophecy from none other than Apollo himself and Laocoön, one of his priests, warned against interfering with it. But their warnings went unheeded and the horse was dragged into the city. At night a Greek task force hidden within it emerged to open the city gates to their comrades, who proceeded to sack the city.

In the Old Testament the story is told of how Gideon was able to rout the much larger army of the Midianites. Gideon divided his force of 300 warriors into three parts, who, each man equipped with a trumpet and a lamp hidden in a pitcher, surrounded the Midianite camp in the middle of the night. On the given order the pitchers were broken to reveal the lamps and the trumpets were blasted for all they were worth. The 300 men sent up a great cry, 'The sword of the Lord and of Gideon', whereupon the Midianites, thinking they were surrounded by a greater army and no doubt confused at being wakened so suddenly, took flight and were pursued by increasing numbers from other cities who joined in the rout.

The spreading of rumours exaggerating the strength of an army has been commonplace, but to have it believed and acted upon needs special care and originality. The Mongols achieved this false impression of strength by virtue of the speed and manoeuvrability of their cavalry, which could give the impression of operating over a much wider area than was really the case. Add to this the fact that each man would come to the battle with as many as five horses, the spare ones being 'ridden' by dummy riders, and the illusion of a much greater fighting force was complete.

To the Byzantine leaders deception in warfare was entirely acceptable. Why shed blood and spend wealth on achieving what could be gained by the skilful use of feigned retreats, stratagems and cunning ruses? Emperor Leo VI (862–912), known as Leo the Wise or Leo the Philosopher, wrote openly in his *Tactica* of elaborate stratagems and recommended one piece of mischief in particular that remained in use into the Second World War, forming the basis of several deception operations considered in this book: the writing of treasonable letters to enemy officers and ensuring they fall into the hands of higher authorities.[4]

More than 2,000 years after the siege of Troy, during a vital phase in the Battle of Hastings, the most decisive battle fought on English soil, it is claimed that Norman cavalry pretended to retreat in the face of the resolute defence of the Anglo-Saxon foot soldiers. This move wrong-footed the defenders, and Duke William of Normandy won the day and became ruler of England.

Over 800 years later the exploits of a relatively obscure British officer in the Second Anglo-Boer War (1899–1902) served to enthral the Victorian public at a time, in the last few months of the nineteenth century, when a number of reversals had caused depression to set in at home.[5] Col Robert Stephenson Smyth Baden-Powell, who later went on to form the Boy Scout movement, was a bit of a dramatist, with a hint of schoolboy mischievousness about him. The details of how he came to be besieged in Mafeking can be found on page 31 of Jon Latimer's book, *Deception in War*. Baden-Powell's preparations for dealing with his predicament included several examples of deception. His intention was to persuade the enemy that they faced a much larger and better equipped force than was really the case. So when he set up a ring of outposts around the town he made sure one of them could easily be construed to be his headquarters. It stood out by having two flagpoles – a little obvious, perhaps, but nevertheless it attracted enemy gunfire as intended, which was of course a waste of effort and ammunition, because it was a dummy. The genuine trenches and prepared houses were all linked by telephone to the real headquarters in Dixon's Hotel. Baden-Powell employed strings of natives to continuously be seen carefully carrying boxes around the town. They were under strict instructions that on no account must the boxes be dropped. Then signs appeared around the town in Dutch and English warning of minefields. These were given even wider publicity by official announcements. If the enemy's informants in the town still had any doubts, they were quickly dispelled by a very public test-firing of a mine. In reality the boxes so carefully handled by the Africans contained nothing more than sand and the mines were a bluff.

Baden-Powell was aware of the Boers' intelligence-gathering capability and decided to turn it against them by writing to an old acquaintance whose home was just inside the Transvaal, warning him of the impending approach of a 'third column' of British troops. But he knew the man was dead and banked on the letter being opened and read by the postal authorities and the contents passed on to the Boers.

Further examples of the besieged force's inventiveness are to be found in their fabrication from old biscuit tins of a large rectangular cone with a highly reflective interior and the intense light of an acetylene torch at its apex. This was fitted to a long pole to form a searchlight to dissuade the Boers from mounting raids under cover of darkness. The one light was moved quickly from fort to fort and is reported to have greatly impressed the Boers when it was shone in their general direction.[6]

Another device was a huge megaphone, again made from biscuit tins, that was said to have been capable of conveying words of command for more than 500 yards. It was used to broadcast orders to the defending ring to prepare for an attack with fixed bayonets. This was said to have greatly scared the Boers, who responded by opening fire on the megaphone location, thus giving away their own positions.[7]

Baden-Powell held out by means of such deceptions for 217 days, until the Boer Gen Snyman withdrew. His audacity had won through and his tactics entered the history books.

A modern variation on the Trojan horse theme occurred in 1940 when innocent-looking merchant ships entered Bergen and Narvik in Norway only to discharge their hidden German troops, who took over the two cities.

There were several dramatic and well-known deception operations during the Second World War. Among the most notable was Operation Mincemeat, when the corpse of a drowned man was disguised as a Royal Marines Officer, taken in a special container by submarine under great secrecy and put into the sea at a point off the coast of Spain where the tides were sure to wash him up onto the beach. Although Spain was neutral, certain of its cities were hotbeds of spying and intrigue, so the chances were that German agents would hear about the corpse of a British officer and make arrangements with the authorities to examine its papers. Attached to the corpse were documents ostensibly in transit between London and the Mediterranean HQ. Among the papers were carefully drafted letters from which the enemy could construe that Sicily was the cover (i.e. false) objective for the forthcoming invasion of Greece, the reverse of what was really planned. The Allies, it seemed, would attack Greece two weeks after an attack on Sicily had been launched. A week later further assaults were to take place against Corsica, Sardinia and the south of France. Exactly as anticipated, the corpse and its documents were reported to the local Germans, who examined them before the body was given a funeral as 'Major Martin'. The enemy was deceived and was concentrating its forces well away from the genuine invasion area when the Allied troops landed in Sicily.[8]

In the lead-up to the D-Day invasion of the continent of Europe on 6 June 1944 the Allies were intent on keeping the Germans guessing about where the Overlord landings would take place. To achieve this, dummy aircraft, tanks, lorries and landing craft were deployed to give the impression to any Luftwaffe aerial reconnaissance sorties that the build-up of equipment was taking place in areas that indicated the Pas de Calais was to be the point of landing. Broadcasts by the Political Warfare Executive (PWE) and by the German spies who had been 'turned' and were transmitting to their masters under the control of the Twenty Committee also introduced subtle hints as to the target for the Allied assault. The Twenty Committee (so named because the Roman numerals for 'twenty' form a double cross, and by running the captured German agents the Committee was double-crossing the enemy) was part of the counter-intelligence security service, MI5. This was arguably the most successful deception of the war. It ran the entire German spy network in Britain from the fall of France in 1940 up to the return of British armies to France in summer 1944.

Not all the deception plans of the Allies in the Second World War were successful. PWE became involved in the planning of three operations as part of Operation Cockade, which suffered from serious political pressures before being set in motion. In 1943 the Combined Chiefs of Staff had decided that there would be no important operations outside the Mediterranean area. In order to help our own forces in Sicily and Italy, and our Russian allies in the east, it was highly desirable to keep as many German divisions as possible on standby in the west. To do this by means of Commando raids was not regarded as sensible. Apart from the possibility of heavy losses such as had been borne in the ill-fated Dieppe raid of August 1942, such attacks tended to give the enemy as much experience in defending targets as the Commandos gained in attacking them. Moreover, if such raids resulted in the reinforcement of the heavily fortified West Wall at points where the Allies were, in reality, planning to breach it, the exercise would have been counter-productive. At this time one of the chief objectives of British air strategy was to weaken German fighter strength before the date of the invasion. With this in mind, precision low-level attacks were made on factories making parts and assembling aircraft. To further reduce the German Air Force's (GAF) numbers of aircraft and pilots, Fighter Command sought every opportunity to lure the enemy into combat. But GAF aircraft numbers were being reduced by superior Allied air forces, so it was enemy policy to refuse combat until the invasion had started, unless they had local tactical superiority. In addition to keeping enemy forces tied up where the Allies had no intention of engaging them, a secondary objective of these pre-Second Front deception plans was therefore to bring about an air battle and inflict heavy losses on German fighter aircraft.

Three strategic plans were drawn up as part of Operation Cockade: Tindall, Starkey and Wadham.

Tindall involved preparations for an attack on the key German base of Stavanger in Norway by forces based in Scotland. German forces in Norway were only sufficient to hold the country, and any additional threat would cause the redeployment of troops from other parts of Europe where the Allies planned genuine attacks.

Starkey concerned preparations for a British and Canadian expeditionary force to establish a bridgehead at Boulogne. Once again, the hope was to initiate large-scale German troop movements but also to lure the GAF into combat where Allied superiority could inflict heavy losses on it.

Wadham was a plan for an American airborne assault resulting in the capture of the Atlantic port of Brest.

The preparations for Tindall were arranged to culminate in late August 1943, after which the Germans were to be made to believe it had been a feint. A week or two later Starkey and Wadham would finish, and once again the Germans would have to acknowledge they had been feints. Then Tindall would be remounted a few weeks later to give the impression of an invasion of Norway.

PWE and the Special Operations Executive (SOE) were charged with drawing up detailed plans to counter the political disadvantages of the operations, for they would be taking place at a time of desperate need for liberation of the Nazi-occupied territories. In the midst of all their privations, and with the prospect of yet another winter under the Nazi jackboot, the enslaved populations would be very disappointed if they were led to believe the real invasion was at hand, only to find it was a feint. Furthermore, the enemy propaganda service would make the most of a failure to invade.

The lengths to which the deception went illustrate the necessity of covering every conceivable angle in the planning of an operation such as Starkey.[9] Genuine troops were supplemented by 60,000 non-existent men whose presence had to be allowed for. PWE sent simple instructions to resistance groups on the use of small arms. The BBC broadcast talks on 'Resistance and Security', 'Enemy Troop Dispositions and Plans' and (most tellingly) 'Recognising Allied Troops'. There was a flurry of meaningless code messages put out on the BBC French, Belgian, Dutch and Norwegian services: all activities that could be expected prior to a real invasion.

Shipping and landing craft, many of them dummies, were moved along the south coast of England from Falmouth to Rye, radio deception being used to give the illusion of far greater numbers than was really the case. Some 400 gliders, 128 Spitfires and 64 Hurricanes, all of them skilfully made dummies, were inserted into airfields in the south of England, care being taken to ensure the fighter aircraft were moved from time to time to give them some semblance of life.[10] Decoy lights and fires were set up, and lighting schemes were installed to give the impression of illumination to facilitate troop embarkation.

Even after all this preparation it was decided that a few German prisoners snatched for interrogation purposes in Commando raids on the French coast would add verisimilitude to the exercise. After eight raids the only enemy property brought back were two samples of barbed wire! The leaks through agents in enemy territory and the former German spies now controlled by the British went ahead; they contained information about things that could not be spotted by reconnaissance aircraft, plus some, of course, that could, for the sake of authenticity.

The Allies continued to be concerned about the effect of this deception operation on the morale of the populations of the occupied countries concerned, and in particular on their resistance movements, whose actions were going to be crucial when the real invasion took place. To be seen to be raising the hopes of these people, only to dash them a few days later, was a risk that had to be taken. The historical records do not indicate whether the governments-in-exile were made privy to the secret. The prickly Général de Gaulle would have been a difficult leader to persuade. For security reasons the Allies felt unable to reveal to the resistance on the ground in Europe that Starkey was a fake. In the end a somewhat subtle announcement in the general style of many other messages to the overrun peoples was agreed upon:

> Be careful of German provocation. We have learned that the Germans are circulating inspired rumours that we are concentrating armies on our coasts with intentions of invading the continent. Take no notice, as these provocations are intended to create among you manifestations and disorders which the Germans will use as an excuse for repressive measures against you. Be disciplined, use discretion, and maintain order, for when the time arrives for action you will be advised in advance.[11]

What of the British press, which could not fail to see the build-up and hectic activity along the south coast? Selected members were to be told it was a rehearsal for the real thing.

Suggestions were made for leaflet drops during the week before the operation, advising the population that the activity was a rehearsal – this would further mislead the enemy while hopefully maintaining the confidence of the patriots. Instead, a warning or Avis was broadcast, which resulted in an extremely bad reaction from France. This raised serious and vociferous objections in the French region of PWE and in the BBC. Alternative warnings were drafted in an effort to retrieve the situation, but in the end none was broadcast, and at the appointed time the ships of Operation Starkey sailed. They stood ten miles off the French coast without encountering any opposition before turning for home. The GAF stayed firmly on the ground, and by all accounts the enemy ignored what was going on.

Deception operations throughout the ages have made use of the available technology of the time. From the wooden horse of Troy to the fake horse riders of the Mongols, from remotely fired muskets to Baden-Powell's 'searchlight', current technological developments have been used to deceive the enemy as the opportunity presented itself. Some people in the First World War retained vestiges of Victorian morality that regarded deception as unpalatable, but by the total war of 1939 there were no restraints on the use of technology to achieve success by any means, overt or covert. Two fields in particular had developed greatly during the interwar years and now presented many opportunities for the deceivers on both sides: wireless and aircraft. But wireless had the added advantage that, if it could be received by the enemy, it could be used to subvert his armed forces and general population. Its use in this way required great skill. The Germans tried such subversive tactics with Goebbels's Propaganda Ministry broadcasts by the American-born traitor William Joyce. Joyce employed an exaggerated English upper-class drawl when he introduced his broadcasts with 'Garmany calling, Garmany calling'; nicknamed Lord Haw-Haw, he quickly became the butt of schoolboy humour. Although his broadcasts could be (and were) easily picked up in England on normal household wireless sets, he was never taken seriously. As a subversive operation he was a failure. In Britain subversion was handled chiefly by PWE and SOE, the former broadcasting carefully scripted programmes from secret transmitters in the south of England. Thus deception could now go to the very heart of the enemy.

One of the most ambitious and imaginative deception plans of the Second World War had its origins in the concern felt by the Supreme Commander of the Allies, Gen Dwight D. Eisenhower, about the German people's will to resist. With the exception of a few weeks' setback caused by von Rundstedt's Ardennes offensive in December 1944, the Allies had been steadily advancing towards Germany since the invasion of Normandy in June. In Germany the population itself was still enduring round-the-clock air bombardment, as it had done for some considerable time: daylight raids by the Americans and night attacks by the RAF. Targeting of military and industrial installations was not always accurate. To add to the Germans' misery, Air Marshal 'Bomber' Harris, the head of Bomber Command, had adopted a policy of area (as opposed to strategic) bombing, as part of which the heart of Hamburg was destroyed in July 1943 by a huge firestorm that caused appalling numbers of civilian casualties. Many other cities had also suffered devastating raids. The culmination of this kind of operation took place in February 1945 with the controversial bombing of Dresden. Yet despite this onslaught on the German people and their consequent privations, they showed no signs of a major revolt against the Nazi regime.

On the ground the American, British and French forces advanced relentlessly throughout early 1945 to the German border and then into the 'Fatherland' itself. In the east the Soviets had driven the German invaders from their land and were through Poland and into the eastern states of the Reich. Everything indicated a bleak future for Germany. The obvious and sensible thing for the German forces to do was to sue for peace. But the Allies' demand for unconditional surrender would strip both the military and the civilian population of any semblance of an honourable defeat. Some feared a repeat of the humiliation that Germany felt after its defeat in the First World War and the imposition of the Treaty of Versailles. For most of the traditional German officer class who had sworn their oath of loyalty to their Führer, a repetition of this was unthinkable. The will to resist remained steadfast in most cases.

The Allies, in the form of SOE and PWE, argued that, had there been an organised and effective opposition to Nazism at this time, as there had been in the occupied countries, they could have nurtured, supplied and helped it to rise up against the German authorities, thus assisting the incoming forces. But there was no evidence of an organised and cohesive resistance movement capable of being rapidly mobilised.

Then someone had an idea: 'If there isn't a resistance organisation in Germany, let's create an imaginary one!'

Operation Periwig was conceived.

Chapter 2

WHAT WERE SOE AND PWE?

THE SPECIAL OPERATIONS EXECUTIVE

The Special Operations Executive (SOE) was formed in mid-July 1940 at the height of the crisis following the evacuation of the British Expeditionary Force from Dunkirk and the fall of France. It brought together three existing secret organisations: Section D of the Secret Intelligence Service (SIS), otherwise known as MI6; the Military Intelligence Research unit (MI(R)) of the War Office, formerly known as General Staff (Research) or GS(R); and Electra House, a clandestine body attached to the Foreign Office mainly concerned with propaganda.

As early as March 1939 the existence of three organisations tackling much the same work was seen as an anomaly. A certain duplication of effort was taking place between MI(R) and Section D, something the country could ill afford, both being concerned with offensive clandestine operations. The first paper to address this problem was prepared in June 1939. Over the next few months there followed various initiatives attempting to solve the problem of coordination. Reorganisation was discussed in a complex series of meetings held in June and July 1940 involving, in various combinations, the Chief of Imperial General Staff (CIGS), Lord Gort; the Foreign Secretary, Lord Halifax; the Chief of GS(R), Col Holland; the leader of the Labour Party, Clement Attlee; another Labour rising star, Dr Hugh Dalton; and representatives of SIS. They dealt among other things with the sensitive problem of whether to have military or civilian control of any merged organisation. The solution was to some extent a compromise between political interests, but the details of the discussions leading to agreement, said to have been acrimonious, cannot (according to Mackenzie in *The Secret History of SOE*) be traced from the papers available. The final document proposing the setting-up of an organisation to be called the Special Operations Executive under the chairmanship of the 53-year-old Minister of Economic Warfare, Hugh Dalton, was signed on 19 July by Neville Chamberlain (then Lord President of the Council following his resignation as Prime Minister on 10 May 1940). The leader of the wartime coalition government, Winston Churchill, had already, on 16 July, offered the headship of SOE to Dalton, with the now much-publicised exhortation to 'set Europe ablaze'. Ironically, it was on this very day that Hitler signed his Führer Directive No. 16 for the planning of Operation Seelöwe (Sea-lion), the invasion of Britain. The SOE Charter was finally approved by the War Cabinet on 22 July.

In retrospect it seems somewhat anomalous that it was placed not under any of the parent ministries but under the Ministry of Economic Warfare (MEW). The reasons were a consequence of the complicated political negotiations that preceded its formation. Each of the constituent organisations had been set up independently before the war in 1938 with objectives that were loosely defined and overlapping. The new organisation was given a more specific task of promoting sabotage and subversion through its own covert agents, and of supplying arms, equipment and agents to resistance movements throughout occupied Europe and beyond. When these old organisations were amalgamated to form SOE they each brought with them a good deal of historical baggage which, throughout the war, coloured relations between SOE and its parents. These political problems were of major importance in the general progress of SOE throughout its existence. Implementation of the Charter took a little time. Control of Section D and Electra House passed from the Foreign Office to the MEW on 16 August 1940, while the formal dissolution of MI(R) followed in October. Meanwhile, SOE's London headquarters was moved in October to 64 Baker Street, where it adopted its public cover name of the Inter-Services Research Bureau. It was quite separate from the MEW in Berkeley Square. Dalton remained as head until he was replaced in 1942 by Lord Selborne, also aged 53. The formal relationship between Section D (MI6) and GS(R) (later known as MI(R)) is difficult to disentangle, but some of their technical work certainly overlapped. Electra House, which had been set up in 1938 by Lord Hankey and headed by Sir Campbell Stuart, was inspired by a successful propaganda organisation in the First World War.

SECTION D

In April 1938 the then head of the SIS, Adm Sir Hugh Sinclair, arranged for the secondment of Maj Lawrence Grand, RE, from the War Office to the SIS to carry out a study and to report on the possibilities of creating a British organisation for covert offensive action. Germany and Italy had already conducted such operations in countries that they later overran, and the possible existence of a fifth column in Britain was not entirely ruled out. (The term 'fifth column' applies to enemy sympathisers who might provide active assistance to an invader and originates from Spanish Civil War rebel collaborators in Madrid in 1936, when four rebel columns were advancing on the city. The fifth column were the sympathisers already in the city.) Grand had no experience of secret service work but he had ideas, enthusiasm and a persona that earned the admiration of all who worked with him. His personal energy was much needed, for time was not on his side – by now Austria had been annexed by Germany. Grand was promoted to colonel, given the symbol D and set up the Devices Section of MI6, to be called Section D but with the cover name of Statistical Research Department of the War Office. Section D's terms of reference were to:

- study how sabotage might be carried out
- produce special sabotage ammunition
- make experiments on carrying out sabotage
- train saboteurs
- study methods of countering sabotage.

The use of aggressive action was precluded as long as peace held. At first the Section consisted of only two officers.

Among those recruited by Grand in December 1938 was Cdr A.G. Langley, RN, who set in motion and pursued energetically work on the research and development of ideas and stores needed to meet the above objectives. In particular his small group was concerned with the design of time fuses and switches of various types and of explosives and incendiary devices. Section D was originally based at the SIS's head office in London at 54 Broadway but soon expanded to the adjacent Caxton House. In the early months of 1939, as the threat of war grew ever closer, Horace Emery of the SIS arranged for the manufacture to Langley's design of the first batch of 'time pencil' fuses. Articles made in Germany and Italy that might be suitable for concealing or camouflaging weapons were collected, and contacts were established with organisations that could be of use in war, such as various service departments, the research department at the Woolwich Arsenal, the British Scientific Instrument Research Association, the Royal Society, Imperial Chemical Industries (ICI), the Shell Oil Company, the Railway Executive, etc. On the outbreak of war most of Section D's staff moved with the Government Code and Cipher School (GCCS), the forerunner of GCHQ, to Bletchley Park in Buckinghamshire (Station X – 'ex', not 'ten'), although some went to The Frythe, a requisitioned private hotel at Welwyn in Hertfordshire.

By the middle of 1939 a small magazine for explosives and incendiaries had been built at Bletchley and work had started on full-scale experiments with weapons.[1] This was not universally popular, because it was judged incompatible to have explosives and decoding work on the same site. Furthermore, GCCS's work was expanding rapidly, and Section D was forced to find accommodation for Langley's work elsewhere. In November 1939 it was moved to Aston House at Stevenage in Hertfordshire, which was given the title of Signals Development Branch Depot No. 4, War Office. In 1941 it became War Department Experimental Station 6 (ES6 WD) in recognition of its parent, MI6. On the formation of SOE it became known also as Station XII. Langley took with him a small group of about seven officers, two laboratory technicians, five other ranks and secretarial staff.

Also recruited by Grand was a group of distinguished amateur sailors from the Royal Cruising Club, including Frank Carr, the assistant librarian of the House of Lords, Roger Pinckney, the architect of Melbourne Cathedral, and Augustine Courtauld, Arctic explorer. They had all been recruited to familiarise themselves with parts of the continental coastline that could be of strategic importance in wartime. Attached to this group was Gerry Holdsworth, who was later to set up the Helford Base in Cornwall.[2] Meanwhile, Section D had established agents and offices in Sweden, Norway, Holland, Spain and France. However, within a few months of the outbreak of war it had lost contact with nearly all of its overseas agents, and it was soon apparent that most had been arrested by the Germans. Its work was, inevitably for such a novel enterprise, largely a process of trial and error which was overtaken by the progress of the war before significant results could be obtained. As a consequence, by the time of the fall of France in 1940 neither Section D nor any other Allied covert organisation had any agents on the western European mainland, although a number remained in the Balkans and the Middle East.

GS(R)

In 1938 a section was set up in the War Office by the Deputy Chief of Imperial General Staff (DCIGS), Sir Ronald Adam, known by the innocuous title of General Staff (Research), or GS(R). It was to research into the problems of tactics and organisation under the DCIGS. It produced a number of papers, two of which are of interest but have not been found: 'Considerations from the Wars in Spain and China with Respect to Certain Aspects of Army Policy' and 'An Investigation of the Possibilities of Guerrilla Activities'. In December 1938 Lt Col J.F. Holland, RE was appointed head of the group. He had had experience of irregular warfare in Ireland and India which had influenced the writing of the second paper mentioned above. With Col Grand of Section D, Holland produced a joint paper dated 20 March 1939 dealing with the possibility of guerrilla actions against Germany if they over-ran eastern Europe and absorbed Romania. The formal objectives of GS(R) were similar to those of Section D, namely to:

- study guerrilla methods and produce a guerrilla Field Service Regulations Handbook incorporating detailed tactical and technical instructions as they applied to various countries
- evolve destructive devices suitable for use by guerrillas and capable of production and distribution on a wide enough scale to be effective
- evolve procedure and machinery for operating guerrilla activities if it were decided to do so subsequently.

As the Military Intelligence Directorate expanded in response to the increasing threat of war in the spring of 1939, GS(R) changed its name to Military Intelligence (Research) or MI(R). Holland's Section was first housed in Caxton House, adjacent to Grand's Section D, but on the outbreak of war it was moved to the War Office Building. Also in the spring of that year Holland was authorised to appoint two Grade II staff officers to MI(R). The first was another Royal Engineer, Maj M.J.R. Jefferis, later Sir Millis Jefferis, to work on guerrilla devices. His unit was based initially at 36 Portland Place, but when they were bombed out in autumn 1940 they moved to The Firs, a Tudor mansion at Whitchurch near Aylesbury which became known as MI(R)c. Also known as 'Winston Churchill's Toyshop',[3] it produced a string of inventions, several of which, like those from Section D, became the basis for the development of devices that were later adopted both by SOE and the

Regular Army Engineers. However, this unit became increasingly concerned with larger-scale military hardware such as anti-tank weapons, the destruction of concrete pill-boxes and the clearance of minefields. On the formation of SOE it was specifically excluded from the transfer of MI(R) to SOE and remained independent as MD1 under the patronage of Churchill and his friend and scientific adviser, Prof Frederick Lindemann (later Lord Cherwell).

For the second of these posts Holland chose Maj Colin Gubbins, RA. This appointment was to prove crucially important in the later development of SOE. Gubbins's first task was to work on a series of pamphlets: *The Partisan Leader's Handbook*; *How to Use High Explosives*; and *The Art of Guerrilla Warfare*. The last of these was written in collaboration with Holland. They drew heavily on the experiences of T.E. Lawrence (of Arabia) and of operations in Palestine, Ireland, the North-West Frontier and Russia. Surprisingly, there was not at this time a single book to be found in any library in any language on these subjects. In fact, none of these books was published in England, although they were distributed widely in Europe and South-East Asia. *The Partisan Leader's Handbook* is reproduced as Appendix 2 in Prof M.R.D. Foot's *SOE in the Low Countries*, but copies of the other two have not been located.

With the formation of SOE, MI(R) was combined with Section D.

THE BIRTH OF SOE

SOE had a difficult birth and suffered recurring post-natal pains. The incorporation of Section D with MI(R) to form one body responsible to an executive director, to be called CD, required many changes both in structure and personnel. There were hard decisions to be taken, and several heads rolled. Both Grand and Holland had made internal enemies and returned to pursue their distinguished military careers; they both ended up as major-generals. Many other staff left or were transferred to other duties.

The first to fill the post of CD in August 1940 was 58-year-old Sir Frank Nelson, who had to build up SOE almost from nothing. Nelson was a businessman, a former Conservative MP and former Vice-Consul at Basle in Switzerland, where he had had some involvement with SIS. He undertook his task with great enthusiasm and dedication, but he ruined his health in the process and was obliged to resign in May 1942 after less than two years' service.

SOE was initially divided into three branches: SO1 (Propaganda), SO2 (Active Operations) and SO3 (Planning). SO1 was soon taken over and incorporated into the Political Warfare Executive (PWE), controlled by the Foreign Office and closely assisted by the Ministry of Information (MoI) and the MEW. (Useful sidelights on the early years before SOE and PWE parted company are contained in *The Secret History of PWE* by David Garnett.) SO3, in the words of Prof M.R.D. Foot, 'proceeded to strangle itself in festoons of paperwork'[4] and had disintegrated by the end of September 1940. This left SO2, which now took on the mantle and title of SOE. At this stage, with the exception of a few Regular Army officers, the whole staff was amateur. Mercifully the organisation was free from the minor bureaucracy of a government department. This led to a looser and more flexible arrangement, which was not, however, without its disadvantages.

SOE was financed by secret funds from the MEW, and for some time (certainly until the end of 1942) its officers were paid monthly in crisp, white £5 notes – until the Inland Revenue became aware that some people were not paying income tax. It is sometimes said that those paid from SOE funds were exempt from tax. This may well have been true of its agents, but not for the rest of its personnel, as many of its survivors recall.

Nelson inherited two deputies. Maj (later Col) George Taylor from Section 6 was in charge of operations, including the establishment of country sections, while Col F.T. (Tommy) Davies from MI(R) took control of 'facilities', which included training, supplies and stores. Both were ruthless and efficient and played important roles in SOE throughout the war.

George Taylor was an Australian business tycoon who had joined the SIS and Section D before the war. He influenced the organisational structure and was later to play a major role in Balkan and Middle Eastern affairs.

Col Davies, the son of a general and a director of Courtaulds, had joined MI(R) as a captain in the Grenadier Guards shortly before the outbreak of war. In 1939 he was a member of the MI(R) mission (No. 4 Military Mission) to Poland, which arrived at its destination on the day war broke out but returned within a few days, since there was little it could actually do. In May 1940 Davies paid a hasty trip to Amsterdam to destroy or remove certain securities, and a few weeks later led a raiding party on the Courtaulds factory in Calais, where he succeeded in removing large quantities of platinum before the Germans arrived. As well as being deputy for Nelson, he was also his personal assistant and, as such, was responsible for setting up the training sections. By the end of 1941 he had become Director of Research, Development and Supplies, with the code symbol AD/Z, a post he held for the rest of the war.

On Nelson's retirement his post as CD went, early in May 1942, to his then deputy, Sir Charles Hambro, a successful city banker and a director of the Great Western Railway and the Bank of England. He had been in charge of the Scandinavian Section for two years. His many other responsibilities meant that he was unable to spend as much time on SOE business as the post demanded. By the spring of 1942 Dalton had been replaced as head of SOE by Lord Selborne. Following personal difficulties with Selborne, Hambro was sacked in September 1943. His replacement as CD was Brig (later Maj Gen) Gubbins, who, as recorded above, had joined SOE in November 1940 and been Hambro's deputy.

Colin McVean Gubbins was in many ways the ideal leader of SOE. A professional soldier, he had seen service in the First World War and in northern Russia and gained valuable experience when he fought as a major against the Irish Republican Army in the Irish Civil War in 1921. He was a small, wiry Scotsman who was described as 'Quiet-mannered, quiet-spoken, energetic, efficient and charming', 'a still-waters-run-deep sort of man' and 'a born leader of men'. (Biographical details are given in Chapter 4; a full biography, *Gubbins and SOE*, written by Peter Wilkinson and Joan Bright Astley, was published in 1993.)

Gubbins's influence on the direction and overall policies of SOE was crucial. Throughout his association with the organisation from 1940, his period as deputy to Hambro, and his own period as CD to the end of the war, his personality and drive played a major role in developing and executing SOE policies.

THE POLITICAL WARFARE EXECUTIVE (PWE)[5]

During the First World War the British Propaganda Department had been set up at Crewe House in London's Mayfair. It gained a favourable reputation, even being held by Germany's FM Ludendorff as a contributory factor in his country's defeat (wrongly, in the eyes of some commentators). Its deputy director had been the Canadian-born former military attaché, Sir Campbell Stuart. After the end of hostilities the development of propaganda for military purposes seems to have fallen by the wayside, but during the Munich Crisis of September and October 1938 certain progressive civil servants and senior officials of the BBC, chiefly Sir Stephen Tallents, suggested the creation of a body to coordinate British foreign propaganda which, with the improvements in broadcasting and air travel, showed promise as a useful weapon of war. But if Tallents had imagined the rapid adoption of his suggestion, he had not reckoned with the interdepartmental territorial squabbles in Whitehall which were to delay the birth of such an organisation for another three years.

During the Munich Crisis Tallents had plans to drop millions of anti-Hitler leaflets on Germany but, not surprisingly, this met with opposition from the appeasers in government and the civil service. He believed that the MoI, which would be set up at the outbreak of war, should contain a department that could immediately disseminate publicity material to enemy countries. Furthermore, he proposed another department in this ministry specifically charged with studying public opinion in such countries. This idea was opposed by the Foreign Office, which regarded it as encroaching upon one of its own traditional areas of interest, and by the Treasury, on the grounds of cost. These two departments of state put up stiff resistance to the creation of a British propaganda organisation until the head of the Foreign Office's News Department, former diplomat Reginald 'Rex' Leeper, was offered a major role in the proposed new executive.

While this was going on the Prime Minister, Neville Chamberlain, asked Sir Campbell Stuart to set up his own secret propaganda department but, for some inexplicable reason, decided not to tell Tallents. The new department was housed in a building on the Victoria Embankment known as Electra House. Stuart chaired the Imperial Communications Committee which met at this venue and gave the new venture some initial cover. The official title of the clandestine body was the Department of Propaganda in Enemy Countries, but it is generally referred to in the records of the time merely as Electra House. Its activities declined after Munich, but when Hitler invaded Czechoslovakia in the spring of 1939 and war looked inevitable, it was re-activated.

When war broke out in September 1939 Electra House came initially under the control of Lord Macmillan, the first Minister of Information. A month later overall responsibility for it was transferred to the Foreign Office. Then, in June 1940, it was given back to the MoI, now under Alfred Duff Cooper, a friend of Churchill's. He had resigned over Munich but was now brought back to the Cabinet by the new Prime Minister, who would shortly approve the charter of the Special Operations Executive.

When its first minister, Hugh Dalton, divided SOE into SO1 (Propaganda), SO2 (Operations) and SO3 (Planning), SO1 took over the secret propaganda role of Electra House and was placed under Leeper's immediate control, Stuart disappearing from the scene. Dalton also had an eye on Electra House's 'open' propaganda role, but for the time being it was left with Duff Cooper at the MoI.

Departmental differences surfaced again at the end of 1940, when SOE challenged the MoI over the control of 'open', 'white' or 'non-subversive' propaganda. This – mainly BBC broadcasts – did not attempt to hide the fact that it originated from the United Kingdom, whereas the 'secret', 'black' or 'subversive' propaganda that SO1 had been putting out from transmitting stations set up at the Marquess of Tavistock's Woburn Abbey in Bedfordshire and elsewhere was said to originate from resistance groups in occupied Europe.

Duff Cooper and Dalton continued their battle for control, the former arguing that he saw no real difference between subversive and non-subversive propaganda activities, while the latter considered that all the BBC's broadcasts to the half of Europe now controlled by the enemy should be transferred totally to SOE. Both these ministers had important supporters, so Churchill appointed the Lord President of the Council, Sir John Anderson, to adjudicate and arrive at a compromise. It was suspected that Churchill did not have any real interest in propaganda; he certainly did not have much time to waste on interdepartmental bickerings. A ministerial meeting in May 1941 resulted in Duff Cooper keeping control of 'open' propaganda and Dalton the 'secret' work. Yet within a month Duff Cooper was complaining to Churchill that the arrangement was not working and arguing that if his ministry did not control all of Britain's propaganda, its existence was redundant. The Prime Minister asked his friend Lord Beaverbrook to look into the matter for him. Beaverbrook had been Minister of Information in the First World War, and so he was not without experience for such a task. But even Beaverbrook was unable to come up with a workable solution, the main sticking-point being the control of foreign propaganda. It was left to Churchill to take the bull by the horns, remove Duff Cooper from the MoI to report on the military situation in the Far East, and confirm the tripartite Standing Ministerial Committee, whose charter he approved on 19 August 1941.

The three officials appointed to this committee were well suited to their task. Robert Bruce Lockhart represented the Foreign Office. He had been a British secret agent during the Russian Revolution, and so he knew the workings of the SIS. He was also the editor of a popular column in Beaverbrook's *Evening Standard* newspaper. Representing the MoI was Rex Leeper, who was of course sympathetic to the Foreign Office point of view. A former soldier who could stand up to his minister if necessary, Maj Gen Dallas Brooks represented Dalton's MEW and SOE. These men were to act 'as a General Staff for the conduct of political warfare'.

It was not long before tensions surfaced once more. Dalton soon realised that PWE was interested in acquiring SO1 operations, which accounted for about half his domain, so he put up fierce resistance. After serious complaints from the committee Dalton finally gave way when it became clear that the new Minister of Information, Brendan Bracken, was not about to allow SOE to have a completely free hand in political warfare. With Dalton acquiescing, PWE was allowed to get on with its job of fighting the political and psychological war against Germany. The formation of PWE was publicly announced on 11 September 1941 in a ministerial answer to a parliamentary question. The country headquarters of this new clandestine organisation were to be at Woburn Abbey.

PWE was engaged in spreading propaganda by two main activities: leaflet-dropping and broadcasting. As early as 25 September 1938 a secret memorandum on the employment of aircraft for dropping leaflets on enemy countries included the statement, 'In view of the well-known and widespread opposition in certain quarters in Germany to the present regime . . .'.[6] This false conviction that there existed a powerful anti-Nazi faction in Germany remained among those in Electra House and its successors for some years. Clearly, the truth or otherwise of this information was vital to PWE, and one can only speculate as to how they obtained it.

They were, of course, sure of the opposition in the occupied countries, and throughout their existence sent millions of leaflets and made thousands of broadcasts, many purporting to come from within Germany or German-held areas. Some of the most successful broadcasts were those to German troops giving information on their comrades' misfortunes in other theatres of war. The German High Command denied their forces in the West truthful situation reports from the eastern front; but PWE provided them, to the detriment of the troops' morale.

PWE enjoyed good relations with SOE as a whole, but in the last year of the European war most of their cooperation was with the German Directorate. They had developed highly sophisticated forms of propaganda: white, which was mainly broadcast, although in the early days dignified leaflets dropped by the RAF over civilian areas gave carefully argued reasons for opposing Hitler and Nazism. Later, when the tide of war had turned in the Allies' favour, the broadcasts gave factual information to the Germans about Allied successes, information denied to them, of course, by Goebbels's Information Ministry, and also coded messages to resistance movements in occupied countries.

Black propaganda, on the other hand, tried to differentiate between villainous Nazis and other, deceived, Germans and made use of leaflets, posters and pamphlets carrying rumours, slanders, forgeries and lies interspersed with items of truth for the sake of authenticity, all purporting to come from the Nazi-controlled civilian or military authorities or by German groups hostile to Hitler and Nazism. In reality they originated in Britain and were printed by PWE at its own secret works or at other clandestine locations. Black propaganda was also the purpose of two bogus broadcasting stations known as Research Units or RUs that claimed to emanate from within German-held territory but were in fact in England: *Soldatensender Calais*, broadcasting to troops in Europe, and *Kurzwellensender Atlantik*, which targeted U-boat crews. At first these broadcasts were made from twenty-nine short-wave transmitters distributed across the hills of southern England, but after the USA entered the war the Americans provided a powerful medium-wave transmitter. This was code-named Aspidistra, and its 600kw output was sufficient to reach much of Germany itself from its site in the Ashdown Forest in Sussex. This powerful tool had the additional advantage that it could break into German and Vichy French propaganda broadcasts and make them unintelligible.

PWE faced many arguments with fellow organisations, particularly during the early period when in-fighting and interdepartmental bickering seemed a feature in the background of the clandestine sections of the Allied war machine. But winter 1943/4 marked a turning-point in its fortunes. As the preparations for Operation Overlord, the invasion of France, gathered pace, psychological warfare was made the responsibility of the Supreme Headquarters Allied Expeditionary Force (SHAEF), and the Psychological Warfare Branch (later Division) was created (PWD). But the branch could be formed only by transferring men and materials from PWE and its American opposite number, the Office of War Information (OWI). PWE never recovered from the effects of this move.

Detailed plans for Overlord were prepared by Gen Morgan, Chief of Staff to the Supreme Allied Commander, known by the acronym COSSAC, and were revealed to selected officers of PWE from September 1943. PWE studied three contingencies:

- a weakening of German forces that would permit an attack in the West with existing Allied forces before the date fixed for Overlord
- the Germans withdrawing from the western-occupied countries to shorten their lines of communication
- the unconditional surrender of German forces, with the cessation of organised opposition in the West.

The third contingency would present PWE with an entirely new set of urgent problems simultaneously in all theatres. They involved the control of populations, resistance movements and workers in the Todt ('Death') organisations in friendly countries as well as the problems within Germany itself. The Todt organisations were involved in the construction by forced labour of the West Wall defences, U-boat shelters on the Atlantic coast of France and roads, from northern Norway to southern France and in Russia.

Underlying the plan drawn up by PWE to render maximum assistance to Overlord was the concept that political warfare must exploit and canalise the political ferments behind enemy lines, which could only be done effectively if the highest authorities gave their support to such movements. Included in its aims was 'so to affect the will of the German people and the German armed forces as to make them refuse to continue the war'.

In January 1944 an internal crisis arose within OWI which was eventually referred to President Roosevelt, who rebuked the two adversaries and refused to allow resignations. News of this reached Brendan Bracken, the Minister of Information, who thereupon refused to agree to the integration of PWE and OWI. The result was a period of considerable confusion in both organisations, the effective loss of three months' time, and the loss by PWE of leadership in the political warfare field.

By July the paper shortage that had plagued Britain for years had now reached such proportions that sufficiently large quantities of leaflets could not be stocked to take advantage of the increased airlift now available. Attention was forced to more efficient ways of targeting the leaflets, and at long last the RAF agreed to adopt the Munroe leaflet bomb, which the Americans had been using for some time. The effect was to reduce the scatter of leaflets in the countryside, where they would be less likely to be picked up, and to concentrate them in urban areas with a much greater potential readership.

At the end of 1944 proposals were tabled for messages to be broadcast by enemy prisoners of war (PoWs) as an incentive to make German troops surrender to the Allied armies. The messages, recorded as soon as possible after capture, were to be supplemented with talks by recently converted anti-Nazis, technical talks on the military situation and descriptions of life in PoW camps in Canada. These proposals were developed and led to a special camp being set up at Ascot to house prisoners deemed likely to be useful for political warfare. This in turn led to the Ascot–Brondesbury Scheme, the result of an agreement for the camp to be shared between PWE and MI19, the organisation gathering intelligence from enemy PoWs. Prisoners arriving at Kempton Park Distribution Camp were roughly segregated, those requiring further interrogation being sent to Lingfield Camp. A further selection was made at Lingfield, and those of interest went to Ascot in Surrey, where parties of up to eight willing men were sent to the PWE propaganda working centre at Brondesbury in north-west London.

The German Region of PWE at Bush House in the Aldwych, central London, coordinated the needs of the PWE, BBC, OWI, SOE and OSS (Office of Strategic Services) by arranging access to the prisoners, and MI19, as well as to the Director of Political Warfare (DPW). The talks and songs broadcast by these German prisoners in the BBC German Service grew steadily until the autumn of 1946, over a year after the collapse of the Third Reich, when they were transferred to the Control Commission for Germany. The scheme was deemed a great success, friendly prisoners contributing to the defeat of Nazism and the spread of democratic ideas both in Germany and among their incarcerated comrades.[7]

SPECIAL DUTIES SQUADRONS

The newly formed SOE had to have agents and contacts on the mainland of north-west Europe but was faced with the problem of how to infiltrate them into enemy-occupied countries. The use of fishing and other small boats and submarines was tried in the early days but became too hazardous as a routine method in north-west France and along the English Channel and North Sea coasts. The use of small boats was unpopular with SIS and the Admiralty, which jealously guarded its absolute right to control all seaborne operations. The RAF was reluctant to spare any of its meagre stock of aircraft for the risky task of dropping agents and stores into occupied territory, activities that it saw as of lower priority than bombing. Moreover, the Chief of Air Staff, Lord Portal, wrote on 1 February 1941 expressing strong ethical objections to the methods employed by SOE: 'The dropping of men [*sic*] dressed in civilian clothes for the purpose of attempting to kill members of the opposing forces is not an operation with which the RAF should be associated.'

From September 1940 two elderly twin-engined Whitley bombers were made available to a newly formed corps of airborne troops in a unit called 419 Flight, RAF East Anglia. By February 1941 the unit had expanded to four aircraft, but one was then lost in an accident in April that year. Under pressure from Dalton, SOE's first minister, in the summer of 1941 the flight was expanded again to become 138 Special Duties Squadron, with ten Whitleys and three four-engined Halifaxes. The following March the squadron established itself at Tempsford airfield in Bedfordshire, situated immediately east of the London to Edinburgh railway line and close to the Great North Road. The airfield was shared with 161 Squadron, which specialised in pick-ups from fields rather than parachuting into them.

Tempsford airfield was prone to fog, so operations would sometimes be transferred to other bases. Tangmere on the south coast was the regular departure point for Lysanders going deep into France. From here they could just make the return trip to Lyons.

No. 138 Squadron expanded to twenty Halifaxes, which were then exchanged for twenty-two four-engined Stirlings in May 1944; 161 Squadron had one twin-engined Hudson and seven single-engined Lysanders when it was formed. To these were added five Whitleys and two twin-engined Wellingtons in February 1942, but they exchanged the Whitleys for Halifaxes in November. In January 1944 161 Squadron was equipped with ten Lysanders and five Hudsons, and by May, when it went over almost exclusively to pick-up operations rather than agent- or stores-dropping, it had thirteen Lysanders and six Hudsons.

Chapter 3

THE GERMAN SECTION OF SOE

The German Section of the Special Operations Executive (SOE, or SO2 as it was known at the time) was created on Monday 18 November 1940, and, as was the case with all other country sections of the organisation, it was given a symbol – in this case, X. Just over a year into the Second World War the prospects of infiltrating a victorious and expanding Germany were very poor; indeed, they were never to compare with the opportunities that arose in the German-occupied territories. Reflecting this, the size of the German Section was small: four officers who, till their disbandment, had constituted Section R and Section DZ of the former Section D, the small, unacknowledgeable part of the Secret Intelligence Service (SIS) which, with Military Intelligence Research (or GS(R)) had combined to form SO1, SO2 and SO3, and eventually SOE. The head of the German Section was a Lt Col Brien Clarke, and the group was accommodated at the Inter-Services Research Bureau, the cover name of SOE that was fixed to the sandbag blast wall at the entrance to 64 Baker Street, London.

Among the surviving German Section files is one that deals with an agent who must have been inherited from Section D, for the dates of some of the documents are prior to the formation of SOE in July 1940. What is interesting is that it gives a flavour of the way clandestine operations were being carried out in these early months of the war. The agent, Johannes Jahn, operated through the International Transport Workers Federation (ITF) and had made contact with the British covert organisation in January 1940. 'Y' had informed 'D' (there is no indication of their identities) on 30 January 1940 that an agent had been recruited to sabotage German railways and would require various quantities of flares, signal relays, cigarettes, chlorate of potash, fuses and adaptors. Items such as 'flares', 'signal relays' and 'cigarettes' were obviously code names for forms of explosive or incendiary stores. This parcel, which was to be anonymous and untraceable, had to include simple instructions for use in the German language.

The instructions for delivering the parcel to Johann Eckhardt in Antwerp included his address, the number of the tram from the train station that went near by and the fare of one Belgian franc. The courier was instructed to ring the bell twice, ask for Monsieur Eckhardt and say 'Schöne Grüsse von Brutus' ('Best wishes from Brutus') and, on meeting him, lay a Belgian franc on the table with the king's head face upwards. The two men were then to show each other their respective halves of a cigarette card – the stuff of spy films, but no doubt necessary. Eckhardt's room was in 'the depths of the slums of Antwerp', so couriers were warned to go there shabbily dressed and only in daylight – and certainly not by taxi.

The parcel was duly delivered, and in a letter of 15 April from the ITF representative in Luxembourg that was intercepted in censorship on its way to the ITF headquarters in Kempston near Bedford it was reported that 'During the past week a goods train of 120 axles was completely blown into the air between Aachen and Köln [Cologne].' It added the comment, 'What a good shot!' The statement that a train of around sixty wagons was completely lifted off the rails by an explosion seems very far-fetched, and no doubt the readers in Section D thought so too.[1]

In January 1941 Maj R.H. Thornley joined the German Section as personal assistant to Clarke and within a few months had taken over from him as head of section. Thornley had particular attributes that suited him for this post. Armed with a Cambridge degree in European History, French and German, his pre-war business interests had taken him to Germany, Austria and other European countries. He thus had recent contacts with, and an understanding of, these nations and their peoples.

By November the section had shaken down and responsibilities had been allocated:

- Maj R.H. Thornley – General supervision of German and Austrian Country Sections, liaison with Foreign Office, the SIS and other departments. Supervision of training. Control of 'black' propaganda activities.
- Maj W. Field-Robinson as GSO.2 – Handling of all German contacts, operations into Germany and recruiting of agents.
- Miss E. Graham-Stamper as GSO.2 – Handling of all Austrian contacts and operations into Austria.
- Mrs M. Holmes as GSO.3 – Assistant to Miss Graham-Stamper on all matters, particularly code communications.

Two other men joined the establishment as conducting officers with students at various training schools: Lt Russell and Lt A. Keir.[2]

If the implementation of them was to prove extremely difficult, the aims of the German Section were straightforward: to establish channels of communication into Germany and Austria for the initiation of subversive activities and to build up in these countries a network of agents suitable for carrying out such operations.

The 31-year-old Thornley was soon to encounter a problem that was to hinder the activities of all country sections of SOE. 'C', the traditional designation of the Head of SIS (also known as MI6), proved unable (or unwilling) to give the fledgling organisation any assistance. Early in 1941 the Vice-Chief of the Secret Service (VCSS) had made it quite clear that his organisation could give them neither contacts nor channels of communication into Germany. The VCSS considered SOE's task to be impossible, and as far as he was concerned it followed that there was no point in setting up a German Section. Furthermore, Thornley knew from his own experiences in immediately pre-war Germany that the so-called anti-Nazis were at that time neither willing nor able to undertake subversive activities against the German regime. Now that the Nazi army had been so decisively successful, support for anti-government actions would be even more difficult to muster.

It was clear from the start that the activities of the German Section would be limited compared with those of other sections operating in support of countries occupied by the enemy. There would be no attempt to organise resistance: this was considered bad policy from a long-term viewpoint. The prospects of success for such a venture were poor and suitable personnel too scarce and valuable for the risks involved. Instead, work should be concentrated on subversive activities, sporadic sabotage to alarm the enemy and encourage genuine opposition groups, and administrative sabotage that was thought likely to yield worthwhile results against the methodically minded Germans.

In these early days recruiting agents was particularly difficult. Anti-Nazi émigrés who would at first seem a natural pool of potential agents often proved totally unsuitable, especially those who had left Germany seven or eight years previously and were out of touch with the changed conditions within the Fatherland. The much stronger security apparatus and, following Germany's initial military successes, the support of the general population for

Hitler, presented a more difficult situation within which to work subversively. The first few agents to be trained at this time were faced with the problem of infiltration into Germany. With no help from 'C' and only occasional, reluctant, assistance from the RAF, SOE was forced to arrange its own methods of placing agents through neutral countries bordering Germany and German-occupied territory, in particular Switzerland and Sweden. To achieve this it was necessary to establish German Section representatives in the SOE missions in the important neutral countries. Hence representatives were installed in Berne, Stockholm, Madrid, Lisbon and Istanbul. Special Operations Mediterranean, the infant group to cover operations in this theatre, dealt with contacts in Tangier and Cairo. The German Section's other approach to the problem of establishing channels for the infiltration of agents was to call upon the good services of other country sections to deliver the agent to the resistance in an occupied country for onward transmission to Germany, but this proved understandably difficult, as the groups in both Baker Street and the field had their own, far from insignificant, problems.

From the very start the importance of up-to-date intelligence on Germany and the possibility of establishing links with certain key organisations with access to the country were recognised. As a result, by the end of 1940 the Censorship Department was passing to the German Section copies of all correspondence that came through its hands connected with certain named individuals. One can only speculate who these might have been; but the system worked well. By this same time liaison with the ITF, an essential step in SOE-planned administrative sabotage of Germany's rail network, had been achieved. The following month an officer was attached to the section to liaise between SOE, the ITF and the IFTU, the International Federation of Trade Unions. German trade unions had suffered badly under Nazism, and their master organisation was seen as a likely source of help for the Allies in their efforts to subvert the regime.

In January 1941 the section's first trained agent passed out and prepared to go into the field. But instead of going to Germany, P. Horowitz left Britain for the USA on a special mission, the details of which are not recorded.

One area that was seen as a possible route into Austria and thence into Germany was the Balkans, the volatile region where Serbian nationalist guerrillas were embroiled in a bitter struggle with communist partisans led by Tito. In order to build up communications via Yugoslavia into Austria, two well-qualified agents were fully trained and despatched in February 1941.

But with so much mistrust among the indigenous population, the lives of British agents operating in this wild and mountainous region became particularly precarious. When Germany invaded Yugoslavia in April 1941 Britain offered support to the Serbian guerrillas, who adopted the name of an earlier nationalist movement, the Chetnicks, in their fight against the common enemy.

In their continuing search for recruits, the section set up contacts with MI9, the branch of the War Office Military Intelligence Directorate that dealt with escapes of Allied PoWs. They designed a questionnaire for use when interrogating escaped or repatriated prisoners who might have information of use to them. Arrangements were made for MI9 to keep the section apprised of interesting documents they found during their interrogations – documents that SOE would later be forging for its own purposes.

By December 1941 the German Section acknowledged that it faced three major problems that, for the time being, they could not overcome. Firstly, access into both Germany and Austria, as compared with that into enemy-occupied countries, was extremely difficult; second, organised opposition to the Nazi regime did not exist inside Germany; and third, recruitment of suitable agents was proving almost impossible. The section was therefore forced to temporarily restrict its activities to:

- preparatory work: lines of communication
- administrative and commercial sabotage
- infiltration of subversive propaganda and incentives for isolated dissidents and foreign workers to carry out acts of sabotage.

Ten months later a memorandum from Thornley to CD (or Head of SOE), Sir Charles Hambro, expounded the policy of the section and in particular made the point that direct infiltration on a large scale was considered both costly and useless. Work into Germany would have to be from neighbouring countries. SOE's representatives in Sweden, Switzerland and the Middle East were working under the direction of the German Section in London to establish lines into Germany; and, for the purposes of comparison with other country sections, these representatives and those working under them were to be regarded as part of the London staff.[3]

The section now sought political guidance on its response to an increasing number of clandestine approaches with peace feelers, ostensibly from the enemy, through contacts in various neutral countries. The Allies considered these approaches to emanate directly or indirectly from the German intelligence service anxious to assess the effect on Britain of the Luftwaffe's blitz and the devastating and ongoing U-boat war against Britain's vital transatlantic supplies. For Germany, this assessment had to be seen against the entry into the war against them of the world's most powerful nation, the USA. Although postwar revelations showed at least a few of the approaches to have been genuine and from civilian opposition groups, and some others to be from conspirators in the later 20 July 1944 plot, the decision was taken to ignore them.

Plans were considered for action in the event of a revolution in Germany, an event that was by no stretch of the imagination imminent. Coming at the end of 1942, this could only have been a 'pie in the sky' intellectual exercise, which proposed small guerrilla bands of German nationals, the supply of arms to workers, the use of political propaganda agents and a general appeal to German anti-Nazi leaders.

In September 1943, as plans took shape for the Allied invasion of mainland Europe, SOE was invited by the Chief of Staff to the Supreme Allied Commander (COSSAC) to draft a skeleton directive, part of which was to give 'A general indication of the prospects of developing resistance in Germany and of the lines upon which SOE should work.' SOE's reply was that there was no active, organised resistance in Germany. There had been sporadic examples of resistance, mostly in heavily bombed areas where the normally rigid security was likely to have been disrupted. There had been claims of a number of individual acts of sabotage on railways, communications and minor industrial targets. The same perpetrators also disseminated 'black' subversive propaganda material prepared by PWE. Despite efforts to rouse the huge numbers of foreigners forced to work in Germany, the best that had been achieved so far had been passive resistance and go-slow actions.

The following February Thornley turned his attention to the question of SOE's long-term propaganda campaign against Germany. This presented a serious problem, in that it had to reflect the declared Allied demand for unconditional surrender. At that time SOE and other covert organisations considered that the whole of Germany's high-level fifth column among generals and senior civil servants was being mobilised to create sympathy for their country to bring about the softest peace possible for her. To the German military, unconditional surrender meant deep humiliation; to the civilian population, it meant the fear of a return to a Weimar Republic-type administration and years of hardship and shame. To the German mind as a whole, a rescinding of the unconditional surrender demand would leave the way open to an honourable, negotiated peace. The population at large could not grasp the political reality of letting them get away lightly with the terrible crimes and atrocities committed by the Nazis in the name of Germany. Perhaps they were unaware of the full extent of the torture, death and destruction visited by their regime upon millions of innocent men, women and children throughout mainland Europe.

On 29 July 1944, nine days after the abortive attempt on Hitler's life, Thornley wrote a note to Brig E.E. Mockler-Ferryman, Director of the London Group, within which the German Section operated, on the potential resistance movement in Germany. It is reasonable to assume he was aware of the assassination attempt, since Hitler himself had broadcast to the German nation about it, and Schutzstaffel (SS) and Gestapo sweeps throughout the country cannot have gone unnoticed by Allied agents or neutral newspaper correspondents. In his note Thornley, SOE's expert on German matters,

> pointed out that there was no organised resistance as the Allies understood the term. There were no active resistance groups in Germany such as existed in the occupied countries; nor were these likely to emerge unless the German armed forces suffered a decisive defeat. There were undoubtedly potential oppositional elements that were mostly inactive and unorganised, although minor acts of sabotage had been carried out. These elements may later cooperate to a certain extent with the large numbers of foreign workers in Germany.[4]

He concluded by saying these forced labourers were primarily interested in saving their own lives and ensuring some kind of future for themselves at a time when the security services were in full control and likely to be strengthened. This last observation was to crucially influence the German Section's thinking on operations into Germany.

The likelihood of a viable resistance in Austria was higher, but it would only strengthen and surface if the Allies announced their postwar policy towards that country. Without that, Thornley believed, there was no hope of any large-scale resistance in Austria.

August 1944 saw the German Section no longer part of Mockler-Ferryman's London Group but reporting directly to the Head of SOE, CD, who at this time was Gen Gubbins. He presided over a German Committee that now set out to mobilise all the country sections for work against Germany. At last the German Section was at the forefront of SOE's activities.

Steadily, France was being liberated and the western Allies advanced inexorably eastwards while the Russians drove in towards Berlin. SOE's work in occupied Europe began to be scaled back, allowing more effort to be devoted to its role in the final defeat of Nazi Germany in its homeland. In correspondence Thornley again stressed that there was as yet no organised resistance within Germany but there were undoubtedly latent opposition groups. While these essentially patriotic elements would not wish to undermine their hard-pressed armed forces, if they suffered a collapse the fragmented anti-Nazi groups might coalesce into a cohesive opposition movement. But the experts found it very difficult to forecast what political form such resistance would take.

At this time Thornley's section had a small number of German-speaking coup-de-main parties for small, vigorous attacks and another small number of German-speaking agents under training. Even at this stage, barely three months into the invasion of the European mainland, the German Section was looking forward to the time when the Allies would occupy a defeated Germany. They had several highly trained German and Austrian experts ensconced in neutral countries to build up useful contacts under instructions from London. Thornley visualised these men as being of considerable value in helping to trace and investigate secret German documents and records that would be of essential interest to the proposed Allied Control Commission following the occupation of Germany. In addition, he saw a possible use in organising any counter-action against the German underground movements that were known to be in preparation – a German resistance against the Allies. Through the contacts that they had and would continue to make, these agents and experts were in a position to provide useful counter-intelligence information, especially concerning youth organisations, which were seen as a most likely source of recruits for such subversive underground movements. (It must not be forgotten that SOE worked closely with other Special Forces in the irregular warfare against Nazism.)

In mid-September 1944 Maj Hale of Special Forces Headquarters (SFHQ), the integrated headquarters of SOE and the Office of Strategic Services (OSS) under the Supreme Headquarters Allied Expeditionary Force (SHAEF), submitted a report on the resistance and general situation in Germany based on information supplied by Thornley. This report illustrates the information that was available through agents, neutral sources and the interrogation of PoWs. It dealt with the location of opposition elements in Germany with which SFHQ were in touch; gave examples of the successes achieved in the subversion of German troops by 'black' propaganda methods, including the dropping of malingering instructions; highlighted the disruption to the German economic organisation, stimulated by the dropping of forged ration cards; and tackled the problem of the development of contacts with the millions of foreign workers forced against their will to prop up the Third Reich. This comprehensive report emphasised the need to exploit all forms of discontent in Germany rather than to encourage one particular opposition element which might then get the impression that it, and its further political aims, had the support of the Allies. The internal situation in Germany was still under the rigid control of the Gestapo, preventing serious acts of insurrection. Of equal importance was the general apathy of a civilian population that was becoming increasingly preoccupied with survival against the onslaught of the RAF by night and the US Army Air Force (USAAF) by day.

In the continuing build-up of the offensive against Hitler and his minions, and with the inevitable prospect of bitter fighting across Germany itself, the Chief of Staff asked SOE for a paper showing what the possibilities were of their working into Germany and for a proposed directive to cover their activities up to the end of organised resistance in the Reich. On 21 October 1944, only four days after the Chief of Staff's original request, the Directive for Germany was submitted to SOE.

SOE action into Germany was considered under three phases:

- up to the collapse of Germany or the conclusion of an armistice
- from the cessation of effective German resistance up to the establishment of firm Allied control
- in the postwar phase, starting when Allied control of Germany had been fully established.

During the first phase SOE was to: increase to a maximum its penetration and subversion of Germany; prepare lines of communication from liberated areas; give assistance to Allied governments in preparing their own organisations for combating German underground activity in liberated areas;

seize German documents and records affecting future SOE work and past counter-resistance measures; and prepare for the seizure of similar documents in Germany itself.

In the second phase SOE was to seize documents and records of value for future SOE work; establish contact with elements of the population willing to collaborate with the Allies; and assist Allied forces in organising counter-action against specific German organisations.

Phase three would see SOE officers with the Allied Control Commission supervising counter-action against German organisations and carrying out unacknowledgeable action against underground General Staff or Nazi movement organisations.[5]

Thornley was not entirely happy with the directive, feeling it concentrated too much on short-term activities at the expense of guidance on long-term matters, in particular the threat from Nazi underground movements after the formal end of hostilities. But the end of October saw the climax of the German Section's fortunes, with the formation of the German Directorate, for the further expansion, development and completion of the work it had built up from such austere beginnings.

When the German Directorate was created in the autumn of 1944 the structure was reinforced and the numbers of personnel increased. Five sections were set up, each responding to the director (AD/X): general staff and liaison (X/S), plans (X/Plans), air liaison (X/Air), intelligence (X/Int) and administration (X/AQ). Intelligence was further divided into intelligence, collation and distribution; targets; and preparation of documents.

The deputy director (AD/X1) also responded to the director, but he was responsible for the rest of the directorate. This comprised five sections which had attached to them numerous subsections: German Country Section (X/Ger), Austrian Country Section (X/Aus), Neutral Missions (X/C) and Allied Missions (X/M), the latter's main purpose being to recruit, train and despatch agents to contact foreign workers in Germany.[6] Also answering to the deputy director was the fifth section, dealing with one of SOE's last projects of the war, Deception Scheme Periwig. In direct charge of this was Sqn Ldr H.M. Potter, who was also responsible for the Air Liaison Section. The establishment of the German Directorate had thus expanded tenfold since the initial five persons had set about their difficult and frustrating task almost four years previously.

The German Directorate's objectives were now:

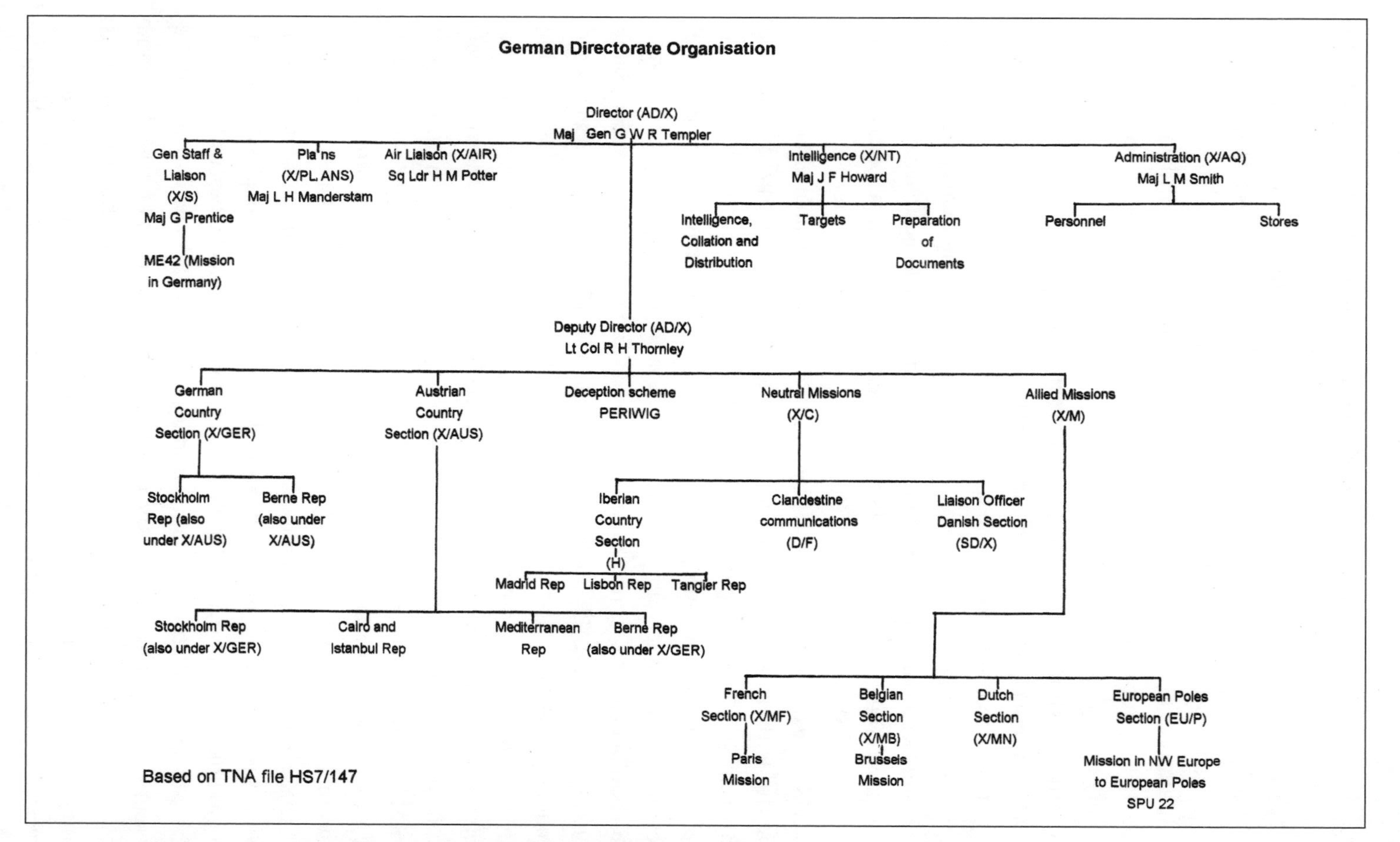

Organisational chart of the German Directorate of SOE. *(Based on TNA file HS7/148)*

1. the 'mass subversion' of Nazi German administration officials in occupied countries
2. subject to SHAEF directives, 'any activity that would cause large movements of people in Germany' or would 'create administrative chaos' through that or other means
3. attacks on Nazi security services, especially the Sicherheitsdienst (SD)
4. the organisation of each country's nationals doing forced labour inside Germany
5. the recruitment from resistance movements of agents who, 'for money or revenge', would be willing later to go into Germany and carry out tasks specifically allotted to them
6. the demoralisation of German troops, ideally leading to mass desertions
7. attacks on any Nazi German assets and holdings in occupied countries
8. the development of new channels to disseminate black propaganda.[7]

With Allied troops now established on the European mainland and headed for the Fatherland, it was important that all operations be coordinated through one body capable of seeing the whole picture. The German Committee set up by Gubbins on 2 August 1944 emphasised this point: all activities by resistance movements, including work into Germany itself, had to be coordinated with conventional military operations, and the responsibility for this lay with SHAEF's SFHQ, whose staff now included members co-opted from SOE and the Office of Strategic Training (OSS). But the OSS was setting up a 'huge' Central European Section on its own. CD therefore considered integration with the OSS impossible if, as he hoped, a purely British SOE was to continue after the war. At the end of September a meeting was held at SHAEF to consider the coordination of SOE and OSS operations in Germany. It was decided that each party was to operate independently under SHAEF, and that Col J.H. Alms of SHAEF should coordinate their activities.

This question of coordination was to present several problems initially. SOE was granted a general clearance for sabotage against German communications, but the coordination of their other activities with those of the SIS and OSS had to come under SHAEF. Thornley was given the responsibility of informing all the other agencies concerned of SOE plans, and Col W.C. Jackson would do the same for the OSS. But the problem was compounded because OSS controlled some of its activities from Paris. To overcome this, a centralised planning and operations staff was set up in

London. But this alone did not solve the problem, since the SIS and OSS were reluctant to reveal details of their future operations, and the latter were in any case subject to last-minute alterations due to weather conditions or military developments. By January 1945, however, the SIS and OSS agreed to provide the German Directorate with full particulars of their forthcoming air operations into Germany, whether mounted from the UK or the continent. With SOE plotting all these on a map and holding monthly clearance meetings, plus being informed daily of alterations to plans, the system eventually worked well enough. Nevertheless, the failure adequately to embrace this directive was to have a serious effect on the execution of Operation Periwig.

From time to time subversive operations of a somewhat special nature emanated from the fertile mind of the head of the German Section and were discussed with other departments concerned. The special nature of these operations seemed to lie in their complexity and political risk. Operation Braddock was not strictly a German Section plan, but since it involved the dropping of very large numbers of small incendiary devices in the hope that disaffected Germans and foreign forced labourers would pick them up and use them, the section was inevitably involved. Only a small proportion of the several million devices manufactured were actually dropped on Germany, the fear being that any drifting close to PoW camps might provoke reprisals against incarcerated Allied men.[8]

Much intelligence was gathered and many plans laid out for the assassination of a few key figures in the Nazi hierarchy in Operation Foxley.[9] The German Section was never in a position to execute the plan, even if it had been sanctioned. What gives an interesting insight into Thornley's character is the statement in the records that 'Despite the contrary view of several members of the Council, Lt Col Thornley and the German Section were strongly opposed to any attempt at a British-inspired assassination of Hitler himself.' This seems to imply that they would not necessarily object to the killing of some Nazi leaders, but not the chief one. The assassination of traitors, collaborators and quislings by SOE agents or SOE-supported resistance groups had gone on throughout the war. In 1942 Reinhard Heydrich, the brutal governor of occupied Bohemia–Moravia, had been killed by SOE-trained Czech agents, but the ensuing vicious reprisals had included wholesale slaughter and the razing to the ground of two entire villages. One wonders what Thornley's attitude would have been to the later proposal of Maj Gen Gerald Templer, head of the German Directorate, to plant important information on agents of German nationality who were then to be infiltrated and deliberately killed to ensure the vital documents fell into the hands of the German security authorities.

Two other special operations are mentioned in the records without any explanatory details. Operation Duffield was supported by all with whom it was discussed but was finally vetoed by the Cabinet Office on the direction of the then Deputy Prime Minister Clement Attlee. The other operation was Longshanks, an attempt to capture enemy shipping in the neutral Portuguese colony of Goa, which failed when the vessels were scuttled by the Germans. However, three anti-Nazi German seamen surrendered to the British and later served on SOE's strength in India, no doubt supplying the German Section with valuable information.

Operation Casement was thought out by SOE's printing expert, Maj Wintle, and his section as part of the campaign to break the German will to resist. It involved the deception of friends, foes and neutrals alike by revealing to the German Army that their leaders had made plans to flee to Eire on a given date. Political sensitivity dictated that Argentina be substituted for Eire. Rumours appeared in the Allied and neutral press concerning preparations for flight by Hitler, Himmler, and others. but they contradicted a major theme of our political warfare against Germany: that Hitler was ruining his country by continuing to fight when defeat was certain, a theme that happened to be true.[10] There was one section (albeit temporary) of the population of Germany in 1944 that appeared to offer the prospect of a very large anti-Nazi and pro-Allied movement. This was the several million-strong foreign labour force that had been uprooted from all the occupied countries and forced to work in mines, factories, agriculture or wherever a need arose due to German workers having been drafted into the armed services. Attempts had been made long before the invasion in June 1944 to contact these workers, but without significant success.

SHAEF was hesitant about laying down a definite policy on foreign workers for the same reasons that Operation Braddock was delayed for so long and eventually mounted in only a token manner: the fear of reprisals. A directive on policy for foreign workers was included in a staff study of the question in November 1944, but it was not issued until the end of the following February. This directed that the clandestine services must at present limit their activities to 'the gradual establishment of communications with foreign workers and their organisation into disciplined bodies'. Foreign workers' action was limited to 'committing undetectable sabotage and presenting a constant threat of overt action'. SHAEF hoped to see these workers in disciplined and organised bodies assisting the Allies in the initial stages of their occupation of Germany.

How justified SHAEF's fear of reprisals was is questionable if the findings of Belgian agents visiting workers' camps in southern Germany are accurate. Their reports indicated that by February 1945 the Germans were already so disorganised that it was doubtful whether they would have been capable of organising large-scale reprisals against foreign workers. But the workers' morale was understandably low, and their general apathy meant they were not prepared to take any action against the enemy. As they saw it, their best chance of repatriation to their families lay in keeping quiet until they were overrun by Allied forces.

Wireless communication with foreign workers was virtually impossible. Instead, contacting agents took with them a list of standard messages to be broadcast on the BBC. It must have been presupposed that someone among the workers had access to a radio that could pick up the BBC Overseas Service. In the event, the speed of the Allied advance meant that the messages were used on only two or three occasions.

Although arms were not to be supplied to foreign workers, the fear of a massacre remained, and at the turn of the year SHAEF suggested that SFHQ might stockpile containers of food and weapons for dropping to the workers if their worst fears appeared imminent. SFHQ was not able to secure all the stores felt necessary; mercifully, none of this reserve supply was needed.

Running through all considerations of the use of foreign workers in Germany was a serious lack of up-to-date intelligence. From December 1944 the German Directorate strove to collect and collate information from various sources. OSS intelligence turned out to be between six and twelve months old; the Polish secret services in London could produce little current information; French and Belgian secret services were encouraged to collate intelligence from their nationals returning from working in Germany or from letters received while they were still held, but it contained insufficient detail to be of use. The Ministry of Economic Warfare (MEW) had little contemporary information to share, but the Political Intelligence Department did manage to provide some. These shortcomings presented a serious limiting factor in making use of what could have been a valuable asset but which was, in reality, a non-starter.

It was now possible to carry out air operations into Germany, albeit on a scale restricted by geographical and political limitations in addition to the disappointing number of volunteers from the German PoW population. The air operations had to be planned with great care and involved a number of different sections within SOE. To reduce the possibility of mistakes, the German Section had drawn up an aide-mémoire or checklist of twenty-four actions needed in the mounting of an air-drop of agents into the Reich. It is interesting to see the steps in the process and the bureaucracy involved in this life-or-death matter. The full document is reproduced in Appendix 4, but in summary the steps were:

1. Decide on priority, technical and tactical possibility of target.
2. Decide availability, training and ability of personnel.
3. Discuss task with operators and ascertain their willingness to volunteer.
4. Complete proposal form and allocate code name to operation.
5. Discuss drop area and procure pinpoints acceptable to Air Ministry and Bomber Command.
6. Discuss with operators their cover identity, documents and personal equipment, including rations, for which 10 days' notice is desirable.
7. Write to X/S with priority in relation to other operations.
8. Attend meeting at Station IX to form technical plan and decide on stores to be taken. [Station IX was the centre of SOE's scientific research and development work at The Frythe, Welwyn.]
9. Arrange conference to formulate complete tactical and technical plan, including withdrawal and communications. Lay on escape arrangements with mission in country of exfiltration.
10. Discuss any specialised preparatory training and establish timetable.
11. Formally advise X/Air at least three days before operation.
12. Formally request star priority.
13. Formally request funds for operation.
14. Formally request packing of stores.
15. Formally request equipment for personnel being despatched by air, including extra ration of chocolate and boiled sweets.
16. Give details of operation to X/Air with date when ready to emplane.
17. Prepare briefing instructions.
18. Send copy of briefing instructions to AD/X and OC Group C.

19. Brief operators and check stores, equipment, documents, etc at least one day before first day of flying period. [A few days either side of the full moon.]
20. Establish at 1100 hr on day of emplanement whether operation is on. If so, arrange for transport and hot meal at aerodrome. Check whether operators can be accommodated at Station 61 [Gaynes Hall, St Neots] in event of late cancellation.
21. Conduct party to aerodrome [RAF Tempsford], carry out final general check and security search immediately prior to emplaning. Remain at aerodrome until after take-off. Remain at Station 61 until confirmation of successful drop. If unsuccessful, stay at Station 61 or return to holding school.
22. If operation is 'off' on first day, submit again for following day.
23. When operation has been completed:
    a) advise Switzerland of exfiltration plans
    b) advise Switzerland/Sweden if postboxes were allocated
    c) send details of operators to SF detachments for records
    d) advise X/S if operators likely to be overrun soon on American front
    e) send copy of financial agreement to D/FIN [Director of Finance].
24. When news is received from the field, send in ATF.15.[11]

The German Section had, of course, to maintain liaison with other official departments of the establishment and the military. Sometimes these relationships were satisfactory; sometimes they were far from it.

Throughout its existence SOE enjoyed less than satisfactory relations with 'C' and the SIS, and the German Section suffered perhaps more than most. They were disappointed by the meagre assistance afforded them, as in the matter of the German identity documents and information concerning German travel regulations, all of which they were eventually forced to obtain through alternative sources. They were also denied information on the German counter-intelligence service in neutral countries, a step that gravely handicapped and put at risk their agents. On the other hand, the German Section was able to catch and hand over to 'C' important German secret service agents who were of great value to him. The section's representative in Stockholm was able regularly to obtain high-value information concerning the activities of the German secret service in both

Sweden and England. The German Section passed this on to an appreciative 'C'. Although Thornley maintained close personal contact with the German Section of SIS throughout the war, and overseas representatives cooperated locally with their officers, there was a general complaint that the information flowed in one direction only, and SOE's German Section received little help in return.

Thornley and Sefton Delmer of PWE enjoyed a close personal relationship in developing 'black' propaganda for Germany. PWE's various Freedom Stations[12] were also used on occasions to pass secret communications, while SOE's man in Stockholm was able to persuade a prominent German émigré to come to Britain where, being under strong suspicion, he was handed over to MI5.

The German Section's relationship with the Foreign Office itself, unlike that with the SIS for which it was responsible, was described as 'close and satisfactory'. They were able to supply the section with information on the political activities of a number of German and Austrian émigrés in various neutral countries as well as England. As is to be expected, very close contact was maintained when the section was dealing with various peace feeler approaches that it received.

OSS was relatively late on the scene and did not set up a German section at their London HQ until early 1944. OSS was not able to be of much assistance to SOE, the reverse being the case. Nevertheless, a good relationship existed both in London and in Stockholm, where OSS had established a mission.

Finally in this list of relationships comes that between the German Section and MI9 and MI19, dealing respectively with PoWs and with escape routes out of German-occupied territories. Both were very satisfactory.

With the end of hostilities in Europe, the German Section, like its fellow sections within SOE, set about the difficult and too-often sad task of tracing the whereabouts, or in many cases confirming the death, of the men and women it had sent into enemy-occupied countries. Officers were sent to 'wander around Europe' examining the records of prisons, concentration camps, hospitals, town halls and anywhere else where a list of those passing through its gates could be scanned for the name of an agent who had lost touch with London.

By June 1945 the following German Directorate agents were still unaccounted for: Koenig, Kuhnel, Mattner, Taplik, Buchtik, Loring, Wiedemann and Penczok, although the last-named was known to be a communist who had probably gone over to the Russians.

Establishing how many men or women were sent into Germany by the German Directorate is not easy. The surviving records of the section list some sixty operations into Germany. Some of the infiltrations were achieved by parachute, some through the lines and some by stowing away on a ship or vehicle bound for Germany. These were by no means solely SOE operations but illustrate the degree of cooperation they were prepared to give to the Army, Special Air Service (SAS) and their American counterpart the OSS, where their particular skills and training could be used. Mackenzie states that during the German Section's existence a total of fifty-four enemy men had been diverted from the mainstream of captives before their existence as PoWs had been officially notified and earmarked to become 'Bonzos' working for the Allies. These men were put under training for relatively simple tasks. Nineteen men took part in eleven operations between November 1944 and April 1945, with a degree of success achieved in nine of them.[13]

Wilkinson and Bright Astley, in *Gubbins and SOE*, claim that twenty-eight Germans were sent into the Reich on sabotage missions, presumably over the full course of the war, and most appeared to have survived.

Angus Fyffe of the Security Section of SOE recalls interrogating two agents who had returned from Germany in late August 1944. With his assistant, Jnr Cdr Skoyles, ATS, he interviewed Weber and Vonderheidt, who had been dropped in the Pforzheim area to destroy railway junctions. With the aid of a 6-inch map Vonderheidt was able to give a very detailed account of their landing, even down to the location of a stream where they had refreshed themselves. After the German surrender Fyffe was sent on an evaluation mission from ME42 throughout Germany and Austria. When he found himself in the Pforzheim area he was able to confirm not only the sabotage to the railway lines but also the accuracy of the agents' reports of their landing near the stream.[14]

As the western Allies advanced across Europe, SOE's experience was put to use in seeking information and securing the buildings in which it might be found. They were very keen to update themselves in all kinds of matters: from the progress achieved by Germany's nuclear physicists to the fate of SOE's missing agents; from any evidence of a German last stand in the redoubt area of Bavaria to details of use in forthcoming war crimes trials of the leading Nazis.

Chapter 4

THE MAJOR PLAYERS

COLIN MCVEAN GUBBINS[1]

Colin McVean Gubbins was born on 2 July 1896 in Tokyo, the son of John Harington Gubbins, the Oriental Secretary at the British Legation. At the age of 6 he was sent to Normanton Grammar School in Yorkshire, a day-boys' school where, as the only non-day-boy, he boarded with the Headmaster, Mr Corbett W. Atkinson. Being the odd one out he came in for some unwelcome attention from the other boys, but this hard period taught him to control his temper, be independent, stand his ground and fight back. After two years Atkinson moved on to Ilkley Grammar School, and the young Gubbins moved with him. Two years later he won an exhibition (award) of £30 a year to Cheltenham College, which had a high reputation for grooming boys for top places at the Royal Military Academy at Woolwich; and this is just what it did for Gubbins. The two-year training course of 1913–14 ended halfway when, sent to Heidelberg to learn German, he discovered Germany was at war with Russia and Austria was fighting Serbia. He found his way back to England the day before war was declared (4 August 1914) and reported back to Woolwich the next day.

Three months later 2/Lt Gubbins, at 18 years old, was posted to Armentières, and in June the following year he was promoted to lieutenant. During the Battle of the Somme (from summer to autumn 1916) he was awarded the Military Cross (MC) for rescuing wounded comrades when a gun was hit by a German shell. In August he was promoted to acting captain; in October he was wounded by a gunshot in the neck and was out of action for eleven days. During the dreadfully cold and wet winter of 1916/17 Gubbins made a number of trips to England for leave and military courses, which culminated in an investiture at Buckingham Palace by King George V.

In autumn 1917, having recovered from being gassed, Colin Gubbins was back in France for the Battle of Cambrai. The war ended for him on 17 April 1918, when an attack of trench fever so weakened him that he was shipped home on sick leave.

The Archangel Expeditionary Force (AEF) had originally been formed to deny Murmansk and Archangel to German shipping, but later it supported the White Russian anti-Bolshevik forces under Admiral Kolchak. In March 1919 Gubbins was appointed aide-de-camp (ADC) to General Ironside, the General Officer Commanding (GOC) of the Russian expedition. This hard, grim and isolated war was almost over by the time Gubbins arrived, and he was fortunate not to experience the worst of the fearsome north Russian winter weather, when river traffic was brought to a halt as the water froze. The evacuation of the AEF began with the thaw in May and continued until 27 September, when the last 5,000 men, including the GOC and his ADC, embarked for Liverpool. Among the things Gubbins acquired during his service in Russia was a deep hatred of communism and all it stood for.

After getting married in October 1919 Gubbins was sent to Ireland in early December. During his three years there he gained valuable insights into guerrilla fighting, was awarded a second-class interpretership in French and was promoted to brigade major. In 1923 he obtained a similar linguistic qualification in Russian at King's College. Then on 2 March of that year, Gubbins, his wife and their young son Michael set sail for India, reporting to Lucknow on 1 April. In the summer he passed another language examination, this time in Urdu.

Gubbins spent two years of his time in India at Staff College, passing out fourth and receiving very encouraging reports. He also used his undoubted ability with languages to assist in some intelligence-gathering. Here he met F.W. Nicholls, later to be his Director of Signals in SOE.

The family, which now included two sons, returned to England in January 1930. After a year Gubbins was sent to the War Office and to MI3(c), the Soviet Section of the Military Intelligence Directorate. From April 1933 to October 1935 he had various training appointments before returning to the War Office and the policy-making branch of the Military Training Directorate.

In July 1938 Gubbins attained the rank of brevet lieutenant-colonel, and, nearing the end of his assignment to the Military Training Directorate, was selected as a member of the British Military Mission that was to monitor the withdrawal of Czech forces from the Sudetenland, which was to be ceded to

Nazi Germany. He found this a distasteful business which confirmed his conviction that Hitler was set on war and left him with a lasting sympathy for the Czechs.

By the autumn of 1938 it was generally believed that Hitler would invade eastwards before turning his attention to the Western powers. In January 1939 the small and obscure War Office section known as General Staff (Research) or GS(R) set up by Gen Adam, the Deputy Chief of Imperial General Staff (DCIGS), as a kind of 'think tank' in 1936, was authorised to expand by the addition of two Grade II staff officers. The first was to be Millis Jefferis, an expert on explosives and demolition; the second was to be in charge of recruitment, organisation and training and Gubbins was selected.

GS(R) was studying guerrilla warfare, its implications for colonial operations and, most secretly, the possibility of providing British support for insurgency in any country of eastern Europe overrun by the German Army. In view of the sensitivity of this subject the studies were carried out under the cloak of the recently formed Section D of the Secret Intelligence Service (SIS).

Gubbins was soon engaged in the writing of secret pamphlets on guerrilla warfare. He found the sheer amateurism, the corner-cutting and the administrative risk-taking of the small group a welcome change from the ponderous procedures and tight purse-strings of the pre-war War Office. He began recruiting men with overseas connections and regular officers with special qualifications who would be useful in any operations behind German lines.

Gubbins made a visit to Poland, Romania and the Baltic States. Training courses were being planned. The tempo was rising as war approached. In July 1939 he was told that on mobilisation he would be chief of staff of a British Military Mission to Poland, responsible, if overrun by the enemy, for the activities of a sizeable Millitary Intelligence Research or MI(R) group (formerly GS(R)). He paid a second visit to Poland, contacted Polish Intelligence and learned that the Germans were expected to invade before the end of August. The problem was now to mobilise the MI(R) elements and get them to Poland in less than two weeks.

The last visit to pre-war Poland was a nightmare. Because of the risks of travelling across Germany the party had to go by ship, plane and train via Marseilles, Alexandria, Athens and Bucharest. On arrival in Warsaw they found that the German invasion had started, the blitzkrieg was in progress and the military situation was changing by the hour. Gubbins had no alternative but to withdraw his Mission. In a little over three weeks since the formation of the Polish Mission in London it had now abandoned its objectives in the face of the lightning German advance and was scattered in Alexandria and Bucharest.

Gubbins arrived back in London with Gen Carton de Wiart on 4 October 1939. The Polish experience had not brought much credit to the Military Mission, and this was reflected in the General Staff's scepticism of the reports submitted. From 20 November Gubbins was in Paris as Head of the No. 4 Military Mission to the Polish and Czech Armies in France. The crucial factor of the procurement and supply of material and its delivery to eastern Europe was being organised in London with the help of Section D. He was recalled to London on 23 March.

At the end of April 1940 Gubbins commanded a force known as the Independent Companies, which was sent to Norway to harass the Germans in their rapid advance northwards. The campaign was a messy affair, brought to an end when the troops were needed for defence of the homeland. Gubbins's command performance and organisation of the evacuation did not go unnoticed, and on his return in mid-June he was appointed to the Distinguished Service Order (DSO).

In the summer of 1940 Hitler launched his air offensive against Britain preparatory to an invasion. While the Battle of Britain raged in the air there was a frantic urgency to provide some defence for our vulnerable isle. As the most knowledgeable groups on subversion and sabotage, MI(R) and Section D had been instructed to create the nucleus of a resistance organisation, but the unorthodoxy and secret nature of the work made them unfriendly with local military authorities, so the C-in-C, Home Forces, Gen Ironside decided that all clandestine operations must be under military control. The job was given to Gubbins.

Estimates of the time available before an invasion would be mounted varied between six and sixteen weeks. Preparations would therefore have to be complete within six weeks at the most vulnerable areas of the country: the south coast and East Anglia. Suitable leaders were recruited from all walks of life, sworn to secrecy and shown how to build hideaways for their equipment and arms. Training in guerrilla warfare was given by officers appointed by Gubbins, and week by week the Auxiliary Units, as they were called, increased. In the end a string of units was set up stretching from John O'Groats to St David's Head, manned by some 3,000 loyal British subjects. The best they could hope for was to delay the enemy and lower his morale.

Their use would be short-lived for their stocks of stores were low and they would be fighting on their own. But these were desperate times and the answers were desperate measures.

As the threat of invasion ebbed, and without any obvious employment prospects in sight, in November 1940 Gubbins was offered secondment to the newly formed Special Operations Executive (SOE), with the rank of brigadier.

Gubbins's initial work in SOE was concerned with training, devising operational procedures acceptable to the Air Ministry and the Admiralty, and establishing close working relations with the joint planning staff. He quickly came to realise that in this immediate post-natal phase of the organisation, training was of paramount importance, and the supervision of day-to-day operations and the establishment of working relations with the Chiefs of Staff Joint Planning Section could be left to Maj R.H. Barry, the head of his Operations Section.

The year 1942 saw changes at the top of SOE, several attempts to abolish it and, in December, Gubbins's promotion to acting major-general and the post of deputy to Sir Charles Hambro, who had succeeded Sir Frank Nelson as chief in May. This appointment carried with it responsibility for operations.

In September 1943 Hambro resigned and Lord Selborne, who headed the Ministry of Economic Warfare (MEW) under which SOE worked, had no difficulty in securing Prime Minister Winston Churchill's approval for the appointment of Gubbins as the Head of SOE (CD) in his place.

Colin Gubbins now became closely involved in the defence of SOE against the sniping and manipulatory manoeuvres of the SIS, the Foreign Office and at times the RAF who were loath to see their aircraft allocated to what they regarded as ungentlemanly warfare whose results, unlike bombing campaigns, were not immediately apparent.

Another development that caused him concern was the rapid growth of the American Gen William J. Donovan's Office of Strategic Services (OSS). This secured ever more influence over areas of traditional SOE involvement, with the associated risks of crossed lines and compromised security.

In February 1944 Gubbins was dealt a devastating blow when his elder son Michael was killed in an SOE operation near Anzio in Italy. His grief was compounded and prolonged by the fact that Michael had no known grave.

After the Allied invasion of France in 1944 it became clear that it would not be long before SOE's work in many occupied countries would be drawing to a close, so Gubbins set about reorganising the German Section of SOE to deal with what he saw as the final challenge in Europe. At the same time, in July 1944, OSS achieved its independence from SOE, an important change that had already happened the previous September for operations in Italy. Donovan had been growing increasingly irritated under the constraints imposed on OSS by both SOE and the SIS for long-standing reasons of operational security.

Gubbins was no doubt disappointed to see the loss of SOE primacy in areas he had worked hard to build up. From mid-1944 work steadily declined. Some members were transferred to South-East Asia, where OSS was establishing a firm foothold. Attention turned to the postwar situation, where he foresaw a need for a clandestine organisation to counter any attempt by residual Nazis or any other faction to initiate another war. All efforts to consider such a body independent of his arch-enemy the SIS came to nothing when Ernest Bevin, the new Foreign Secretary, wrote to Gubbins on 11 September 1945 to say it had been agreed by the Defence Committee that SOE and SIS be placed under a common head, and that head should be 'C' – the Head of SIS.

Gubbins appears to have got on better with ministers than with generals. The Chief of Imperial General Staff (CIGS), Gen Brooke, disapproved of SOE and could not spare the time to deal with matters affecting it. But Churchill's military adviser Gen Ismay did find time to help Gubbins, even while some Whitehall departments were being unhelpful and distancing themselves from SOE. Churchill himself always had a good opinion of Gubbins, although his Foreign Secretary, Anthony Eden, while respecting his ability, was condescendingly hostile to SOE. SOE's minister, Lord Selborne, trusted Gubbins, who also had a good friend in the man he succeeded as CD, Sir Charles Hambro.

Gubbins's appointment terminated on 1 January 1946. For service in both wars he had gained some twenty awards, both British and foreign. He had been appointed CMG in 1944 and was to become a KCMG in 1946. There were now no other jobs in the Army open to him.

On retirement from the Army he became managing director of a carpet and textile manufacturing firm. The contacts he maintained in the countries his wartime work had helped to liberate resulted in an invitation to join the Bilderberg Group,[2] and he was a co-founder of the Special Forces Club. He spent his last years in the Hebrides shooting and fishing and was appointed Deputy Lieutenant of the Islands Area of the Western Isles in 1976. He died in Stornoway on 11 February 1976.

SIR ROBERT BRUCE LOCKHART[3]

Robert Hamilton Bruce Lockhart is a name that crops up in many files connected with clandestine work in the Second World War. He was born in 1887 at Anstruther in Fifeshire and claimed to have not a drop of English blood in his veins. His father was a rugby-playing, Sabbath-observing preparatory schoolmaster. He was educated at Fettes College, where he considered there was too much emphasis on games. As an academic disappointment to his parents he was sent to Berlin instead of Cambridge, where he learned to work, respect institutions and customs other than English ones, and the secret of mastering foreign languages. He then went to Paris, where he cultivated a proper French accent, before returning to England at the age of 20 to prepare for a career in the Indian Civil Service.

In 1908 an uncle who was a pioneering rubber planter in Malaya came home and fired the young Bruce Lockhart with a desire to try his hand at this venture. When he was given an area of land to develop himself, he enjoyed it until he fell seriously ill with malaria and had to be sent home via Japan and Canada.

At 23 he passed the examinations for the General Consular Service and joined the Foreign Office in 1911. The following year he was posted to the consulate in Moscow, the embassy being in the then capital St Petersburg. At the end of 1912 he got married and supplemented his meagre salary by some journalistic work under a pseudonym. He was able to keep his finger on the pulse of industrial unrest in Russia through contacts with British cotton industrialists.

He was favourably impressing his superiors, and at the age of 27 was left in charge of the consulate-general, during which time he sent regular reports on the political situation to the ambassador.

But despite his good work, a romantic association with a Russian woman led to his being 'talked about' in the wrong circles, and he was sent back to England suffering from a 'nervous breakdown through overwork' in order to avoid a scandal. In London in addition to meeting Lloyd George he also encountered Rex Leeper, a Russian expert who was later to work with the Political Warfare Executive (PWE) in the Second World War.

In January 1918 Bruce Lockhart was appointed to lead a small mission to Russia to establish informal relations with the Bolsheviks. He was given no authority, but it was hoped he could obtain diplomatic privileges from the Bolsheviks in return for similar concessions to Maxim Litvinoff, their Soviet ambassador in London, all without any official recognition by the British government. At this time the Bolsheviks were playing the Germans against the Allies and vice versa.

In February Bruce Lockhart met Trotsky for two hours. Two weeks later he had his first interview with Lenin. Amid the confusion reigning in Russia that spring he was also to encounter Sidney Reilly, the British secret agent known as the 'master spy'.

The Foreign Office came under some pressure to recall him but the Foreign Secretary, Arthur Balfour, resisted this, since Bruce Lockhart's ability to get intelligence out of Russia was of more value than his diplomatic talents. The Russians, however, always suspicious, guessed he was primarily a spy and a diplomat second. On 31 August 1918 Dora Kaplan, a social revolutionary, shot and seriously wounded Lenin and the Soviets saw their chance to bring things to a head. Bruce Lockhart and others were imprisoned for alleged complicity in the assassination attempt, which the Bolshevik press referred to as the 'Lockhart Plot'. In reprisal, the British government arrested Litvinoff and held him until Bruce Lockhart was freed.

During his stay in Russia Bruce Lockhart was clearly a valuable contact, fluent in Russian and an astute observer of the Russian character. He sent many warning but unwelcome messages that the revolution was not a temporary phase and there was no chance of the restoration of the Tsars. Some in the Foreign Office considered him 'pro-Bolshevik', others cold-shouldered him; the SIS completely rejected his interpretations of events, even though he was well acquainted with the leading revolutionaries and was even trusted by some until they began to believe he was the tool of a government that regarded them as potential enemies. The information and views he passed upwards were not popular with some influential people and did nothing to further his career. He left the foreign service in 1922 and indulged in some journalism, being the editor of 'Londoner's Diary' in the *Evening Standard* from 1928 to 1937.

Bruce Lockhart rejoined the Foreign Office in 1939. He was the British representative to the Czech government-in-exile in 1940 and Deputy Under-Secretary of State in charge of the PWE from 1941 to 1945. In 1942 he was made a KCMG in the New Year's Honours List in recognition of his work in connection with Operation Torch, the Allied landings in North Africa. Bruce Lockhart's health was not strong during his leadership of PWE. In 1943 he was seriously ill and absent from his duties for a total of five months. The following year he was on sick leave for six months.

Robert Bruce Lockhart died in 1970.

RONALD HOWE THORNLEY[4]

Lt Col Ronald Howe Thornley was born on 5 December 1909 and was educated at Winchester and Clare College, Cambridge, where in 1931 he graduated in Modern European History, French and German. Between university and the outbreak of war his work as a businessman took him to Germany, Austria and other European countries, where he gained considerable insights into these nations and their inhabitants. He volunteered for military service in 1939 and, with his extensive knowledge of Europe, particularly Germany, it is not surprising he was soon on a staff training course at SOE Special Training School 17 at Brickendonbury Manor near Hertford.

When formed in 1940 Section X, the German Section, was led by Lt Col Brien Clarke and run by a staff of only four people, there being thought to be little opportunity for resistance work within Germany. After only a few weeks the leadership was taken over by Thornley, who was to remain there until 30 October 1944, by which time he had fifteen officers and a few other staff. On that date the section became a directorate under Maj Gen Gerald Templer, and Thornley became his deputy. The staff now expanded in anticipation of greater opportunities for work, his central staff rising to twenty-six, others assisting as needed.

After being demobilised on 1 October 1945 Thornley took a position in industry in Hull, becoming the managing director of the Ideal Standard Company. He was awarded the US Bronze Star and the Medal of Freedom with Bronze Palm in 1948. After retiring he lived in the village of Cherry Burton in the East Riding of Yorkshire, where he died in September 1986.

GERALD WALTER ROBERT TEMPLER[5]

Gerald Templer was born on 11 September 1898 in Colchester, where his father was a lieutenant-colonel in the Royal Irish Fusiliers. The young Templer's initial schooling was at home. He was sent to Connaught House School at Weymouth in 1909 and three years later to Wellington College where, as a physically small boy, he was subjected to severe bullying which outwardly he stood up to well but which resulted in his harbouring a life-long hatred of his time there. He applied for entry to Sandhurst and on 16 August 1916 was commissioned as a second lieutenant in his father's old regiment. Although keen to serve in France his youth delayed this, and he was sent instead to Buncrana on Lough Swilly in Ireland.

In October 1917 he served at last in the trenches in France, witnessing episodes of carnage that were to haunt him for the rest of his life. Templer later saw service in Persia, volunteered for secondment to the Egyptian Army (his selection was cancelled owing to the political situation in Egypt), volunteered unsuccessfully for the Iraqi Army and finally sailed for Egypt in 1925.

In 1926 he married Ethel Margery Davie, known to all as Peggie, who was to bear him a daughter in 1934 and a son eleven years later.

After two years at the Staff College, Camberley, Templer transferred to the Loyal Regiment (North Lancashire) as captain in 1930. While in India five years later he was promoted to brevet major and saw service in Palestine before returning to England and promotion to brevet lieutenant-colonel on 1 July 1937.

With the war in Europe looming in October 1938, Templer was given a job as GSO.2 in Military Intelligence at the War Office, a position he was to hold for two years. He could see a place for irregular warfare, especially in the face of the threat to England's freedom. Joan Bright Astley, who worked as his secretary at this time, wrote of him in her book *The Inner Circle*, 'Gerald had a lively interest in irregular warfare, and was one of those who realised and emphasised its potential at a time when many more senior and conventional officers were inclined to regard the whole concept as being in the worst of taste and beneath the contempt of professional soldiers.'

Templer spent some time in France in the desperate days of 1939, returning to raise the 9th Battalion of the Royal Sussex Regiment for home defence duties. It was around this time, mid-1940, that he and key members of MI(R) and Section D helped in the original establishment of Churchill's SOE.

April 1941 saw him appointed Chief of Staff to Gen Montgomery, and a year later he became the youngest lieutenant-general in the British Army. In the summer of the following year he was in command of 1 Division in North Africa, which was soon to start the hard fight up the Italian peninsula.

On 5 August 1944 Templer was commanding the 6th Armoured Division of XIII Corps, the 26th Armoured Brigade, 1st Guards Brigade and the 61st Infantry Brigade in the thrust up Italy towards the Germans' Gothic Line. On his way from Divisional HQ near Arezzo to the front line the edges of the narrow, winding road were strung with white tapes indicating the extent of mine clearance. As the jeep he was driving rounded a corner he was confronted by a 15cwt truck. He hooted and the driver of the truck responded too sharply by easing to the edge of the road. As the jeep drew level with it one of the truck's wheels detonated a mine, and the explosion propelled the wheel into the lieutenant-general's back. He suffered a compound fracture of the first lumbar vertebra and was taken to field hospitals at Trasimene and Naples, where he had two operations before being shipped back to England in a plaster cast. His old friend Gubbins learned of his misfortune and offered him the headship of the new German Directorate of SOE. He formally took charge around New Year's Day 1945 but had already been immersed in the work for several months.

The German Section of SOE, Section X, had been intended to operate as a 'focus for the activity of agents in missions in neutral countries'. Templer, however, knew of many disaffected Germans and saw them as a potential that SOE should make use of. He therefore did not rule out the possibility of SOE operations into Germany following the insertion of the odd one or two, one jointly with the OSS, in September 1944.

According to John Cloake, Templer's biographer, at SOE he felt frustrated by the care that had to be constantly exercised to avoid upsetting the Chiefs of Staff on the one hand and the Foreign Office on the other. He 'couldn't be bothered with all that nonsense' and was outspoken in Gubbins's absence abroad.

Cloake records that a score or so of SOE agents of various nationalities who could pose as foreign workers were dropped into Germany in the closing months of the war. Their brief was to exploit the resistance to the regime rather than indulge in direct sabotage. Most were quickly arrested by the Gestapo. Of more success was the infiltration of German-speaking Danish Army officers run from SOE's representative in Sweden, Ewan Butler. Their task was to lie low and get to know the intricacies of life in western Germany until the Allies arrived, when they would place themselves at their disposal.

Templer's stay in SOE was not long. On 17 March 1945 he reported for duty at Monty's headquarters in Germany. On April Fools' Day the following year he returned to Whitehall. In January 1952 he was sent to quell the communist uprising in Malaya, a job that was to earn him the sobriquet 'Tiger of Malaya'. The climax of his career was when he was appointed Chief of Imperial General Staff in 1955. He retired in September 1958.

Templer was busy with charitable works during his retirement and was responsible for the setting up of the National Army Museum in London. He died in 1979 and was given a fitting military funeral.

'C'

'C', the traditional symbol of the head of the SIS (or MI6), was used during the Second World War by Col (later Maj Gen) Sir Stewart Menzies. Stewart Graham Menzies was born in London on 30 January 1890, the son of a father of independent means. In 1912 his widowed mother married Lt Col Sir George Holford, an officer in the Life Guards, equerry-in-waiting to Queen Alexandra and extra equerry to King George V. Stewart Menzies was educated at Eton, where he was a popular and good athlete but not particularly academic. On leaving school he joined the Grenadier Guards in 1909 but transferred to the Life Guards the following year. While in the Army he acquired a love for horses and hunting which he retained throughout his life.

Menzies came into contact with the intelligence world during the First World War when he was sent to France and, after recovering from a gas attack, he was assigned to an intelligence appointment at General Headquarters (GHQ). His knowledge of European languages helped his flair for the work. He was awarded the DSO and MC and as a brevet major in 1919 was selected as a Military Liaison Officer with the SIS. This was the start of a thirty-five-year career in professional intelligence. He was promoted to colonel in 1932 and retired from the Life Guards seven years later.

He became 'C' and took full command of the SIS in December 1939. The service had been underfunded by successive governments and was ill-prepared for the demands it faced at this time. Expansion and reorganisation had to be embarked upon together amid the complications surrounding the Venlo affair in November 1939, when two SIS officers were captured by Gestapo men in Holland. The whole character of the service changed after Menzies's reorganisation, talented men and women from all walks of life now being recruited. But this was not without its management problems, and he also had some complicated inter-Service relationship problems brought about by the creation of SOE and its American counterpart, the OSS, operating in parallel with and often in the same territories as his own agents.

Menzies was also responsible for the Government Code and Cipher School (GCCS) at Bletchley Park, whose greatest achievement was the breaking of the German Enigma codes. This gave the Allies access to German secrets and was therefore of crucial importance to the war effort, but it was also a highly vulnerable intelligence source which had to be used with great circumspection. In discharging his responsibilities for this security Menzies found himself refusing forceful operational commanders the right to act on leads arising from Enigma decrypts if he thought it might endanger the source. With this incredibly valuable information at his disposal he grew to be influential with the Prime Minister, the War Cabinet and the Chiefs of Staff. He became a member of Churchill's intimate circle of war advisers, which meant he was on call to brief the Prime Minister at any hour of the day or night. As an intelligence man his strength lay in his rapid grasp of operational issues and his discerning management of a network of influential contacts.

Menzies made a significant contribution to the Allied war effort and to establishing Anglo-American and other Allied intelligence alliances. He retired in 1951, by which time the Cold War had accelerated the growth and technological advance of intelligence work. He was appointed Companion of the Bath (CB) in 1942, Knight Commander of the Order of St Michael and St George (KCMG) in 1943 and Knight Commander of the Bath (KCB) in 1951, and he received a number of foreign decorations. He died in London on 29 May 1968.

Due to the secrecy surrounding many aspects of SIS, little information is released about key figures on its staff during their service or even sometimes their lifetime.

Chapter 5

PRE-WAR OPPOSITION IN GERMANY

HITLER'S RISE TO POWER AND THE ESTABLISHMENT OF NAZISM

To understand the difficulties faced by the German Section of SOE in the period following the Allied invasion of mainland Europe in June 1944 it is necessary to look at the situation that had developed in Germany since 1918.

After the First World War Germany considered itself to have been not only defeated by the Allies but also humiliated by the restrictions imposed on it by the Treaty of Versailles. Germany had been forced to accept sole responsibility for the war; to surrender 13.5 per cent of its land including 7 million (10 per cent) of its citizens; its entire Navy; half its merchant ships over 1,000 tons gross displacement and all those of 1,600 tons gross and over; and 75 per cent of its iron-ore deposits. The former provinces of West Prussia, Upper Silesia and Alsace-Lorraine were given up. The Austrian-Germans in Bohemia (the Sudetenland) had to move into Czechoslovakia, and Austria was forbidden from uniting with Germany in spite of both governments being in favour of such a union. The Army was limited to 100,000 men, with very little artillery. A deep zone of fortifications inside Germany had to be cleared away. Germany was banned from stationing troops on its own soil west of the Rhine and from a zone approximately twenty miles east of the river. Germany was permitted neither an air force nor a tank force. In addition, it had to hand over vast quantities of goods and future commercial opportunities. Even private German assets abroad did not escape the harsh demand for reparations. According to John Maynard Keynes, the British economist, the impositions wrought by the Allies were astronomical in their scope and wholly unrealistic of fulfilment.

The new German National Assembly met in the city of Weimar, a city traditionally associated with German literature. The Weimar Republic, as it was known, is widely regarded as having been sympathetic to liberty and emancipation, a flourishing of the arts, and the reconstitution of the German soul after its loss of direction under Kaiser Wilhelm II. It showed itself to be democratic, liberal and pluralistic. Political emancipation and artistic and intellectual liveliness sprang forth.

But the Republic started to buckle under the overwhelming burden of the legacy of the First World War. Some believed those now in government had contributed to the country's defeat, adding to the administration's unpopularity during a time when it attempted to meet the impossible demands on it. In December 1922, when German war reparation payments were in arrears, the governments of France, Belgium and Italy (but with Britain opposing them), determined that Germany was in 'voluntary default'. The following month French and other foreign troops occupied and took control of the Ruhr region, the heart of German industry. Unable to defend itself, Germany saw its economy and currency collapse, causing severe hardship to its people, a significant proportion of them losing their entire life savings through galloping devaluation. In July 1923 an American dollar was worth 353,412 marks; by November it was 4 trillion marks.

Unsurprisingly, amid this hardship was unrest and sedition. Left-wing conspiracies were aimed at turning the Republic into a soviet dictatorship; right-wing putsches sought a fascist regime. Right-wing agitators claimed the ability to restore German independence, honour and greatness through dictatorship, rearmament and conquest; and such claims as these found not a little support at the polls. With the Great Depression of 1929 the right-wing extremists gained increased support against the fear of a communist-Bolshevik alternative. Riots, strikes and pitched battles between revolutionaries and police and Army units added to the deep dismay of the population. The political party most successful in exploiting these conditions was the National Socialist German Workers' Party or NSDAP, the Nazi Party, led by a 40-year-old veteran of the First World War, Adolf Hitler.

The rise of Hitler – 'that Austrian corporal', as President Hindenburg referred to him – and his Nazi Party, with its huge patriotic gatherings with military-style parades and elaborate uniforms, inflammatory rhetoric, displays of flags and even mysticism, appealed to many who wanted change – any change – that might result in a better future for the country. Many powerless democratic opponents of National Socialism felt that Hitler's rocketing rise would soon peak and burn itself out. 'Let Hitler come to power and he will be the first to ruin himself,' they said. When he promised parliamentary rule the Republic virtually collapsed, and he led the Nazi Party into a coalition of power with the German National People's Party: his party had failed to secure an overall majority in the elections. Popular support for the Nazis was less than 38 per cent in free elections and only 43.9 per cent in the face of threats and intimidation at polling stations in the elections on 5 March 1933.[1]

Once in power in 1933, Hitler used an arson attack on the Reichstag building as the excuse he was looking for to take emergency powers. He passed an enabling act that left him free to start the boycotting of Jewish businesses, the disbandment of trade unions and the dissolution of other political parties. His promise of parliamentary rule was quickly forgotten and the concept abandoned. So Hitler had come to power by means of a legal revolution and had set the stage for his totalitarian rule. But his rise was due just as much to the short-sightedness of the voters and the lack of will to oppose him as to his skill in oratory, persuasive propaganda and ruthlessness. In turn this self-generated quietism in the face of government-endorsed violence was tied to Germany's deep-rooted authoritarian heritage and the deferential Lutheran tradition of the Church.

It is not surprising therefore that when the Nazis showed radical initiative and political daring and met with little resistance from a population still trying to eke out a living during a period of severe economic depression, they steadily increased the severity of their political demands and the threats for non-compliance.

Hitler's often stormy relationship with the military could be said to have begun just four days after becoming Chancellor on 30 January 1933. He decided to pay a formal visit to the leaders of the Reichswehr, the German armed forces, men with a reputation for arrogance and remoteness whose allegiance he needed for his imminent plans to seize total power in Germany and for his schemes for future expansion abroad. Many of the younger officers with an eye to their futures were not opposed to his movement, even if unsure of its methods. The old Weimar Republic's home and foreign policies, hamstrung by the rampant economic depression of the time, had lacked resolve and courage, and what the military really wanted from Hitler was a renunciation of the undignified restrictions of the Treaty of Versailles, the restoration of the Army's prestige, real career prospects and significant social change. Many hoped for changes so marked as to be deemed a revolution; this was often the case with young officers who later joined the resistance to Nazism.

Senior officers, to whom the Weimar Republic had never seemed attractive, took a different view. They looked for a regime that would not only sweep away the 'shame of Versailles' but would also reconcile the State and the Army, and once again give the military some political influence. Among these men was Lt Gen Ludwig Beck, the *Chef des Truppenamtes* [Adjutant General] in the Reichswehr Ministry in Berlin, an officer who set himself high standards, endured an austere lifestyle and displayed an exceptional devotion to duty, all of which had contributed to an unusually rapid rise to the rank of general. By 1923 he felt that the social democracy of the Weimar Republic had mismanaged everything and 'stabbed in the back' his beloved Army. To prevent its disintegration a strong leader was needed – a dictator. When Hitler rose to power he had Beck's support; when he became Chancellor in January 1933 Beck said, 'It is the first ray of hope since 1918.'[2] But the political views and professional code to which Beck adhered did not comfortably embrace the new regime, and his support for the new strongman carried with it some latent reservations. Many senior Army officers had serious misgivings about the Nazis' anarchistic behaviour and contempt for the law, the terrorism of the million-strong, brown-shirted Sturmabteilung (SA) and the vulgar ways of their leader, Ernst Röhm, described by one of the officers' class-conscious number as 'not a gentleman but just an ordinary guy'.

Under Hitler's new regime many of the worst features of the Weimar Republic had indeed been quickly abandoned, but in their place were new horrors: the persecution of helpless minorities, growing conflict with the Church (Roman Catholic and Protestant) and censorship of the press, all of which in turn brought increasing suspicion of Germany from abroad, and much more. The police operations of Hermann Goering and Heinrich Himmler in these early months of the Nazi regime put communist and social-democratic leaders under arrest, whereupon their headless parties were helpless. Hitler was received that February by his concerned generals with polite coolness, and despite using all his skills of persuasion he remained ill at ease with them.

The SA under Ernst Röhm extended its violent activities and greatly alarmed not only the 'gentleman generals' of the Reichswehr but the Führer himself. In June 1934, after secret reports spoke of Brownshirts about to stage a revolt, Hitler's private army, the Schutzstaffel or SS, sent out its death squads in the early hours to arrest and execute the plotters, including Röhm himself. The opportunity was taken to kill many plotters and erstwhile opponents of the regime in a demonstration of exemplary terror.

At first the public was horrified by the butchery, but soon it was prepared to dismiss it as the victory of Hitler's forces of order over the savage energies unleashed by the revolution which ended the despised Weimar Republic. Hitler left Berlin and lay low for a while, unsure how the Reichswehr would react to the bloodletting, which had included the murder of two of its generals. There followed demands for an investigation, followed by evasions, prevarications and gagging orders – and then the first signs of the Army's retreat to an emphasis on a soldier's duty to obey. Here started the stillbirth of the embryonic will to resist Hitler's regime. Three weeks later Röhm's ambition for a state built on the SA was replaced by the emergence of a state built on Hitler's SS.

But the events of this period caused a number of Army officers to question their allegiance to the Führer: Col Henning von Tresckow, Gen Franz Halder and Col Hans Oster (see p. 69) to name but three individuals, none yet in a position of power but destined to be influential in later years.

President Hindenburg, Commander-in-Chief of the Armed Forces, died on 2 August 1934 at the age of 87. The previous day Hitler had presented his cabinet with a law combining the offices of president and chancellor; Hitler thus assured his dictatorship. Werner von Blomberg, the Minister of Defence (not yet promoted to the rank of field marshal), on the basis of his power to issue ministerial decrees ordered all officers and enlisted men to swear an oath of allegiance to their new supreme commander, the Führer, Adolf Hitler:

> I swear by God this sacred oath that I shall render unconditional obedience to Adolf Hitler, the Führer of the German Reich, Supreme Commander of the Armed Forces, and that I shall at all times be prepared, as a brave soldier, to give my life for this oath.[3]

The question remains as to whether Blomberg's order was inspired by the Führer and whether either of them realised its likely importance, for it was to have far-reaching consequences in largely emasculating the opposition to Hitler. Henceforth he would have complete power over the Army. In the spring of 1936 he reoccupied the Rhineland, and in so doing he enabled Germans to feel at last some self-respect for the first time since 1918.

November 1937 saw Hitler announce to his top military leaders his intention of invading Czechoslovakia and Austria in the near future and that these were mere stepping-stones to further conquests. He wanted Germany to be self-sufficient which, he claimed, was not possible with the existing population and available land mass. The annexation of these two countries would, it was estimated, provide food for 5 or 6 million Germans. Blomberg, Gen Werner von Fritsch, the Commander-in-Chief of the Army, and Konstantin von Neurath, the Foreign Minister, opposed this proposal, fearing an eventual global conflict. The news of the Führer's plans was said to have 'shattered' the Chief of General Staff, Ludwig Beck, who now for the first time began to criticise his foreign policy in principle as opposed to the detailed objections he had raised in the past through Blomberg.[4] Beck did not agree with Hitler's self-sufficiency rationale and doubted the economic surpluses forecast for the takeover of Austria and Czechoslovakia. His criticism made no difference whatsoever.

The critical reaction of the generals confirmed Hitler's view that he could not rely on the old elite to carry out his plans. In future, meetings with the military leadership would emphasise their oath of allegiance and be solely for them to receive their orders from him.

THE BIRTH OF MILITARY AND CIVILIAN OPPOSITION TO HITLER

In January 1938 a scandal erupted around Blomberg when Goering alleged that the woman Blomberg had recently married had enjoyed a series of lovers. He was soon dismissed. Hitler then assumed 'direct and personal' command 'of the entire Wehrmacht' (formerly the Reichswehr) and transferred over sixty generals in order to bring younger officers to the top. But when he ordered General Staff preparations for the occupation of Czechoslovakia the increasingly concerned Beck started a long-drawn-out duel to dissuade Hitler from going to war.

Then a second scandal descended on the officer corps. Himmler had drawn up a dossier alleging C-in-C Fritsch to be a homosexual. The contents were based upon the highly suspect testimonies of a most unsavoury extortionist named Otto Schmidt. It was later shown to be complete fiction. The injustice meted out to Fritsch marked one of the lowest points in the history of the German military. The spring of 1938 also prompted the first stirrings of organised underground opposition. Groups sprang up in various locations, concerned at the threat posed by Hitler to the country and his blatantly unacceptable behaviour. The groups differed widely but all realised that they were being led towards the abyss and that things could not be allowed to continue.

Although the word was not coined with respect to Germany until after the war, the most prominent officer in these embryonic 'resistance' groups was Col Hans Oster, Chief of the Central Division of the OKW (Oberkommando der Wehrmacht – the German Army High Command) Military Intelligence Office in the autumn of 1938. Another group developed in the Foreign Ministry, led by the lawyers Baron Adam von Trott zu Solz, Hans-Bernd von Haeften, the Kordt brothers, Erich and Theodor, with Otto Kiep and Eduard Brücklmeier. These were joined by Georg Thomas, the OKW Armaments Chief; Gens Wilhelm Adam, Erich Hoepner, Carl-Heinrich von Stülpnagel and Erwin von Witzleben, Commander of the Berlin military district; Chief of Military Intelligence Adm Wilhelm Canaris; and many others. Lawyers Fritz-Dietlof von der Schulenburg and Hans von Dohnanyi agreed with Col Tresckow and many other officers that with the trumped-up Fritsch affair they had passed a watershed. Dohnanyi's concerns at the direction his country was taking went back to Hitler's emergence five years earlier, when he started compiling a secret list of party and State crimes: a list that was to help condemn him when it was discovered by the Gestapo in the late summer of 1944.

The difficulty of releasing the generals from their inhibitions against taking serious action because of their personal oaths of allegiance to the Führer and their ingrained ideals of loyalty and obedience was not lost on Hans Oster. The oath, or *Fahneneid*, had been sworn on the almost sacred regimental colours and carried exceptional weight for an army that numbered the Teutonic knights among its ancestors: men of their word since the late twelfth century. The oath was to prove a serious hurdle for disenchanted officers. If only Oster could demonstrate that Germany stood to be defeated by a major foe, he might persuade the military to act in the interests of the greater whole, regardless of oaths and traditional duties to obey. Oster proposed to inform France and Britain of Hitler's intentions towards Czechoslovakia, in the hope that the West would make clear its opposition to such aggression. His associate, Carl Goerdeler, the former Mayor of Leipzig who had resigned in protest at the anti-Semitism of his councillors, travelled to Paris in March and April 1938 to meet the most senior official in the French Foreign Ministry, Alexis Léger. But the French could not make him out and became suspicious, and he came back with little more than fine words. He caused similar irritation in London, Sir Robert Vansittart, the Chief Diplomatic Adviser to the Foreign Office, pointing out that Goerdeler's action amounted to high treason.

Oster then sent the courageous conservative lawyer Ewald von Kleist-Schmenzin with an assignment from Ludwig Beck. He met Vansittart, Winston Churchill and his very right-wing supporter Lord Lloyd. Prime Minister Chamberlain completely misunderstood Kleist's mission on behalf of the Chief of the German General Staff and missed the last opportunity to prevent war.

Two weeks later, but without any knowledge of Kleist's mission, Oster's second emissary, the industrialist Hans Böhm-Tettelbach, travelled to London and also failed to get his message across. Then Oster asked Erich Kordt, Chief of the Ministers' Bureau in the Foreign Ministry, to draft a letter to the British government requesting a firm declaration of opposition to Hitler's war-mongering. The letter was transmitted verbally to Kordt's brother, Theo, who worked in the German embassy in London. Although Theo Kordt secured an interview with Lord Halifax, the Foreign Secretary, in 10 Downing Street and the matter was discussed with certain cabinet ministers, Britain could not be persuaded to issue a public declaration. The fact was the British were confused and suspicious. These self-declared (to the British) opponents of the totalitarian regime nearly all held posts within it, and the subterfuges and pretences to which they had to resort could not be fathomed by Whitehall.

At the same time Ernst von Weizsäcker, the Secretary of State in the Foreign Ministry, was begging the High Commissioner for Danzig, Carl Jacob Burckhardt, to use his influence to secure a British declaration. In the summer of 1939, at the very last moment, Hjalmar Schacht, Minister of Economics and President of the Reichsbank, had several meetings with Montagu Norman, the Governor of the Bank of England. Fabian von Schlabrendorff (a lawyer and first lieutenant in the reserves), Count Helmuth von Moltke (the lawyer-owner of the Kreisau estate in Silesia), Erich Kordt, Adam von Trott and Capt Ulrich Wilhelm Schwerin von Schwanenfeld (an influential intermediary between military and civilian opposition circles), all made their approaches in London. But without exception their efforts were in vain.

The clearer it became that Hitler was leading Germany into another war, the more numerous his opponents became. The opposition groups in the Military Intelligence and Foreign Ministry were now joined by two more lawyers in the form of Hans Bernd Gisevius, formerly in the Ministry of the Interior, and Count Peter Yorck von Wartenburg of the Reich Price Commission, and by Gen Helmuth Groscurth, chief of the Army intelligence liaison group on the General Staff. All had trusted associates. Lawyer and first lieutenant in the reserves Schulenburg recruited Count Wolf-Heinrich von Helldorf, Prefect of the Berlin police. Oster himself brought Witzleben into this group.

Chief of General Staff Beck's behaviour illustrates the difficulty many of the officer class found in casting aside military tradition and striving to save what was left of the Army's influence over political life. Oster asked Beck, who tried to persuade Gen Walther von Brauchitsch, the Commander-in-Chief of the Army who had succeeded Fritsch, to support a mass resignation of the generals. But Beck was insistent that his name must not be associated with, to him, unsoldierly things like mutiny and government by South American-style juntas. Beck realised the risk that a mass resignation might play into Hitler's hands and give him the opportunity to replace the generals with senior officers of the SS. So he proposed to argue that they were protesting against the party and the SS to save the Führer from them. This was a very risky move when the countrywide popularity of the regime and its leader was considered. The regime, unlike the old elitist order, which struggled to shake off its outmoded conventions, was not constrained by traditional values. Fritsch, privately bitter about the unjust accusations aimed against him, refused to protest because it would have been rude and inappropriate for a person of his social standing. He did, however, plan to challenge Himmler to a duel! Such were the problems of conscience facing the old officer corps.

In August 1938 Hitler took another step to secure his grip on Germany by elevating the SS to a fourth service alongside the Army, Navy and Air Force.

Beck continued his efforts and persuaded Brauchitsch to summon the generals to a meeting at the Berlin headquarters of the Army on Bendlerstrasse on 4 August, at which it became clear that all the commanding generals believed a war would be disastrous for the country. FM Ernst Busch and Col Walther von Reichenau, however, did not consider an attack on Czechoslovakia a prelude to war with the West. Brauchitsch was therefore in such a quandary that he did not raise Beck's idea for mass resignation to pressure Hitler against his warmongering. But Reichenau told Hitler of the meeting: he immediately demanded Beck's dismissal as Chief of General Staff. Eight days later Beck – the 'philosopher general', clever, wise and authoritative – resigned, once again showing the submissiveness and political incompetence of the officer corps. But he was popular and respected, and if there was to be a successful putsch he would almost certainly become head of state.

Beck's successor was Franz Halder, far more capable of taking action than his predecessor, and a man who had personally resolved the conflict between traditional loyalty and the need to topple Hitler. He was soon in discussions with Witzleben, Schacht, Beck, Oster and the Quartermaster-General of the Army, Col Eduard Wagner. Halder was concerned with finding moral and political justification for a coup that would satisfy the general public as well as the Army. He recognised the need for both to be in support if civil war was to be avoided. But Oster and Gisevius had lost patience and were anxious to strike the regime by any means.

Opposition to Hitler and the Nazi regime was by no means restricted to the military. Thinkers among all classes of German society saw where this ultra right-wing administration could lead the country and were fearful. Among them was the Confessional Church, the German Protestant organisation founded in 1934 by Pastor Martin Niemöller in response to Nazi efforts to establish an acquiescent national church. Its clergy, balking at that quarter's deference to authority, spoke out from the pulpit in March 1935 against what it saw as the evils of Nazism. The immediate response, confirming their fears, was the arrest of 700 of their pastors. The following August Hitler's police cracked down hard, with a wave of arrests of the socialist Neubeginnen (Beginning Anew) Group of anti-Nazis.

The spring of 1936 saw the start of Hitler's implementation of his expansionist ambitions with his reoccupation of the demilitarised Rhineland. The world looked on but did nothing. At the same time the Gestapo was engaged in a wide-ranging campaign against monasteries and convents. The conscience of the Church was deeply disturbed: the Confessional Church once again publicly condemned Nazi racial policies. In August the Gestapo continued its suppression of opposition groups with the breaking-up of one of northern Germany's largest groups, the Socialist Front in Hanover, led by

Werner von Blumenberg. Further repression resulted in the arrest of left-wing socialist members of the organisation known as the Red Fighters.

The fate of Julius Leber illustrates the treatment that could be expected by anyone caught opposing the Nazi regime. Born in Alsace in 1891, Leber had a hard, poverty-stricken youth but, with the help of any additional work he could obtain, was bright enough to gain places at Freiburg and Strasburg universities. As a volunteer in the First World War he was decorated and promoted to officer rank. In the so-called Kapp Putsch of March 1920 he led workers in a universal strike during the failed coup.

His working-class origins led him to join the Social Democratic Party (SPD) and from 1921 to 1933 he was editor of the *Volksbote* (*People's Messenger*). During this period he became a member of the SPD parliamentary faction in the Reichstag until the fire of 1933, representing the left wing of the party in debates.

An attempt by Hitler to speak in Leber's home constituency of Lübeck was thwarted by him, much to the annoyance of the Nazis. The day after Hitler became Chancellor there was an attempt on Leber's life, during which one of the attackers was killed. The day afterwards the Gestapo arrested him and thereafter kept him in custody for the next four and a half years, a time he endured with courage, patience and dignity.

On his release in 1937 he tried to make a living as a coal merchant in Berlin but needed to re-enter the political arena in some way so he became involved with the opposition to Hitler, joining the Kreisanerkreis or Kreisau Circle, a group named after the country estate of Count von Moltke. Here he exhibited such high qualities of leadership that he became Col Claus Count von Stauffenberg's candidate for Reich Chancellor if the plot against Hitler succeeded. After years of underground work Leber was betrayed by an informer infiltrated by the Nazis into the banned Communist Party. On 5 July 1944 he was arrested, brought before the notorious People's Court and hanged in October.[5]

Hitler advanced his political aims the following year with his public withdrawal from the Treaty of Versailles. One wonders why, with such obvious signs of the blatantly aggressive nature of the Nazi regime, the international community chose not to exert pressure to bring the dictator into line. The Vatican did speak out (but has been condemned for its silence in later years) by issuing a papal encyclical in the spring of 1938 entitled 'With Deepest Anxiety' attacking Nazi policy towards the Church. The result was the mass arrest of German clergymen and the expropriation of their printing presses and publishing houses.

In November 1936 Hitler had announced his proposals for the annexation of his native Austria to the Third Reich and for 'embracing' Czechoslovakia. The following month any protests from the civilian population were cut short by large-scale operations against left-wing opposition organisations in major cities. Hitler had always opposed communism, the ideology at the opposite end of the political spectrum to Nazism, which he saw as spreading through western Europe as a result of the Spanish Civil War, the Front Populaire in France and many underground groups. He regarded his leadership as a barrier to this menace and used almost any methods to crush left-wing opposition.

1938: ANSCHLUSS, THE SEPTEMBER PLOT AND THE MUNICH AGREEMENT

In Hitler's first demonstration of his power as Supreme Commander of the Wehrmacht, German troops marched into Austria on 12 March 1938 in what was referred to as the 'Anschluss' or political union, in most cases to a warm welcome. Austria-Hungary had been dissolved after the First World War and the Allies forbade Austria's unification with Germany. In his ambition to create a Greater German Empire Hitler was not prepared to let such prohibitions stand in his way. This bloodless invasion proved popular. Cardinal Innitzer and the Head of the Austrian Evangelical Church immediately paid public allegiance to Hitler and called a referendum on the question of the Anschluss: the Austrians voted 99.75 per cent for Hitler. Encouraged by the lack of any effective opposition to this annexation, at the end of May the Führer issued a directive announcing his plans for the invasion of Czechoslovakia. Alarmed at this escalation of dangerous adventurism, and despite a general shrinking of opposition during the heady enthusiasm for a Greater Germany following the Anschluss, committed elements within the military set up links with depleted civilian opposition groups in an attempt to work out a plan of action.

Chief of General Staff Halder asked Oster in the OKW to devise a plan for a coup, providing a focus for the otherwise aimless activities of the conspirators. Adam, Gisevius, Schacht, Schulenburg, Weizsäcker and Witzleben all became involved in the detailed planning, such that by

14 September Witzleben declared the military preparations for the coup completed. But there was disagreement about what to do about Hitler himself. Halder, as Chief of General Staff, held the right to order the coup, but he disagreed with those who wanted Hitler murdered openly. Witzleben did not wish to see their scheming wasted and threatened to take action without Halder's orders.

Around 20 September the inner core of conspirators met to finalise plans. The details were now revealed to a subgroup commanding a force tasked with taking over the Reich Chancellery and arresting Hitler. At a very late stage it was decided that if he was put on trial he would probably be able to portray himself from the dock as the stalwart champion of Germany. A hard core within the inner ring of plotters therefore resolved to create a scuffle during the arrest and to shoot Hitler there and then. Everything stood ready, awaiting the order from Halder.

Then came a bolt from the blue: British Prime Minister Neville Chamberlain announced his willingness to meet Hitler for personal discussions about the crisis. The conspirators' plans crashed around them, and internal doubts and squabbles arose. But no sooner had the plotters been on the verge of dissolution than news of Hitler's reaction to Chamberlain's approach infused them with renewed vigour. Throughout Europe war preparations began. German armour moved up to the Czechoslovakian border. On seeing a copy of Hitler's note to Chamberlain rejecting Britain's offer, Chief of General Staff Halder informed Commander-in-Chief Brauchitsch, who was equally outraged but insisted on seeing the situation in the Chancellery for himself.

During interrogation before the International Military Tribunal in Nuremberg after the war Halder stated that when Hitler had brought this crisis to its peak he would, in agreement with Brauchitsch, have issued the code word leading to Hitler's arrest. Brauchitsch, however, maintained after the war that nobody had approached him with a plan to depose Hitler. Nothing, he claimed, was further from his thoughts than the issue of an order to initiate an uprising against the Führer. He had no intention of allowing himself to be drawn into an anti-Hitler conspiracy. In his view the German people had elected Hitler and were at that time very content with his political successes. Brauchitsch further maintained that before the war neither Beck nor any other general would have had any support from the troops in an attempt to overthrow Hitler.[6]

At the very last moment Hitler yielded to pressure from his Italian fascist ally, Benito Mussolini, to agree to a high-level meeting with Chamberlain in Munich. This news threw everything the conspirators had worked for into question. The result was an agreement allowing the annexation of the Sudetenland by Germany, while the lands inhabited by the Polish and Hungarian minorities were attached to Poland and Hungary respectively. The Munich Agreement was seen by the plotters as a crushing indictment of their political judgement, and in their bitter helplessness the bonds that had drawn them so closely together were broken amid feelings of mutual distrust. Only a small core remained to harbour thoughts of another coup.

Any success of the September 1938 coup attempt would have been contingent upon Hitler going to war against Czechoslovakia, and Britain and France making a firm military response. Later opposition activities suffered from both Hitler's victories and defeats: victories made him popular with the German people and therefore unlikely to be toppled, while defeats gave the opposition the appearance of assisting in the downfall of their own country. The German people at large would have to be convinced of the inevitability of their country's descent into utter chaos under Hitler, a situation that seemed extremely remote to them at this time.

CZECHOSLOVAKIA AND THE DESPERATE DAYS LEADING TO WORLD WAR

On 14 March 1939 Hitler's armies invaded the rest of the Czech lands and the Führer revealed to his generals his plans for the invasion of Poland, the final act that would plunge the country into another world war. Both civilian and military opposition circles renewed their talks of plans to remove the Führer from power and prevent the catastrophe. Among left-wing opposition to Nazism was a group that formed around Luftwaffe 1st Lt Harro Schulze-Boysen and Arvid and Mildred Harnack. Schulze-Boysen had rebelled against his upper-middle-class background by joining minor semi-revolutionary organisations, during which time he edited an anti-Nazi news-sheet. This was to bring him to the attention of the SS and cause him to suffer severe beatings and incarceration in a concentration camp. As a means of avoiding the unwanted gaze of the regime's watchdogs he enlisted in the Naval Air Service. Soon he realised that his work in this arm of the military gave him the opportunity to penetrate the secret departments of the Ministry of

Aviation and establish influential contacts with access to highly classified information.

Schulze-Boysen gradually gathered around him a group of dissidents, mainly communists, who by 1937 were tired of their regular discussion meetings and were looking for more positive ways of acting against the hated regime. They began by assembling secret information about Germany's support for the fascist Franco in the Spanish Civil War and posting it into the letterbox of the Soviet Trade Delegation in Berlin. This found its way to Moscow, which was supporting the other side in Spain.

These hard-core communists, visionaries and dreamers formed primarily an opposition group that printed and distributed anti-Nazi leaflets, posters and news-sheets; as a side-line they also indulged in espionage. But other opposition groups recognised the similarity between Hitler and Stalin and declined to establish ties with them. No doubt as a result of their passing information to Moscow, in the autumn of 1939, under the urging of Alexander Erdberg, a GRU (Glavno Razvedyvatelno Upravlenie) or Soviet Military Intelligence recruiting officer, Schulze-Boysen's group were transformed into a spy ring which the Gestapo were to name the Red Orchestra.[7]

After the failure of the September plot and Hitler's easy occupation of Czechoslovakia, the groups dissipated in deep gloom. When he announced his intentions with respect to Poland, it was almost as if Hitler sensed the dissolution of the opposition in the Army and was intent on denying them the opportunity to regroup. The hard core clung to the notion that a coup would be justified only if Hitler was clearly intent on going to war and had issued the necessary orders. In other words, it would have to be staged at short notice immediately before the troops moved. Oster, Goerdeler, Gisevius, Ulrich von Hassell, the lawyer and diplomat, and the others persuaded former Chief of General Staff Beck to involve his successor, Halder. These two had similar feelings about the basic nature of the regime, Hitler's determination to provoke war and the need to overthrow him. But they disagreed strongly on when to strike, Halder maintaining there would be time enough to depose Hitler once the Polish question had been settled.

Beck maintained he was no longer prepared to watch Hitler accrue piecemeal successes, moving ever closer to the inevitable catastrophe. He considered that when war came, so would more draconian laws, making a coup more difficult. Beck and Oster persuaded Ian Colvin, the Berlin correspondent of the *News Chronicle*, to convey a message to London revealing Hitler's plans to attack Poland. Colvin met Halifax and Chamberlain on 29 March 1939, and a guarantee was given to Poland shortly afterwards.[8] The central conspirators gradually reassembled, only to get bogged down in debate. Gen Witzleben, a practical man with little patience for prolonged arguments, felt there was little chance of a successful coup at that time but had no doubt Hitler would present an opportunity before long and wanted the plotters to be ready. So he set about finding like-minded officers who would be prepared to strike when the moment was right and soon recognised the difficulty presented by a widening rift within the Armed Forces engineered for his own security by Hitler. Witzleben also worked to re-establish opposition links that had been lost following the Munich agreement and managed to succeed in building a broader support for the conspiracy than had existed at the time of the September plot. But his plan had one fatal flaw: war was imminent, but he did not expect to have his network of conspirators ready until the following year. Once the war had started his contacts could be widely scattered and the task of coordinating such a network would be more difficult. On 22 August 1939 Hitler summoned a meeting of Army chiefs to tell them he intended to attack Poland in four days' time, a date that was shortly afterwards postponed when Mussolini revealed his unpreparedness. To warn the British of Hitler's imminent intentions Beck obtained a copy of the minutes of the conference which he passed to Louis Lochner of Associated Press, who gave it to the British and American embassies. By 25 August the papers were in London.

At the time of the rescinding of the order to attack, Schacht, Gisevius and Gen Georg Thomas were on their way to pick up Adm Canaris and drive to general headquarters at Zossen, east of Berlin, where they planned to force Halder and Brauchitsch either to arrest Hitler and his government or arrest the three of them, at which point they would reveal the involvement of the Army chiefs in the opposition. On arrival they encountered Oster happily announcing the rescindment of the order. But did he know it was a postponement rather than a cancellation? Confusion and disagreement once again took over but the predominant feeling that peace had been preserved led to great relief. It was premature, however, and based on a clouded judgement of the situation. Although Hitler had suffered a major diplomatic defeat, his obsession with prestige would force him to go to any lengths to repair the damage.

Among most conspirators there was a mixture of relief that war had been avoided and a sense of deliverance from having to take any action. But as Gisevius maintained, the belief that war had been avoided was totally misguided. The following days saw the opportunity that the conspirators had always dreamed of, but now they were not prepared. Even the written plans for the September coup had been burnt in Witzleben's fireplace when the conspirators feared imminent unmasking. The elation was utterly shattered when, on 31 August, Hitler reissued the invasion order for the following morning. Canaris forecast that this meant the end of Germany.

Ludwig Beck had at first more than acquiesced in the advent of the assertive Hitler. In the prevailing circumstances of despondency and humiliation felt by the German people under Weimar he did not object to his aggressive foreign policy. Nor was he averse to an authoritarian domestic policy if it kept crime under control and provided a foundation on which to build an economic recovery. What did alarm the then Chief of Staff was Hitler's irrationality in strategic military matters that Beck's training, experience and analytical approach told him would not provide the essential prerequisites for a successful war. As his power had increased, Hitler's pronouncements began to exhibit a haphazard quality that convinced Beck of an eventual disastrous conclusion for Germany. Furthermore, the regime's crimes and misdeeds sickened him. If Hitler embarked on war it was, said Beck, bound to end in the country's defeat: therefore he was impelled to do everything in his power to prevent it. He had been unable to persuade Brauchitsch to spearhead a threat of mass resignations of leading Wehrmacht officers to make it impossible for Hitler to carry forward his war plans. He had therefore proffered his own resignation as Chief of Staff in August 1938 in the hope that the gesture would spur others to action. Beck had hoped subsequently to be given command of Heeresgruppe 3, but Hitler decided not to confirm this or any other posting and made it known that Beck lacked the Führer's trust and that he would actually welcome his retirement. Beck formally retired on 19 October.

During these anxious years leading to conflict the civilian opposition included opponents from the political left; members of the aristocracy and bourgeoisie who sought a state based on the rule of law; nonconformists from every corner of the population who had grown to detest the realities of the criminal regime; those who had been persecuted on racial, religious and political grounds and those by reason of their sexual proclivities; and not least the Church, whose opposition was touched on earlier. But however vehement their opposition, it was as nothing in the face of Hitler's complete control of the Wehrmacht, the police and the armed party organisations. The only possibility of action was in cooperation with the opposition within the military and, as we have seen, this was not sufficiently well organised and was unable to renounce its deep-rooted principles. The non-military faction represented a wide variety of professional, political and religious ideals. Many became known only after the war.

One such group operated under the cover of the Mittwoch-Gesellschaft or Wednesday Society, originally formed by Wilhelm von Humboldt as a forum for the exchange of views every other Wednesday between distinguished men from various fields, a kind of think tank. Its members were of mainly conservative background and with experience in senior positions in the economy, the administration, the diplomatic service, the sciences, the churches or from the land-owning aristocracy. Many of these had not initially recognised the criminal nature of the Nazi regime; bitter experience had turned them against it.

Beck became a member of this elite club as a result of having been introduced by Professor Johannes Popitz, the administrative and financial expert who had been appointed Finance Minister of Prussia, a position ranking as a Reich Minister. Beck here met Goerdeler, Dr Erwin Planck, son of the famous physicist, Carl Langbehn the lawyer, Albrecht Hanshofer, a professor of geophysics, retired ambassador Ulrich von Hassell and a number of other well-known people.

These men could see the relentless approach of war more clearly every day. Hitler was bent on taking over Poland, and even an alliance between Britain, France and the Soviet Union was unlikely to change his mind. But the opposition argued that if Hitler was strategically surrounded, an early military defeat was probable and this would provide the right psychological conditions for a military uprising. But before any such alliance was possible, Hitler had outwitted Chamberlain by concluding a non-aggression pact with Stalin, a deal that was to prove worthless when he launched his invasion of Russia in the summer of 1941.

Chapter 6

WARTIME OPPOSITION IN GERMANY

PROPAGANDA, CONSPIRACIES, VICTORIES AND ATROCITIES

The outbreak of war in September 1939 was a huge setback for both military and civilian opposition to the Nazi regime. However intensely they feared the descent into war, the numerous disparate anti-Nazi factions within Germany – including the Solf Circle, the Stürmer Group, the Saefkow Group, the International Socialist Fighting League and the group led by the former Freikorps leader 'Beppo' Römer – had been unable to make any moves to prevent it. Three reasons stand out: the lack of a coordinated nationwide organisation; the failure to gain the majority support of the Army which alone had the necessary power to act; and the inability of any of them to offer the German people a credible alternative to Nazism.

The German people had been 'strung along' by their own militarist propagandists before and during the Nazi regime, showing at that time a surprising readiness to believe the incredible and give importance to the trivial in all matters concerning German national honour and German national guiltlessness for the First World War. Germany was already rearming in the twenties in contravention of their Treaty of Versailles obligations. This was known to the Allies, who did nothing, because France was exhausted and disunited, Britain was in economic depression and the United States did not feel threatened. What was more, the Allies did not consider the aspirations of the militarists were shared by the mass of the population. For example, the revelation that German aircrews were being trained in Russia caused a very hostile reaction among ordinary Germans. Then, when a perfectly legitimate proposal to build a new battle-cruiser was put before the Reichstag, it was forced through only with difficulty: the militarists did not seem to have much support.

The ordinary German wanted peace but at the same time was humiliated by and resentful of the defeat of 1918. The pro-militarist propagandists seized on this. They claimed Germany had been treated shamefully and must reassert herself to restore her honour. They attacked the alternative forms of government: communism as evil in some vague but sinister sense; and democracy as inefficient and weak. By the end of the twenties this propaganda had led to widespread scepticism of the existing system and doubt that Germany could be run efficiently on the lines of the Weimar Republic.

The leaders of the Nazi Party were in the main relatively unlearned men, unaware of the importance of education in governing to achieve national standing in the world. They saw the academic pursuit of truth as a threat to their hold over the German people: anyone who thought for himself was unlikely to support them. Therefore intellectualism had to be discouraged by prohibitions and penalties, and the German people forced to depend on what National Socialist views were fed to them.

The National Socialists were aware of the need to convince the German people of the justice of their cause and their right to wage war in its pursuit. They felt that until any views contrary to their own were eliminated Germany as a country was not entirely ready for action. So they made emphatic and persuasive propaganda about such emotive subjects as the stab-in-the-back legend, the continuing blockade legend, the Fourteen Points legend,[1] and reparations, inflation and world-slump legends. Germany had, according to this propaganda, been 'monstrously ill-used by envious and unscrupulous foreigners' and it was her right and, indeed, her duty to avenge herself.

The propaganda that flooded the consciousness of ordinary Germans at this time glorified war as the best way to avenge their defeat; depicted Germans as a master people, their racial purity giving a sense of pride, strength and unity; and sent anti-Jewish, anti-communist and anti-plutocrat messages to provide a tangible victim for the righteous wrath and also to provide a scapegoat for the National Socialists' own failures. It warned of foes outside their frontiers preparing for a new attack that would threaten their very existence; pointed out that war would therefore be entirely justified on grounds of self-defence and self-preservation; and emphasised that these foes were weak, so the successful outcome of a just war was not in doubt.[2]

Nothing so damaged the credibility of the opposition groups as their failure to take any action before 1 September 1939 when Poland was invaded.

It says something about the attitude of the population at large and the burgeoning police state that only three of these opposition groups formed closer ties and ever posed even a remote threat to the regime: the conservative circle round Carl Goerdeler, the former Mayor of Leipzig, and Ludwig Beck, who had resigned as Army Chief of Staff; the Kreisauerkreis or Kreisau Circle of Count Helmuth von Moltke, with Christian and socialist philosophical views; and opponents within the military with whom were loosely linked other small isolated cells of dissent, sometimes in high places, such as that of Adm Wilhelm Canaris, Head of Military Intelligence, and Ernst von Weiszäcker, Secretary of State at the Foreign Ministry. Indeed it was Canaris who had agreed that Col Hans Oster and the lawyer Hans von Dohnanyi should make preparations to organise the military faction and the political opposition into a proper conspiracy in the event of war. When hostilities broke out Dohnanyi was appointed to OKW Ausland/Abwehr with responsibility for the policy desk of the Central Directorate, putting him very close to the intelligence chief. Oster became Canaris's Chief of Staff and was to coordinate the military faction. Thus on the outbreak of war there was a nucleus from which grew a widespread conspiracy to overthrow the Nazi regime. Col Gen von Hammerstein-Equord, who had resigned as Commander-in-Chief of the Army in January 1934, was known to be a vehement opponent of Hitler and was approached with a view to leading the growing number of dissidents. Now in command of one of the armies stationed along the Rhine, he proposed to Hitler that he should make a visit of inspection to his sector of the front, intending to use this opportunity to assassinate him. In another example of his apparently uncanny nose for danger, Hitler did not accept the invitation: instead he relieved Hammerstein of his command, having long feared him as a resolute opponent.[3]

But nowhere was there to be found a leader who could both evade the all-seeing, all-hearing eyes and ears of the Gestapo and rally the separate groups into a cohesive resistance offering the prospect of a peaceful and prosperous regime. Apart from the three aforementioned groups which did form ties, it is not known to what extent the bands knew of the existence of other opposition factions. The elite Wednesday Society (see p. 80) certainly had widespread contacts throughout Germany, some of which were with other opposition circles. They were even able to select capable and honourable men to replace the regime in the event of Hitler's overthrow. But none of the civilian groups, nor even a combination of them, had the power to do this without the active participation of the Army. And the Army was inhibited from acting by its own principles.

As is usual once war has started, feelings of patriotism, loyalty and other powerful emotions took precedence, and not long after the beginning of September 1939 the will to resist Hitler evaporated. But soon the sheer brutality and the atrocities committed on the eastern front by the Einsatzgruppen (the SS's notorious death squads), which systematically began a policy of indiscriminately wiping out Jews, aristocracy and clergy, caused great concern among the generals there. The senior officers in the forefront of the campaign could not fail to see the horrors being perpetrated; the civilians on the home front knew nothing. Some high-ranking officers complained to higher authority. Gen Johannes Blaskowitz sent a memorandum to Hitler describing the abuses being perpetrated in the name of Germany and expressing his utmost concern. Hitler rejected the complaint, calling it 'childish'. Gen Karl von Rundstedt (not to be confused with Gerd von Rundstedt, who led the German attacks on Poland and France) became horrified at what he found himself involved with on the eastern district and managed to arrange a posting after a short period. Soon afterwards Blaskowitz wrote to Gen Walther von Brauchitsch, the Commander-in-Chief of the Army, about the intolerable moral burden being placed on his troops and officers opposed to the Nazi regime, including Gen Helmuth Groscurth, now Chief of Military Affairs in OKH (Oberkommando des Heeres or the German Army High Command), and then distributed the document to commanders-in-chief of the western districts, arousing great agitation.

Brauchitsch, although alarmed at what was being reported, refused to take any effective action and delegated responsibility for resolving discord to lower-ranking officers, where by chance opposition members were attracting new men to their cause. In January 1940, when Blaskowitz presented him with another, more critical, memorandum, he refused to forward it to either Gen Wilhelm Keitel, now head of the OKW and later to be promoted to field marshal after the successful western offensive, or to Hitler. By May, Hans Frank, the new governor-general of the conquered territories, had Blaskowitz replaced.

The activities in Poland proved a turning-point for many, even if they did not become active in the resistance. But there were also many younger officers who succumbed to Hitler's management of the overwhelming German victory. Nevertheless the haemorrhaging that the resistance had endured between the Munich Agreement and 1 September 1939 was staunched, and a slow recovery began. Furthermore, the opposition to Nazism was no longer based solely on its reckless foreign policy and military risks but also on fundamental moral questions.

RENEWED OPPOSITION, DISMAY IN THE EAST AND TWO FAILED ASSASSINATION ATTEMPTS

After the Polish campaign a protracted dispute arose between Hitler and the Wehrmacht which resurrected the plans for a coup. On 12 September 1939 Hitler informed his adjutant, Col Rudolph Schmundt, of his decision to launch an offensive in the west as soon as possible. Fifteen days later he notified his commanders-in-chief and ordered them to start planning. The entire corps of generals was appalled and inundated Brauchitsch with protests. Nevertheless, the military arguments put to him by, among others, Col Walther von Reichenau and Rundstedt, cut no ice with a reckless Hitler. But these serious political and military concerns, now reinforced by moral issues, led to the rejuvenation of erstwhile conspirators still harbouring thoughts of a coup.

By the end of September Canaris had gained some idea of the officers' attitude to the planned western offensive and the support for the overthrow of the regime. Generals Brauchitsch and Halder discussed the alternatives of either delaying Hitler's offensive as long as possible or working for a coup. Brauchitsch chose the easier, more practical option of delay. Two days later Hitler told him the new campaign would be launched between 15 and 20 November. He replaced some of the generals in the High Command with more competent men and then pursued them in his frenzy to get the next offensive under way, ignoring the tactical advice of highly qualified and experienced officers in favour of his own intuitive decisions and dismissing all objections out of hand. But this very pressure was the catalyst for a group of younger General Staff officers to renew their old connections with opposition figures in the Foreign Ministry and Military Intelligence, where Col Oster had continued to work with support from a now-impatient Canaris. Oster had earlier recruited Dohnanyi and a number of his friends, including Justus Delbrück, son of the historian, Baron Karl-Ludwig von und zu Guttenberg, publisher of the Christian-monarchist *Weisse Blätter* (*White Pages*), and Dietrich Bonhoeffer, the theologian and representative of the Confessional Church, who provided a link to Christian opposition circles. Gen Groscurth, the lawyer Gisevius and former Mayor of Leipzig Goerdeler also remade their connections. But all these conspirators were prepared to subordinate themselves to the retired Chief of Staff Beck, and even their nominal head, Canaris, approved of this arrangement. Such was Beck's stature among this group that further support was forthcoming from Stülpnagel, Col Wagner, OKW Armaments Chief Col Thomas and Hammerstein. Furthermore, confidence in his standing was such that the civilians Goerdeler, Popitz, Schacht, Hassell and Professor of Political Science Jens Peter Jessen all agreed to designate him future head of state of a country that would initially be ruled by a temporary three-man directorate, with Goerdeler and the lawyer-diplomat Hassell, followed by a hard-line government that would not be democratic, that would not have a parliament and would not support the free exercise of civil rights. They rejected the pluralistic system on the grounds that a parliamentary democracy had been partly responsible for the rise of Hitler.

At about this time opposition groups proposed a number of absurd schemes, ranging from missions to Britain and France to discuss peace conditions and working with 'open-minded' circles in the SS, to the restoration of the monarchy. Impatience at the lack of any real revolutionary activity prompted these proposals.

Gens Halder and Stülpnagel insisted that the time was not ripe for action, neither of them, it appears, knowing of a resistance cell within the High Command known as Action Group Zossen, formed in mid-October 1939 by young staff officers in Wagner's circle. This group seems to have been both radical and determined and had drawn up plans for killing Hitler, eliminating the SS and Gestapo, isolating the main centres of power and forming a provisional government. Their co-conspirators appealed to Halder and Brauchitsch to make their move. Arguments were once again marshalled and support for a coup appeared to be rising. Oster, Kordt (in the Foreign Ministry) and Beck spent the evening of 31 October discussing the attitude of the generals. They concluded that Hitler's death was essential. Next morning Kordt volunteered to 'throw the bomb and liberate the generals from their scruples'.[4] Once Hitler was dead their oaths of allegiance would no longer apply and the major hurdle to action would have fallen.

There followed days of hectic activity. When everything was ready all that was required to set the coup in motion was Hitler's command to attack in the west, the order that the generals were convinced would bring about the eventual defeat of Germany. On 5 November Brauchitsch went to see Hitler in one final attempt to dissuade him from giving the order by emphasising the unanimous opposition of the generals. Halder expected the Commander-in-Chief to return from the Chancellery to issue the order for the coup, which only he could sign. Brauchitsch began his presentation with Hitler quietly listening. Before long, however, the Führer flew into a rage, hurled accusations and made veiled references to the 'opposing generals who would be destroyed'. He then left the room, slamming the door. On his way back to Zossen a weary Brauchitsch recounted his stormy meeting, and at the references to the 'opposing generals' Halder panicked. He had been warned by his chief signals officer that Hitler suspected something about the Army High Command. Fearing their plan had been betrayed, he ordered all related documents destroyed immediately. Not long afterwards the order to launch the offensive in the west arrived from Hitler.

The November plot failed because once again the generals involved had not really convinced themselves that a coup was the right action to be taken. In an apparent lack of awareness of, or lack of confidence in, the plans drawn up by the civilians Goerdeler, Hassell and Kordt, they were undecided about how to deliver the fatal attack on Hitler and who should do it; and they could not agree on an alternative government to the one that, regardless of the atrocities being committed in its name, was gaining in popularity with each military victory. The endless debates trying to justify an action became almost an end in themselves. If only one of them who regularly met Hitler – and Gen Groscurth claimed to have taken a pistol in his pocket but could not bring himself to commit murder – had taken the plunge, some change would have occurred and the opportunity the generals were so desperately seeking would have presented itself. As Otto John wrote: 'As a result of the false hopes placed in these "great commanders" the retired generals of the military faction and the dignitaries of the civilian opposition groups held their hands for years until eventually Stauffenberg acted on his own initiative.'[5]

From 1940 a new generation of conspirators emerged, generally younger, less bound by the traditional values of oaths and obedience, and not so concerned about the possible accusation of high treason. In broad terms colonels took over the reins from generals, and in the civilian arena the aristocracy, no doubt fired by pleasant memories of bygone days of influence now virtually lost, formed a substantial proportion of the resistance.

Col Hans Oster agonised long over the inability of the opposition to achieve any success. He came to the conclusion that no coup stood much chance of success while the German people were under the spell of Hitler, for whom political or military defeat seemed so distant. In his desperation he decided to engineer such a defeat by revealing the date of the German invasion in the west to a friend in the Dutch embassy in Berlin. Once more his efforts and the great risk he ran came to nothing: the Dutch, Belgians and British were sceptical of the information and when the date was postponed time after time (a total of twenty-nine times) it was not surprising that their doubts became near certainties. Then, on 10 May, the German troops moved. On 17 June the French government capitulated. In a typically dramatic move, Hitler ordered the same railway coach that had been used for the signing of the 1918 Armistice to be taken to the same spot in the forest of Compiègne, and there a French delegation signed the surrender. In Hitler's eyes, and indeed in those of millions of Germans, the deep humiliation that had descended on them – 'the deepest disgrace of all times' – was expunged. The German population was elated. A Sicherheitsdienst or security service (SD) report on their mood spoke of unprecedented social consensus. Although church groups still showed some opposition, the communists had ceased their activities, partly owing to the recent Hitler–Stalin pact. The remnants of the Social Democratic Party had disintegrated, and a few party leaders joined various civilian opposition groups which offered merely intellectual resistance. Hitler and the Nazi Party were at a high point.

In the absence of any possibility of a broad-based coup, consideration returned to assassination attempts. The lawyer Fritz-Dietlof von der Schulenburg joined his reserve regiment in order to serve the resistance more effectively from within the Army. With theologian Eugen Gerstenmaier of the Kreisau Circle he planned a substantial Commando unit to kill Hitler. But he failed to recruit the 100 soldiers required, and with unit transfers and official business movements exacerbated by Hitler's unpredictable travel arrangements, the plans could not be completed.

In Paris, newly promoted FM Witzleben, with Maj Alexander von Voss and Capt Ulrich Wilhelm Schwerin von Schwanenfeld, hoped to have Hitler killed by a sniper during the parade of German troops down the Champs Elysées. But after many delays the parade was finally cancelled, partly to spare the

French further humiliation and partly for fear of a British air attack. Schwanenfeld also proposed to kill the Führer with a hand grenade when he visited the western front, but he never went to Witzleben's headquarters.

In the summer of 1940 the civilian opposition in the form of Goerdeler, Hassall, Moltke and Beck was increasingly convinced that the Third Reich would not last long. Although they could not deny their impressive military victories, they felt Hitler was being carried away by his success and was unaware that he was seriously overstretching the country's resources. This national conservative opposition began to recover its strength, with Goerdeler at its centre.

There was at this time a great deal of secret discussion about the structure of a system to replace the NSDAP (the Nazi Party); and there was also much disagreement. But for all this the civilian opposition was united in its desire to see the rapid end of Nazi tyranny. The draft constitutions considered at this time form an interesting study in themselves. In some an underlying feeling of helplessness seems to run through them, a legacy from the Weimar years.

While the Goerdeler, Beck, Popitz group was committed to a *coup d'état*, the other main civilian opposition faction, the strongly religious Kreisau Circle led by Moltke, rejected violence and looked towards a post-Hitler Germany. Needless to say, these different views caused some discord between the two groups. Both spent much of their time in intense discussions; neither found an opportunity to do anything of a practical nature.

In spite of the continual disagreements between the two main civilian opposition groups, contacts slowly developed further. Ulrich von Hassell did not embrace the Kreisau Circle's utopianism, but neither did he agree with all that Goerdeler stood for. He believed the two most important opposition groups should not waste effort in arguing about their differences when they and the country were in such dire danger. Hassell's skill as a negotiator drew the groups closer, in the end the majority of conspirators accepting Goerdeler as Chancellor-in-waiting for a transitional government.

While the celebrations over the victory in France and Hitler's self-adoration as 'the greatest general of all time' were still a recent memory, without any warning the research office of Military Intelligence told Adm Canaris the disturbing news that the timing of the western offensive had probably been revealed to the enemy by a German officer. The monitoring service had eavesdropped on Dutch embassy telephone conversations with the Hague and had decoded telegrams from the Belgian ambassador containing incriminating references. Suspicion fell first on Josef Müller, a Munich lawyer who, at Col Oster's request, travelled several times to the Vatican in attempts to contact the British government; and then on Oster himself.

Canaris was deeply upset by the mounting evidence against Oster, but he continued to protect both men, even though Hitler had taken a personal interest in the matter and had ordered him to conduct an investigation with Reinhard Heydrich, Chief of the SS. With incredible skill Canaris, the master of the art of obfuscation, manipulated the inquiry into his own hands and then, at great personal risk, allowed it to quietly drop.

On 21 July 1940 Hitler ordered the High Command to begin thinking about renewing operations in the east by the autumn. He was dissuaded from such an early date and was obviously concerned about the problems of wars on two fronts at once. He later told OKW Gen Alfred Jodl the problems in Europe would have to be ironed out in 1941, as the United States might well intervene in 1942. He met with 250 senior officers on 30 March 1941 to outline the type of war he proposed to wage.

Col Henning von Tresckow was headquartered at Army Group Centre at Posen (Poznan) at the time. At first he had been an admirer of National Socialism but very soon realised what a mistake this had been. Earlier in his career it had been said that he would end up either as Chief of General Staff or a mutineer. When the western offensive had been under heated discussion he urged his uncle, FM Fedor von Bock, Commander-in-Chief Army Group B, FM Gerd von Rundstedt and the strategist FM Erich von Manstein to take action against Hitler. They didn't want to hear about it.

It is an interesting commentary on the long-established loyalties between members of the officer corps that many must have known of the intense anti-Hitler feelings of their colleagues and wrestled with the knowledge in the light of their oaths of allegiance to him. But denunciations were rare, the exceptions being FM Manstein and Gens Wilhelm Keitel and Heinz Guderian, who were prepared to betray their fellow officers provided the fact of their having harboured the knowledge was not used against them.

Tresckow began his plans for a coup when preparations for the attack on the Soviet Union had got under way. He arranged for the transfer of like-minded officers to all the key positions in the Army Group Centre staff. In addition to Fabian von Schlabrendorff, Col Baron Rudolph-Christoph von Gersdorff and Maj Alexander von Voss they also included Maj Count Carl-Hans Hardenberg, Maj Bernd von Kleist and Lt Count Heinrich Lehndorff, all three of Prussian descent. They were later joined by Lt Col Georg Schulze-

Büttger, 1/Lt Eberhard von Breitenbuch, and Georg and Philipp von Boeselager. Thus the largest and most tightly knit resistance group of the time was in the General Staff of Army Group Centre.

Tresckow, along with many other officers, had been appalled when Hitler issued the decree on military law and the so-called Commissar Order,[6] decrees that would transform military justice for the civilian population of conquered Russia into a mockery. When he saw the decrees Tresckow immediately flew with Gersdorff to appeal to FM Bock to take Gerd von Rundstedt and Gen Wilhelm Ritter von Leeb, Commander of Army Group C, to see Hitler and disavow their obedience to him. Bock considered such a venture useless. Instead he sent Gersdorff to OKH headquarters in Berlin with a message protesting against the orders. There he discovered the High Command agreed with him and that Gen Brauchitsch had tried to get them rescinded or altered on several occasions. Each time the Führer had flown into a rage.

Opposition from the Army would not, of course, prevent the infamous SS Einsatzgruppen from operating behind the front line. Lt Gen Dr Arthur Nebe, who had had loose connections with opposition circles since 1938, was now leader of Einsatzgruppe B in Army Group Centre area, a post he had finally accepted in order to act as a resistance mole in the innermost sanctums of power in the SS. Nebe proposed to report his missions as carried out when in fact they had not been.

After almost a year FM Bock agreed with FMs Kluge and Weichs and Gen Guderian, even though the latter has been described as 'a narrowly professional soldier of the worst sort',[7] that it was 'undesirable' for the decrees from Hitler to be carried out. The Commissar Order was officially rescinded. But what was important to many opposition officers was that Hitler had attempted to make the Army an accomplice to his murderous crimes and they had not been able to muster sufficient feeling to give him a definitive refusal. Now the Army and the *Einsatzgruppen* became inevitably involved one with the other, criminalising everyone.

Another opportunity for the generals to demonstrate to Hitler the limits of his power had passed them by. Although the majority were aware of what criminal activities were being imposed on them, there was no senior commander determined enough to gather fellow generals and protest as a body.

Hitler launched Operation Barbarossa, his campaign against the Soviet Union, in the early hours of 22 June 1941. Despite his string of victories so far the mood of the German people was one of shock and dismay that their leader had torn up his pact with Stalin in such a cavalier fashion, and many recalled the fate of Napoleon, whose campaign succumbed to the vast Russian spaces and unbelievably harsh weather.

The atrocities continued even more brutally than in Poland. Officers besieged their superiors with demands for a halt to the massacres. Relations between the officer corps and their Führer, never more than cool at the best of times, deteriorated rapidly. The resistance gathered strong new support, and it was at this time that Stauffenberg decided he must do everything possible to remove Hitler and overthrow the regime (see p. 97).

The professional soldiers and Hitler were at loggerheads about how to pursue the Russian campaign after the initial swift advance had started to open up long lines of supply. Rumours spread of tensions at Hitler's headquarters, and this buoyed the resistance further. Gens Thomas and Alexander von Falkenhausen, military commanders in Belgium and northern France, went to Brauchitsch and found him at last receptive to their ideas. But then, late in 1941, the terrible Russian winter engulfed the troops, and the General Staff had to devote all their time to providing for their survival. Planning for a coup was forgotten for the time being, even when Hitler dismissed Brauchitsch and took over supreme command himself.

In the middle of this dreadful Russian winter Hitler declared war on the United States on 11 December 1941, and it became clear to the conspirators that the worldwide coalition of forces now available must inevitably overwhelm the Third Reich. The old questions of when it would be best to strike, after a victory or after a defeat, met the same answers: the most favourable time externally was necessarily the least favourable internally.

During the summer of 1942 German forces once again made significant advances in the Soviet Union. After further heated exchanges Hitler dismissed Gen Halder and the resistance felt they had lost their last contact within the highest levels of the military. Despite having many experienced officers in its ranks, most of its time had been spent on theorising and very little on planning and organising – the familiar story throughout the German opposition movement from the very outset.

Resistance at this time could be seen as having three main centres: the field army, the home army and the civilian groups; and all were working under the tremendous difficulties created by the police state. But in spite of these problems notable recruits were still found, such as Gen Friedrich Olbricht, Head of the OKW General Army Office and Acting Commander of the reserve army.

A civilian protest that so alarmed the Nazis that they subsequently executed four of the ringleaders and others in the group was staged by a small band of Munich students who went by the name of the White Rose. They finally acted, albeit not violently, by speaking out vehemently against the regime and the moral paralysis of the German people by daubing slogans on walls calling for the overthrow of Hitler. They found like-minded students in Berlin, Stuttgart, Hamburg and Vienna. On 18 February 1943 Hans and Sophie Scholl were detained after throwing leaflets headed '*Die Weisse Rose*' (The White Rose) from the gallery of the atrium in Munich's Ludwig-Maximillian University. The leaflets protested against the senseless continuation of the war and the tyranny of the German 'subhumans'. The Nazis were stunned by this outrage and convened the People's Court under its notorious President, Roland Freisler, for a special session. The Scholls, Christoph Probst and their music mentor the crippled professor Kurt Huber, plus other members of the group were sentenced to death and executed. Sophie Scholl believed her death would trigger a popular rising against the regime. There did follow another demonstration – of loyalty to the regime, just two hours after Sophie's death.

Throughout 1942 Col Tresckow planned not only the assassination but the follow-up coup, assisted by Gen Olbricht, former Mayor Goerdeler, Col Fritz Jäger, Capt Ludwig Gehre, Col Alexsander von Pfuhlstein, the lawyer Gisevius, FM Witzleben, Lt Gen Beck and Capt Friedrich Wilhelm Heinz, who was to have led the attack on the Chancellery in September 1938. Although Treskow had at least three assassination plans prepared, the opportunity that presented itself was to get a time bomb aboard Hitler's aircraft. The Führer visited the Army Group Centre at Smolensk, about 250 miles west of Moscow, on 13 March 1943, and during lunch Treskcow asked Lt Col Heinz Brandt, one of Hitler's entourage, if he would mind taking a package containing two bottles of Cointreau back to headquarters on the flight. They were, he said, part of a bet he had made with the diminutive Col Helmut Stieff at Hitler's eastern headquarters in Rastenburg. At the airfield the delay device, a 30-minute time pencil, was activated and the package handed to Brandt by Schlabrendorff just before the four-engined Focke-Wulf FW 200A 'Condor' aircraft departed. The conspirators went back to Smolensk to await events. But nothing happened. All their test firings of the device had come to nothing. Tresckow had somehow to recover the package. He telephoned Brandt to tell him there had been an unfortunate mix-up and Schlabrendorff would come on the daily courier flight next day to exchange the packages. This he did, and on examination of the bomb the most likely reason for its failure was thought to be that the package had become unusually cold in the cargo hold when the heater failed, and although all the other components appeared to have operated correctly, the explosive, which was sensitive to low temperatures, had failed to detonate.

Gen Olbricht's plan for a coup following the assassination was based upon Operation Valkyrie, a strategy that had been devised by Olbricht's staff for dealing with the possibility of internal disturbances by the millions of foreign workers compelled to prop up Germany's industry. The plan called for the rapid mobilisation into fighting units of the reserve army, soldiers on leave, trainees, training staff and cadres. Now it was to be used to take over key positions in the country in response to an announcement of Hitler's assassination 'by a treacherous group of party leaders in order to seize power for themselves'. This plan relied on a great hoax to be carried out by officers and troops obliviously following orders.

Eight days after the failed attempt Hitler was due to open an exhibition of captured arms and ammunition as part of the annual Heroes Memorial Day ceremonies. Col Gersdorff was at that time a counter-intelligence officer at Army Group Centre headquarters and had demonstrated his commitment to the cause by procuring the explosives for Tresckow's attempt and testing them with him. He was prepared to go to extreme lengths to rid Germany of its tyrannical leader. As he was to lead a small group accompanying Hitler round the exhibition he decided to carry in his overcoat the bombs that had failed to explode on the aircraft the previous week, this time fitted with 10-minute fuses. But Hitler had a habit on such tours of inspection of making a sudden detour from the official route. Whether this was to try to catch out his hosts by appearing unannounced in an unprepared area or was the result of a highly developed sense of security, one will never know. The fact remains that he spent only two minutes in the exhibition. The horrified would-be assassin managed to take the device into the toilets, where he had to defuse it rather quickly.

THE TIDE TURNS AND TRESCKOW MEETS STAUFFENBERG

In November 1942 the war reached a turning-point: as Churchill said, 'not the beginning of the end' but more 'the end of the beginning'. Montgomery was victorious in the Battle of El Alamein and the Allies landed in Morocco and Algeria. It was also plain that Germany's U-boats were being defeated in the Atlantic. By February 1943, when the German Sixth Army capitulated at Stalingrad, Hitler's mood became ominously quiet, and the population at large realised at last that he was not a superman.

On the eastern front Tresckow had befriended FM Kluge to the extent that he tolerated the opposition activities and sometimes supported them. Kluge began to discuss the removal of Hitler, although he preferred the deed be achieved by an 'accident' or a civilian, or at least an officer from outside his area. While strolling with Kluge, who now agreed that Hitler must be eliminated, Gersdorff confessed to him that he had made an attempt only recently. Kluge was astonished, and throughout that summer did more than ever to support the plotters. He sent Gersdorff to try to persuade FM Manstein to take part in a joint action. Although Manstein fully agreed with Kluge's concern about the course of the war, he refused to cooperate, trotting out the old clichés, such as 'First and foremost I'm a soldier', and 'Prussian field marshals do not mutiny'. But when at the end he was asked if he would agree to become head of the Army General Staff after a successful coup, with Prussian rectitude he replied, 'Field Marshal Manstein will always be the loyal servant of a legally constituted government.'[8]

In addition to rumours that had come his way, Adm Canaris had been given several warnings about the suspicions harboured by Himmler concerning the loyalty of Military Intelligence. On 5 April 1943 a legal officer and an SS *Untersturmführer* arrived unannounced to arrest the lawyer Hans von Dohnanyi on suspicion of currency violations, corruption and even treason. But in the course of the arrest he was heard warning Col Oster to destroy some notes. This immediately placed suspicion on Oster, who had failed to destroy incriminating papers as ordered by Canaris when he became aware of the risks of being unmasked. Oster was placed under house arrest and dismissed from his position in Military Intelligence. This was a great shock to the resistance, made worse by the arrest the same day of Dietrich Bonhoeffer, Dohnanyi's wife, Josef Müller and another Military Intelligence officer. Among the papers seized during Dohnanyi and Oster's arrests were notes about the relations between the German opposition and the Allies, and the possibility of contact to negotiate a last-minute peace agreement.

As we have seen, the late thirties saw several attempts to initiate peace negotiations and avoid the war. Amid confusion, suspicion and fear Britain had studiously ignored all approaches, even going so far as to ungraciously refuse to acknowledge some of them. Since the early forties fresh attempts had been made by Theodor Steltzer, a key member of the Kreisau Circle, via contacts in Stockholm. When it became known that Bishop George Bell of Chichester would be attending a church function in Stockholm, Dietrich Bonhoeffer and Pastor Hans Schönfeld independently travelled to meet him on behalf of Helmuth von Moltke, the 35-year-old great-grandson of the Field Marshal, Chief of Staff in the war of 1870. He was half-English in upbringing, a sincere Christian gentleman, but also a serving member of the Abwehr and hence able to make frequent visits abroad, possible only with official sanction. He was far from the type of person to be a conspirator. Bell submitted a report to the Foreign Office on his return, but Foreign Secretary Anthony Eden decided it would not be in the national interest to respond to the approach. Bell made a second attempt to interest the Foreign Office but was again met with a rebuff. Alas, Bell was an unsuitable emissary in Churchill's eyes because the cleric publicly disapproved of the policy of area bombing.

These approaches must have meant that the British government was well aware of the existence of an opposition in Germany, and yet it decided to ignore it. Perhaps it was seen as a political complication. One commentator maintains that the British could not free themselves from the suspicion that those attempting to establish contact were traitors, and therefore untrustworthy, or Nazis in disguise. But Britain's alliance with the Soviet Union was indeed a problem in this respect, and they were keen not to jeopardise it. This aspect of Anglo-Soviet relations was to resurface in deliberations about Operation Periwig in the latter months of the war.

The Casablanca conference of January 1943 marked a turning-point in the political stance adopted by the Allies and consequently in their attitude to the German opposition to the Nazi regime. US President Roosevelt and Winston Churchill publicly declared they would pursue the war relentlessly until they achieved unconditional surrender. In effect they were closing the door on any form of negotiated peace.

This was another serious setback for the opposition in Germany. They could well recall Ludendorff's efforts to avoid the German Army being labelled 'defeated' in the 1918 armistice negotiations. Once again key members were consumed by guilt: this time that to support Germany's unconditional surrender was to betray their own country. Only a few members could bring themselves to go that far in wartime. Desperate as they were, the resistance realised at last that they should stop looking westwards for help: they were on their own. To the reasons for their eventual failure – errors, inhibitions, over-theorising, clumsiness, indecision and the much greater power of the Nazi regime – must be added this abrupt dismissal of what it mistakenly believed must be on offer from the Allies: moral support.

Canaris had narrowly avoided exposure in the enquiry by the SS into Military Intelligence. Dohnanyi, Bonhoeffer and Oster escaped with being indicted for a few non-political offences. But despite his undoubted skills at covering up the incriminating evidence, Canaris sensed that the regime still harboured misgivings about his fiefdom and it must only be a matter of time before fateful changes would be imposed on it. There followed a period of intense depression for the movement, many members dropping out in despair. But Tresckow, Olbricht, Hassell, Popitz and Goerdeler continued to inspire others, and now that the tide of war was clearly turning, with the failure of the panzer offensive at Kursk, the Allied landing in Sicily and the overthrow of Mussolini, all within July 1943, they took renewed hope. Tresckow managed to convince Col Stieff, with whom he was supposed to have had the 'bet' that resulted in the 'Cointreau bomb' being placed in Hitler's plane, and the only conspirator with regular access to Hitler, to renew his pledge to take part in an assassination attempt. But Goerdeler, once again leaning on his unshakeable belief in the power of reason, now argued against such an attempt.

In August 1943 Tresckow met a young lieutenant-colonel, Count Claus Schenk von Stauffenberg, who had lost a hand and several fingers and wore a black patch over one eye following a low-level attack by an Allied plane in North Africa the previous April. He was due to take up the duties of Chief of Staff of the German Army Office on 1 October. He was just what the resistance lacked: a man of infectious energy, idealism and pragmatism. He was familiar with the reasons action so far had been somewhat limited but had not lost sight of the basic point that under a totalitarian regime there must be limits to loyalty and obedience to authority. He firmly believed that when the German government had been overthrown the Allies' insistence on unconditional surrender would be set aside and an honourable peace could be negotiated. Buoyed up by this, he was determined to act at all costs.

Chapter 7

THE GERMAN OPPOSITION'S FINAL FLING

FOUR FAILED PLOTS AND DISAGREEMENTS AMONG THE GROUPS

Col Henning von Tresckow and Count Claus Schenk von Stauffenberg started planning in earnest in early September 1943. They worked at great risk, for they had to involve an increasing number of officers in their plans so that at the appropriate moment the relevant forces would rise up and carry out the orders allotted to them in this grand strategy. No sooner had the preparations been completed than Tresckow was transferred back to the front. Thus it was left to Stauffenberg to take the initiating action. The problem he faced was to find an officer who had both access to Hitler and sufficient determination to kill him. Col Helmut Stieff took possession of the explosives but tended to cool to the idea and asked for an accomplice. While Stauffenberg searched for a suitable person Stieff proposed an attempt using two young men on his staff, Maj Joachim Kuhn and 1/Lt Albrecht von Hagen. As they looked into the practicalities in more detail, Stieff again backed off, considering it impossible to carry the explosives into a meeting with the Führer without being noticed.

Stauffenberg made contact with a reliable young officer who had been deeply affected by witnessing a massacre of Jews in the Ukraine. Capt Axel von dem Bussche did not hesitate to accept the invitation to kill Hitler. He proposed to initiate the fuse on the bomb, leap on Hitler at a uniform presentation ceremony and hold him till the device exploded. Bussche travelled to the Führer's headquarters at Rastenburg in East Prussia (the so-called Wolf's Lair) to await the presentation. But repeated delays and the destruction of the uniforms in an air raid meant an unacceptable postponement and the attempt was abandoned, Bussche returning to the front where he was to be severely wounded and so disqualified from further attempts. During his long hospitalisation he carried the bomb in his suitcase until a friendly comrade threw it into a lake for him in the autumn of 1944.

Stieff's explosive also proved embarrassing. He delegated its disposal to Kuhn and Hagen, who buried it beneath a watchtower in some woods. They were spotted by a military police patrol but managed to evade them. The subsequent enquiry was, fortunately, assigned to a close confidant of Oster and so came to nothing.

Stauffenberg persuaded Lt Ewald von Kleist to make the next attempt, again during the presentation of new uniforms. This officer's father was none other than Ewald von Kleist-Schmenzin, who had travelled to London in 1938 to meet Vansittart and Churchill, and who, so strongly did he feel, was enthusiastic about this proposed suicidal action of his son (see p. 70). Once again the plan failed owing to the repeated postponement of the presentation. Next, Stauffenberg's adjutant agreed to do the deed but was dissuaded by his brother on religious grounds.

Yet again the plotters were beset by pangs of conscience, concerns about the Führer's security arrangements, and difficulties in obtaining explosives and disposing of them if the plans failed, all of which led to anguish and despair among the conspirators. In their desperation some of the plotters advocated just getting on and shooting Hitler, accepting the remote chance of survival or escape afterwards. Cavalry Capt von Breitenbuch agreed to do this, and when he was summoned at short notice to a briefing meeting at Hitler's headquarters on the Obersalzberg (the so-called Eagle's Nest) in Bavaria he took a pistol in his pocket. But at the last moment the SS man admitting the party to the room announced that adjutants were not to be present.

There were a number of other attempts that failed, but little is known of their detail as almost all the participants were discovered and executed. One account relates how Stauffenberg proposed to take a bomb into the Wolf's Lair at Rastenburg on Boxing Day 1943 but was dissuaded by Beck and Olbricht. As it happened, the meeting was in any case cancelled at the very last moment.

Stauffenberg joined the active opposition after the best opportunities for an assassination had passed. Now he had to struggle against a State security apparatus that was taking a much greater interest in the opposition following its raid on Military Intelligence, as well as pessimism and fatigue among the plotters.

Tresckow, desperate to escape from his inactivity as a conspirator, applied for several posts that would bring him into contact with Hitler. But his reputation in personnel quarters for a 'negative attitude' prevented his serious consideration for any of them.

Meanwhile, in December 1943 the Gestapo had homed in on the Solf Circle, a group that supported persecuted people and those forced to live underground. This was a group formed around Hanna Solf, the widow of the former ambassador in Tokyo. Arrests of group members occurred on 12 January 1944. A week later Count Moltke (of the Kreisau Circle – see p. 73) was arrested. On 11 February Canaris was dismissed and imprisoned while Himmler began dismantling Military Intelligence preparatory to taking it over for his own purposes. The State security apparatus had started an intense clamp-down.

Popitz, the Prussian Minister of Finance, now attempted to engineer a coup from within by discussing with none other than Himmler, who was beginning to doubt Germany's ability to win the war, the possibility of his taking on some of the Führer's work in order to lighten his load when it was so clear he needed his talent to deal with the most pressing crises. Himmler absorbed the subtle blandishments and suggested another meeting soon. It did not occur. It is not known what Himmler thought of the proposal. It is possible that the head of security initially regarded every suggestion as suspicious. Perhaps he discussed it with Hitler who continued to show an apparent sixth sense about his own safety. Popitz did not have another meeting with Himmler, but the anti-Nazi attorney Langbehn was arrested and Popitz was subsequently increasingly marginalised within the civilian resistance. The coincidence of Popitz's extremely risky meeting with Himmler to attempt to 'help' the Führer and Langbehn's arrest cannot have gone unnoticed in opposition circles and no doubt raised questions, however far-fetched, about his loyalty. In the end Popitz, like so many others, was to pay the ultimate price for his resistance to Nazism. Goerdeler, at Stauffenberg's urging, abandoned Popitz. Morale was again at a low. The circle had been 'blown apart' according to Hassell, and everything was 'going to hell'.[1]

Carl Goerdeler, forever confident in his powers of reasoned argument, maintained his opposition to an assassination and even requested the Chief of General Staff Kurt Zeitzler, Gen Halder's successor, to arrange an interview with Hitler, or a radio broadcast debate between them, during which he would persuade the Führer to resign merely by the forcefulness of his arguments. This naive and unrealistic initiative failed and aroused contempt from the determined and practical Stauffenberg.

The disagreements that spread throughout the opposition produced serious and pronounced divisions within it. Little by little the resistance tore itself apart in controversies that bore no relation to the world they were trying to change. The majority support Goerdeler had enjoyed a year before had now evaporated.

Discussion during the early summer of 1944 concerned foreign policy and how the Allies would respond to a coup. The conspirators found it difficult to believe that Britain and the United States would not enter into some kind of negotiated peace. For a while they pinned their hopes on the Soviet Union and a comment by Stalin that 'the German people would remain' after individuals like Hitler had gone. The Soviet leader had made an encouraging move by approaching the German resistance through contacts in Stockholm and through the National Committee for a Free Germany established in the previous summer near Moscow by German PoWs and emigrants. Like the abortive attempts to make worthwhile contacts in the west, these were soon undermined by suspicion and distrust. This inherent difficulty with the Soviets would surface again when it was decided by the British and Americans not to make Stalin aware of certain SOE operations which it was felt were likely to be misunderstood in the east.

The communist-inspired opposition was largely separate from the rest. Many of the most ardent anti-Nazis equally feared the possibility of a regime at the other end of the ideological spectrum and hence distanced themselves from the group that became known as the Red Orchestra (see p. 77). This group grew from small beginnings in the mid-thirties to be taken under the wing of the GRU (Soviet Military Intellence), whereupon it spread through Germany to Belgium, Holland, France and neutral Switzerland as a solely intelligence-gathering organisation. In August 1942 117 Red Orchestra members were arrested by the Gestapo; 76 were accused and 46 received death sentences. Such was their alienation from other resistance groups that these events aroused little feeling among them.[2]

By the end of the war the Red Orchestra had had 217 agents and informers arrested, of whom 143 met untimely deaths through execution, murder, suicide or in concentration camps; 74 members survived to experience the problems of a divided Germany.[3]

In June 1944 Germany's military fortunes took two devastating blows: the Allies invaded occupied France, and four Soviet groups broke through the

German line between Minsk and the Beresina river and destroyed twenty-seven German divisions.

Tesckow was once again urging immediate action against Hitler while Stauffenberg believed they had lost any bargaining position they may once have held. They had reached the point of no return, beyond which a coup would be a futile gesture without any hope of a negotiated peace. Tresckow returned a messenger to Stauffenberg with the exhortation that assassination must be attempted, come what may. The German resistance 'must take the plunge before the eyes of the world and of history'.[4]

STAUFFENBERG'S FINAL ATTEMPT

Stauffenberg began his final planning for the assassination. He was promoted to colonel on 1 July 1944 and took on his new duties as Chief of Staff to the commander of the reserve army, a position that gave him access to Hitler. Despite the obvious risks, when Stauffenberg first met his new boss Gen Friedrich Fromm, he intimated that he was considering a coup. Was this a sign of lax security within the resistance or was the unspoken desire for a coup almost universal in the officer class? Fromm was an opportunist but could not be persuaded to join the conspiracy. On 7 June Stauffenberg had accompanied Fromm to the Berghof in Obersalzberg, where Hitler seemed 'in a daze' following the Allied invasion of Normandy. A month later he returned to the Führer's headquarters and this time took a bomb with him. Goering and Himmler, whom the conspirators wanted eliminated along with Hitler, were not present, which may have explained why the bomb was not detonated. Stauffenberg discovered that Col Stieff would be presiding over the long-postponed presentation of new uniforms the following day, but when he invited him to resume his role, Stieff declined. Stauffenberg's resolve hardened, until he believed himself to be the only person to carry out the deed.

The plans called for meticulous preparations, absolute security and complete obedience by all involved. And yet even at this late hour Stauffenberg's fellow conspirators started to engage yet again in deep philosophical discussions, becoming entangled in a hopeless web of professional codes of honour, ethical maxims and religious strictures. Stauffenberg, on the other hand, had lost patience with this debating and had convinced himself that it was his duty to liquidate Hitler and his loathsome regime by any means. There were still some, notably Goerdeler, who wished at this desperately late hour to try to negotiate an armistice in the west. If only he and the retired Gen Beck could go to France he would use his talents to persuade German commanders there to offer a truce to the Allies, allowing them to pour into Germany. This, he hoped, would stop the advance of the dreaded Red Army from the east. Beck and Stauffenberg both turned down the plan as impractical, a decision reinforced by the news that the British ambassador in Madrid had reiterated the Allies' position that hostilities would cease only with the unconditional surrender of German forces on all fronts. The total military disaster so long forecast by the opposition now looked inevitable.

As the plotters completed their plans with an ever-widening circle of contacts they became only too aware of the growing security problem. For example, Wilhelm Leuschner, the leading socialist conspirator and trade unionist, and non-socialist leaders Jakob Kaiser of the Christian trade union movement and Max Habermann, the President of the German Office Workers' Association, had been setting up a broad network of opposition cells throughout Germany to give support for the coup. The larger the network became, the greater the risk of the security services, who were now very active, discovering a member. Death sentences had been passed on members of the Solf Circle; Col Wilhelm Staehle, a close contact of Goerdeler's, had been arrested; Julius Leber, the determined left-wing conspirator who had spent over four years in a concentration camp, and Adolf Reichwein, educator and leader of the opposition's youth movement, were arrested in early July. These were people 'in the know', and it was impossible to say how much they might be forced to divulge to their police interrogators.

On 11 July Stauffenberg once more took a bomb with him to the Führer's headquarters at Obersalzberg. The other conspirators were put on the alert, but when Himmler failed to show up the attempt was called off again. The next four days were spent in refining the plans. Numerous Army units had to be ready to swing into action immediately, and this placed enormous importance on rapid communications for the conspirators and a shut-down in communications for the regime.

The next meeting with Hitler was on 15 July at the Wolf's Lair in Rastenburg. Both Stauffenberg and Gen Olbricht were desperate to carry out the assassination this day whether or not Himmler was present. But Chief Army Signals Officer Gen Erich Fellgiebel, Col Stieff and Col Wagner were adamant that the *Reichsführer-SS* should be present. There are differing accounts of why this attempt joined the list of failures, but no attempt was made to detonate the bomb. Faced with the resistance from Fellgiebel, Stieff and Wagner, Stauffenberg had phoned Berlin to speak with other members of the group in the hope of getting a consensus to carry out the attack despite Himmler's absence. After wasting a precious half-hour on uncoordinated exchanges, illustrating yet again how much his fellow plotters were obsessed with endless discussion and debate, the majority voted for a postponement.

The next evening a group met in Berlin to explore once again various aspects of the plot. At the end Stauffenberg pledged to act next time, come what may. Almost immediately the group was alarmed to learn that the State security apparatus had become interested in various members: from within the SS Lt Gen Dr Nebe warned Gisevius that Goerdeler was about to be arrested; a rumour was circulating in Berlin that the Führer's headquarters was to be blown up that week; and Schulenburg reported that two men who he did not think were harmless had been enquiring about him in his neighbourhood. These reports must have put the final seal on Stauffenberg's determination to waste no more time. At the next opportunity he would act.

At the Wolf's Lair on 20 July 1944 two bombs were available, and one can only speculate why Stauffenberg placed only one beneath the heavy conference room table. Some accounts state he was disturbed while preparing them and only just managed to conceal one in his briefcase. The building in which the meeting with Hitler took place was of light construction, which also helped to dissipate the energy of the explosion. Had both bombs been detonated simultaneously it is estimated that almost all those present would have been killed. As it was, several were badly injured but Hitler escaped with minor injuries.

The most frequently cited of the many reasons for the failure of the 20 July plot is the 'amateurism' of the leaders: ineffective planning, blind trust in the chain of command and poor coordination among the participants. However much analysts examine the plans and the actions which did and did not take place after the explosion, the success of the plot depended on two things: the assassination of Hitler and the interruption of all communications from the Wolf's Lair. When the assassination attempt failed, the second condition could not be maintained for long.

The brutal and far-reaching consequences for the conspirators and for many innocent people are well known. Stauffenberg, Olbricht, Haeften and Mertz von Quirnheim, a friend of Stauffenberg who was deeply involved in

Operation Valkyrie and present at Bendlerstrasse that evening, were all arrested and shot on the night of 20 July. Four others committed suicide rather than be arrested. Around thirty men were subject to show trials by the People's Court and most were hanged within a few days. The families, including children and grandparents, of the key members of the plot were rounded up and sent to concentration camps.

But what was the immediate reaction of the German people and particularly of the military? Given the widespread criticism within the Army of Hitler and the Nazi regime, it is surprising that not one officer who had been aware of the plans for an uprising decided to join the conspirators on impulse. When the radio announcements proclaimed Hitler's survival and that 'legal' authority remained in his hands, most officers turned on the plotters as insurgents or traitors.

The widespread manhunts and endless trials that followed 20 July were well publicised. A second wave of arrests in mid-August took the number of alleged opponents of the regime detained to around 5,000. But the publicity surrounding the trials was revealing the reasons behind it, something the regime did not wish. On 17 August Hitler forbade any further reporting of the trials. Eventually, not even the executions were publicly announced.

But now a curious and indeterminate thing happened. Just as the conspirators were resisting barbaric torture and interrogation, the Allies appeared to offer the Gestapo answers to its questions. 'British' radio began regularly broadcasting the names of people alleged to have been involved with the coup. Moreover, Capt Schwanenfeld was shown a leaflet claimed to have been dropped by the Allies that heaped scorn on the plotters. Both of these events just might have been hoaxes by the Gestapo aimed at making the prisoners feel they had nothing to lose by confirming the details of the broadcast and leaflet.

In September Ernst Kaltenbrunner, Head of the Imperial Security Headquarters (RSHA) and responsible to Heinrich Himmler, reported that his investigations into the 20 July plot were largely completed and he did not expect any fresh revelations. Within a few days more papers were discovered dating back to 1938 that clearly showed the conspiracy not to be the work of a few disillusioned officers, unhappy with the way the war had swung against them. The roots were within the highest ranks of the Wehrmacht, and their motives were far more complex than had previously been thought. Kaltenbrunner's second report was far more enlightening and caused an alarmed Hitler to place severe restrictions on its use. One of the conclusions reached by the Gestapo was that the attempts of the diverse resistance circles to build a united front had produced 'a political monstrosity', and the only matter in which they were united was their rejection of National Socialism.[5] Direct attempts on Hitler's life were many, as we now know, and he survived them all. Peter Hoffmann, the German historian, cites at least twenty planned attempts between 1935 and 1945. Some were made to combine opposition groups into more powerful units, but they never succeeded.

According to Joachim Fest in *Plotting Hitler's Death* the German resistance was virtually ignored by the Allies. In the House of Commons Winston Churchill went further by referring to the failed plot as 'a murderous internecine power struggle'.[6] Yet at this very time SOE was examining in detail methods of assassinating Hitler in Operation Foxley and had, indeed, considered such a plan for the previous three years.[7] Was Churchill's condemnatory dismissal of a major event in the war an attempt to dissuade any other would-be assassins from killing the dictator whose irrationality was now playing into the hands of the Allies? The plot has been described as an expression of possibly widespread feelings on which only a tiny minority was prepared to act. It is also said that Nazi propagandists and Allied spokesmen disparaged both its motives and accomplishments. But however brave the plotters were, what exactly did they accomplish? Fest writes that the arguments which demanded to be resolved among the resisters and the endless rounds of discussions resulted in 'inaction that in retrospect makes the German resistance look like nothing more than a passionate debating society'.[8] A further illustration of the Allies' apparent contempt for the German opposition was the fact that after the end of the war many Army officers who had been involved with it were kept in captivity for longer than those who had played no part in it. It was apparently felt that a person who had strong enough feelings to operate against Hitler could just as easily make trouble for the Allies in the initial stages of their struggle to set up a democratic Germany.

In attempting to understand these attitudes it has to be borne in mind that anti-Nazi Germans were rarely pro-Allied. Furthermore, it is almost impossible sixty years later to appreciate the ethics, traditions and ingrained loyalty that prevented these men from simply killing the despicable Nazi leadership early in the war. The conspirators' clear sense of conscience and morality gave them a black-and-white outlook on the issues at stake. With their partiality for abstract theorising and elaborate intellectualism this, as we have seen, led to indecision and inaction.

There was lack of support for the military plotters among the general population, much to the disappointment of many Army generals. But these were men of high social rank who had little to do with the common people. The attempt to bridge the gap by means of the network of former trade union members was insufficient to break down the social isolation of the resisters. They were also unsuccessful in finding a way to make the general population aware of the regime's criminality.

When one compares the German resistance with that in the Nazi-occupied countries it is clear how the latter succeeded. They represented only a tiny minority of the population but managed to build movements that could count on support from the rest. They had a clear purpose. They did not have to wrestle with torn loyalties, broken oaths or concerns about treason, and they had no need to indulge in interminable debates about the form of a future government.

Just how accurate was the information assembled by Lt Col Ronald Thornley, SOE's expert on Germany and the Germans? It is fair to assume his information from SIS and German PoWs who had encountered opposition groups would have shown a picture of some fragmented dissidents. But it is clear that in his view the situation within Germany was not conducive to an attempt by SOE to set up and exploit a resistance movement. If he had had to hand the picture we have today, would it have made any difference to his judgement of the situation? With the benefit of hindsight one can see that there were a number of disillusioned Army officers, many hamstrung by the oath of loyalty to Hitler, but the likelihood of their taking any spontaneous action against the State was questionable. There were even fewer civilians in opposition to the regime, and the vast majority of the population were not interested in overthrowing it. Thornley's assessment that there was absolutely no chance of raising an active, organised resistance movement within Germany seems to have been correct.

Chapter 8

CONTACTS AND INFILTRATION

From 1938 until Section D was absorbed into SOE in July 1940 Col Grand had been busy contacting and testing refugee organisations. Three of the most important official groups were of no significant use for subversive activities: the German Social Democratic Party, the Neubeginnen Group and the Reichsbanner Section of the Social Democrats. But the Internationaler Sozialisticher Kampfbund (ISK) was a small, unusual, multinational, though mainly German, socialist party that was more inclined to action. The ISK also provided one or two valuable contacts and was particularly useful in the marshalling yards at Basle, where destination tickets on wagons were exchanged, resulting in supplies going to anywhere but their intended places.

Two eccentric old gentlemen had formed an active and lively organisation known as Lex or Probst. Although they didn't make exorbitant claims, they did appear able to achieve what they undertook. Contact with Karl Otten and Karl Groehl started in December 1938, when the latter lived in Paris, and was maintained by Section D after the outbreak of war.

Groehl was arrested by the French in September 1939 but his release was secured after a deal was struck involving the dissemination of propaganda and the collection of information. Groehl escaped to London but maintained contact with his friends in Switzerland, where his main representative was Karl Gerold, a romantic, incalculable and tedious man. Sabotage activities were proposed at the Tullinger Hügel, an important control centre for the southern part of the defensive Siegfried Line. Explosives were passed to Lex's agents in Basle, and an explosion took place on the expected date in February 1940. But it was not at the agreed target, because the agent had seized a convenient opportunity to attack an important munitions dump. Still in 1940, the group supplied SOE with plans of the important Zeiss optical works at Jena and of factory sites in Berlin and Dresden. They were doing useful work and were asked to obtain more information, including maps of German cities.[1] Lex claimed responsibility for a number of sabotage attacks in

Germany, some on aircraft factories, Gestapo barracks, a factory in Hamburg and numerous railway targets in 1942 and 1943, but in October 1943 Gerold was betrayed to the Swiss police by his mistress, and that virtually ended the organisation's usefulness.

Another contact established by Section D in 1939 was the International Transport Workers Federation or ITF, a left-wing trade union organisation. Despite early disappointments, contact with them remained alive throughout the war and paid dividends in terms of substantial strategic activities at the time of Operation Overlord (the allied invasion of Normandy).

From the outset SOE in Baker Street strongly advocated what they termed 'administrative sabotage', and there were no greater supporters of the concept than the German and Austrian Sections who, by the very nature of the conflict, were in a totally different situation from those controlling operations into occupied territories. By 'administrative sabotage' was meant the disruption of the bureaucracy of German government, the demoralisation of its officials and the fostering of distrust among the civilian population. The more chaotic they could make the reputedly efficient Nazi system appear, the better.

Work into Germany and its ally Austria was a daunting task. One of the least difficult ways of sabotaging the highly organised system was by forging and distributing ration cards for both food and clothing. In a trial run in a period when intelligence reports spoke of the supply situation in Germany suffering a seasonal decline and the incidence of criminally forged ration cards increasing, the German Section embarked on Operation Rosebush to drop 100,000 clothes ration cards forged by the SIS (Secret Intelligence Service) on Hamburg and the Ruhr in July and August 1941. SOE's own forgery facilities had not at this time been established, but despite prevarications and the eventual grudging acceptance of the forgery task by the SIS, the operation, though launched later than intended, was a success. Obviously, it took some time for information on the effects of the operation to filter out to the German Section, but PoW interrogations, newspaper reports in April 1942 and a report from a Norwegian student in the autumn of the following year all indicated that the clothing trade in the towns affected had been driven into chaos.

In 1940 Briggens, the home of Lord Aldenham near Roydon in Essex, was Special Training School (STS) 38 for Polish members of SOE. Three of them took over part of the cellars to set up their own unit for the production of forged documents needed by their compatriots about to be dropped back into their homeland. The quality of this work was not, however, high enough to fool the Germans, so in the spring of 1941 an experienced British officer took over the entire station. At this time there were several sources of forged documents, but the value of a central forgery facility for the whole of SOE was soon recognised and the unit and its reputation expanded (with a certain amount of assistance from Scotland Yard) as Station XIV. By All Fools' Day 1942 the Poles had been transferred elsewhere and the entire house became the False Document Section.

When news of the effectiveness of Rosebush reached SOE it was emboldened to plan a much bigger and potentially more damaging operation. Operation Grog involved the printing of about 250,000 forgeries, this time by the Political Warfare Executive (PWE), of special food ration cards used by soldiers on leave. They were dropped by the RAF between February and April 1943. Shops in the towns targeted, which included Essen and Eupen in Belgium, were reportedly cleaned out of food by people picking up and using the cards, while the authorities had to take special measures to recover the situation.

In the next project, Operation Pack, 100 million food ration coupons of the type used by travellers were dropped in August and September 1943 over a large area of Germany and caused great concern to the Nazi administration. Then, with Operation Sleuth, SOE went one better and had about 500 million travellers' food coupons dropped by both the RAF and the USAAF between December 1943 and August 1944. It is easy to understand how such a widespread and continual rain of such forgeries for eight months caused enormous disorganisation to the rationing system.

These kinds of operation continued with Cleveden, Caldwell, Catfoss, Plateau and Fradswell all distributing great quantities of forgeries of various descriptions right up to the beginning of March 1945. The quality of PWE's forgeries was extremely good. In some cases it took a scientist's careful examination of the document to spot a tiny imperfection – not something a shopkeeper could be expected to do. But, of course, the authentic samples had to be procured and passed safely to London by SOE and SIS agents on the ground and by careful recovery from enemy PoWs.

Another activity enthusiastically fostered by SOE with the help of PWE was the perpetration of so-called 'insaisissable' sabotage: small-scale destructive actions that could be carried out during one's normal work and that did not appear to have been done deliberately. These included such acts as inadequately lubricating machines on war work until they overheated and were damaged; running precision machinery at the wrong speeds to affect their accuracy; adjusting transmission belts wrongly, causing them to fail prematurely; and allowing lathe tools to overheat when being sharpened by grinding, destroying their hardness. Transport workers were encouraged to waste fuel, inadvertently expose perishable goods to the ravages of the weather, and change consignment labels, especially on military supplies. Anti-Nazi workers in practically every industry were given advice on how to inflict this unacknowledgeable damage. More obvious sabotage was encouraged where such acts could be perpetrated: a German Section progress report in June 1941 spoke of a captured U-boat crew member revealing to his interrogators that a shipyard worker had sabotaged a submarine in harbour by putting cement 'in the diving compartments'.[2]

Just how much damage had been done is not clear, but SOE had been working on a 'weapon' that could inflict insaisissable harm to a U-boat crew. In November 1941 the first consignment of SOE's own brand of itching powder, developed from the barbed seeds of the Mucuna plant and packaged in talcum tins, was infiltrated into Switzerland for onward transmission to Germany. A report of June 1942 states that the powder had been introduced into the clothes of German ships' crews. Another claimed at least one U-boat had to return to port with its crew in a distressed state. Lord Selborne's quarterly report to Churchill in July 1943 said 7,000 German uniforms had been sprinkled with the powder; three months later he claimed 25,000 uniforms had been treated, resulting in 'great discomfort to the tender parts of the human body'.[3]

Agents, contacts and sympathisers within Germany were necessary to distribute many of the items of black propaganda produced by SOE and PWE. This was a hazardous activity demanding the utmost care and security, for, in the eyes of the Nazis, this was a capital offence. The first recorded instances of subversive propaganda being infiltrated into Germany date to the summer of 1941, when citizens opposed to Nazism were encouraged to adopt passive resistance methods of working slowly and inefficiently in factories engaged on war work and to generally give the authorities the minimum of cooperation conducive with not arousing suspicion.

Railway workers could carry out insaisissable acts of sabotage using SOE's lubricating grease substitute, indistinguishable from the real thing but in reality made with finely ground carborundum, a very aggressive abrasive substance. A wagon bearing treated with this product could be expected to develop a 'hot-box' or overheated axle bearing within 50 to 100 kilometres.[4] The grease guns and the abrasive grease were smuggled into Switzerland from the beginning of 1942 and passed to contacts recommended to the German Section by the ITF.

The same year, normally suppressed descriptions of Allied air-raid damage in northern and western Germany were being distributed. When a number of German and Austrian troops fled from Norway in April 1943 to sanctuary in neutral Sweden it was thought that SOE's campaign of encouraging desertion had had a hand in it. The following month large-scale printing of black propaganda began in Switzerland. But these positive signs were more than offset by a number of arrests in Sweden and the dispersal of an active group of collaborators in Hamburg following air-raid damage to their homes.

By late 1943 Allied propaganda was paying off in its objective of undermining the morale of the enemy. The German Army was so concerned that it issued stern warnings to its troops in the January 1944 issue of *Mitteilung für die Truppen* (literally 'Information for the Troops') published by the German High Command. They quoted a dozen instances of Allied propaganda collected in recent weeks, admitting it was only a small percentage of the 'countless poisoned arrows' shot at them in one month by London and Moscow.

One leaflet asserted that the State could divorce a wife from her husband after his death in action in order to rob her of her inheritance. Another claimed to be from 'a community of bombed-out Germans' and graphically warned of serious diseases among evacuees. It also claimed that using transport from the big cities was inviting 'rides of death' and the spreading of infectious diseases.

A fake edition of 'Information for the Officer Corps' with a convincing exterior took the reader in by copying part of an earlier, genuine issue before embarking on a text that was full of vulgarities about the Nazi Party. Three leaflets, claimed by the authorities to have originated in Moscow, were reported to have been directed at turning the Austrians against Germany, and another entitled 'News for the Wops' highlighted problems with German steel production. In addition, the Nazi authorities expressed serious concern at the 'barrage of slanderous leaflets' against the SS.

In a somewhat back-handed compliment – 'one must grant these fellows [the Allied propagandists] that they are unscrupulous' – the High Command warned that the battle against subversion was very important.[5]

One must not discount the complexities of working a clandestine organisation in a neutral country. The political sensitivity of the situation made operations in the early part of the war difficult, for both Sweden and Switzerland feared German invasion, but by the autumn of 1944, with the final outcome of hostilities beyond doubt, a distinct improvement in favour of the Allies was apparent. The draft of a Chiefs of Staff directive of 20 October explained the way the situation had developed:

> The SOE mission in Sweden was established initially with the object of preparing, without the knowledge of the Swedish authorities, a subversive organisation to operate only if Sweden was invaded by Germany or otherwise came under German control. Recent developments in the war have rendered these eventualities unlikely and it has been possible to make use of the SOE mission in Sweden:
>
> a) To assist the development of Danish and Norwegian Resistance.
> b) To obtain the unofficial support of the Swedish authorities for activities in Sweden designed to help Resistance in Norway and Denmark.
> c) To operate from Sweden into Germany.
>
> The increased disposition of the Swedish authorities in favour of the Allies – illustrated by their action in training and arming Norwegian and Danish police . . . makes the development of the activities outlined above possible. . . .[6]

In the late spring of 1944 SOE's efforts were almost totally devoted to the preparations for Operation Overlord. Their contribution to Operation Bodyguard/Fortitude, the strategic deception plan, helped to mislead the Germans into thinking that the main landings would be in the Pas de Calais. Soon after the invasion Gen Gubbins, head of SOE, lost the political battle for control over the French resistance to Gen Koenig, the French hero of Bir Hachim, the fort in the Western Desert that had held out under siege by Rommel, giving the British time to re-form at El Alamein. Another blow for Gubbins, who had had a long affinity with the Poles, was the failure of the Allies, and in particular his own organisation, to assist them in the Warsaw Uprising in August 1944. Britain was now keen to improve Anglo-Soviet relations, while the Soviets were open about their suspicions of the intentions of the Polish Home Army that was leading the uprising. The provisional Polish Administration was distinctly anti-Soviet, and SOE was forced to admit how little control it was able to exert over this eastern European resistance organisation. The problem with Poland was one of distance. Attempts were made to deliver supplies to the Home Army in specially modified long-range Whitley bombers. But the extra fuel carried meant an equivalent reduction in payload. The weather forecasting for such a distant dropping zone was largely a hit-or-miss exercise, and if the reception committee could not be identified quickly, there was insufficient fuel to search around and still get back to England. Stalin would not listen to pleas to allow British aircraft to fly on to Russian bases to refuel for the journey home. Following a particularly bad period when there were only two successful supply drops from the UK in a four-month period, a Polish Special Flight was established at Brindisi in southern Italy, which had the double advantage of not only a shorter distance but also a safer route to Poland over less heavily defended territory.

News of the Polish Uprising reached London on 1 August 1944. The Polish government-in-exile made representations at all levels up to King George VI, but they were to no avail. The gallantry of the Polish resistance, the heroism of the aircrews attempting to supply them and the cold-blooded refusal of the Soviets to offer any help are all recorded elsewhere. Gubbins felt the plight of his friends acutely.

One of the most important achievements of the Polish underground was the capture of a German V2 rocket which had fallen to earth in a swamp without exploding, presumably on a test flight. It was dismantled and key parts were smuggled to London by SOE. This gave the entrée for Gubbins to be appointed to the Crossbow Committee chaired by Duncan Sandys of the Ministry of Supply and reporting to the Prime Minister, the Secretary of State for Air and the Chiefs of Staff. Its object was to form policy to counter the threat presented by Germany's new and indiscriminate airborne 'vengeance' weapons. When the first of these, the V1 or flying bomb, began to fall on England on the night of 15/16 June 1944 they were not entirely unexpected. Intelligence and aerial reconnaissance had revealed some strange structures pointing towards London and what looked like tiny aircraft associated with them. Three weeks later X, Lt Col R.H. Thornley, suggested to AD/E, Director of the London Group Brig E.E. Mockler-Ferryman, that SOE should not over-react to the new weapon: SOE's representative in Istanbul had reported that German diplomatic circles were referring to the V1 as *Versager Eins* or 'Misfire No. 1'.[7]

Gubbins attended his first meeting of the Crossbow Committee on 14 July and, such was the importance he attached to it, subsequent meetings took priority over his other engagements.

At about this time Gubbins decided to focus his attention on Germany and what SOE could do as the Allied armies advanced towards its borders. Naturally, the revelations of the 20 July plot to assassinate Hitler raised the hope that there existed in Germany a significant movement of disaffected members of the aristocracy, military and industry. It was to Thornley that Gubbins turned as he considered his reaction to the news of the assassination attempt.

From some eight months after its formation in November 1940 the German or X Section, with Thornley in charge, had formed part of the London Group within SOE. It remained a relatively small body until August 1944, but it served also as a focal point for a network of representatives working with SOE missions in the most important neutral countries.

Most important among these missions were probably the SOE representatives in Switzerland, who included from September 1941 to December 1943 Miss E.M. Hodgson and from August 1944 Sqn Ldr Matthey. In Sweden an increasingly influential mission was run by Maj Threlfall from January to August 1942 and subsequently included Miss Forte and Maj Ewan Butler. Mr G.E.R. Gedye was SOE's representative in Turkey from May 1943, while Maj Darton looked after the organisation's interests in Italy from March 1944. These people covered the main political lines of access to Germany. In other neutral countries, for example in Lisbon, that hotbed of intelligence intrigue, the German Section worked through its ordinary SOE contacts.

The organisation of the German Section, although staffed by able men and women, was clearly on much too small a scale to make significant inroads on the great practical difficulties of work into Germany. In addition, its embryonic work suffered from misinformation: a continuing feature of British government policy since 1940 had been the mistaken belief that an *effective* anti-Nazi faction existed in Germany. It would be several years before this view was modified. There had, indeed, been scattered cells of resistance to Hitler ever since he came to power in 1933. It was known that there were notional German resistance groups on the Austrian–Yugoslav border, and throughout Germany a large number of bands of youths were loosely organised into rowdy anti-Hitler Youth groups similar to the 'Edelweiss Piraten' ('Edelweiss Pirates') and Catholic youth groups such as the 'White

Rose' (see p. 93). For years SOE's German Section had maintained most secret contact, through its representative in Switzerland, with a railway workers' organisation that had carried out some administrative and physical sabotage to rolling stock in Basle's marshalling yards. But the effect of these groups was nowhere near what was needed to precipitate a serious uprising. In addition, the German Section's scope was severely limited by political considerations, the chief of which was that the later Allied policy of unconditional surrender meant that, from SOE's viewpoint, no free use could be made of feelers from Germans purporting to be disenchanted with the Nazi regime. These approaches were not peace feelers but enquiries about embarking on subversive action against the Nazis: they had to be kept at arm's length.

There were many such feelers of various degrees of importance and their development would have been possible only by the most careful and surreptitious follow-up. Some Germans for certain motives might have been induced to commit some action against their government. But this would have involved grave risks: both political, with a backlash of German propaganda aimed at creating dissent within the, in places, rather fragile coalition of Allies either during the war or after it; and technical, in that a large number of the feelers were put out by the Gestapo in an effort to trap Allied representatives and sympathisers into betraying themselves. It was decided at the highest level that these risks were too great, a decision that the German Section endorsed. Any German approaches must be mocked, contact must be broken off, and the matter must be reported to the Foreign Office or its representative.

There appears to have been contacts in early 1944, for prior to the 20 July plot to kill Hitler SOE had gained considerable information on the main intentions of the attempt. But it refused to be involved in assisting the plotters, being unsure of their sincerity and lack of Gestapo penetration. After the attack their official view was that there was no real resistance in Germany: merely petty jealousies and arguments as to how best Germany should proceed.

Three incidents in the records concerning contacts from Germany bear repeating here. In April 1942 an approach was made by Dr Willem Visser t'Hooft, later to become Head of the World Council of Churches, when he visited London from Switzerland. He brought with him a memorandum written by Baron Adam von Trott zu Solz and addressed to Sir Stafford Cripps,

General Colin Gubbins, SOE's chief from September 1943, with Gladwyn Jebb (left, Private Secretary to the Permanent Under-Secretary to the Foreign Office) and Dr Hugh Dalton, the first Minister of Economic Warfare. *(IWM H8185)*

General Sir Stewart Menzies. One of the few images of 'C', the Head of the Secret Intelligence Service (SIS) during the Second World War. *(IWM HU66608)*

Ernst Röhm, who built the Sturmabteilung or SA into a Nazi Party army of almost a million men which frightened the general public and alarmed the Reichswehr. In 1934, a year after this parade in Berlin, he and important associates were murdered in the Night of the Long Knives. *(Ullstein Bilderdienst)*

General Ludwig Beck, Chief of General Staff, who in 1938 resisted as 'unsoldierly' attempts to persuade key generals to resign in protest against Nazi policies and methods. *(AKG-Images)*

Field Marshal Erwin von Witzleben, a long-term plotter against Hitler who would have had high office had he succeeded. *(IWM HU17282)*

Hans von Dohnanyi (seated), lawyer and member of the opposition within German Military Intelligence. With him are Baron Karl-Lugwig von und zu Guttenberg (left) and Justus Delbrück (standing). *(Bildarchiv Preussischer Kulturbesitz)*

Carl Goerdeler, who resigned as Mayor of Leipzig in protest against the Nazi treatment of Jews in the city. (IWM HU17358)

Julius Leber, the charismatic Social-Democratic Party deputy in the Reichstag who spent four years in a Nazi concentration camp. *(AKG-Images)*

Count Helmuth James von Moltke, one of the founders of the Kreisau Circle, appearing before the People's Court in January 1945. He was opposed to a violent overthrow of Hitler but nevertheless was sentenced to death. *(Bildarchiv Preussischer Kulturbesitz)*

Hans Bernd Gisevius, one of the few to escape arrest after 20 July 1944. *(Ullstein Bilderdienst)*

Adam von Trott zu Solz, a member of the Kreisau Circle and Foreign Office who attempted several times to start discussions with the Allies. He is seen here in the dock in the People's Court in Berlin, where he was sentenced to death. *(Bildarchiv Preussischer Kulturbesitz)*

Walther von Brauchitsch, C-in-C of the Army until dismissed by Hitler in December 1941. Hitler then took over supreme command. *(IWM HU17308)*

Franz Halder suffered from both hating Hitler and not being able to ignore his duty as a soldier. Nevertheless, he participated in two failed coup attempts. *(IWM HU7683)*

Admiral Wilhelm Canaris was chief of Military Intelligence and protected several opposition figures within it. His opposition to the Nazi regime was eventually discovered and he was sent to Flossenbürg concentration camp, where he was executed in April 1945. *(AKG-Images)*

Hans Oster worked in the Military Intelligence Office and was close to its chief, Canaris. He met the same fate as his superior. *(Bildarchiv Preussischer Kulturbesitz)*

Count Schenk von Stauffenberg, who led the final attempt to overthrow Hitler. *(Ullstein Bilderdienst)*

Colonel Henning von Tresckow, whose bomb on Hitler's plane in 1943 failed to explode. *(By kind permission of Uta Freifrau von Aretin)*

Helmuth Stieff (centre) with Hitler and Albert Speer at a presentation of new uniforms in July 1944. *(Ullstein Bilderdienst)*

Plaque to the 20 July 1944 plotters, Bendlerblok courtyard, Berlin. It reads: 'You did not bear the shame/You resisted/You gave the great signal to turn back/Sacrificing your ardent lives for freedom, justice and honour.'

Stauffenberg (left) with Hitler and Field Marshal Wilhem Keitel (right) on 15 July 1944 at the Führer's headquarters at Rastenburg, East Prussia. Stauffenberg made his first abortive attempt on Hitler's life that day and the final attempt just five days later. *(Ullstein Bilderdienst)*

General Gerald Templer, Head of SOE's German Directorate for a few months, during which time he was enthusiastic for Periwig. He was later to become Chief of Imperial General Staff. *(IWM H19217)*

Lieutenant-Colonel Ronald Thornley, Head of SOE's German Section for most of the war. His knowledge of Germans and Germany made him uncertain of the wisdom of Periwig. This post-war photograph was taken when he was Managing Director of the Ideal Standard Company in Hull. *(By kind permission of Ganton Golf Club)*

Lord Privy Seal in the War Cabinet and later Minister of Aircraft Production. This was passed to Churchill, who refused to take the matter any further.

Trott, who was to be executed in the wake of Stauffenberg's failed attempt on Hitler's life, had been a Rhodes Scholar at Balliol College, Oxford, in the early thirties. His undoubted charm and intelligence had brought him into a wide circle of English friends including, in addition to Cripps, Lord Lothian, Lady Astor and her son, David. He had stayed at the Astors' home at Cliveden just before the outbreak of war and had had conversations with Neville Chamberlain, then Prime Minister, and Lord Halifax, the Foreign Secretary, in which he stressed that he was strenuously opposed to the prospect of war between Britain and Germany. But some of his earlier activities, notably his ardent German patriotism, had been regarded with great suspicion by both the British and American intelligence authorities. The memorandum brought by Trott's emissary contained features quite unacceptable to British public opinion at the time. Memories of the blitz were still very vivid and the British saw no distinction between good and bad Germans; nor did they have an interest in plans for a postwar Germany. The fact that Trott was a junior member of the Auswärtiges Amt (Foreign Office) and, like Moltke, often travelled abroad did not endear him to the British authorities. Furthermore, his pre-war association with the so-called 'Cliveden Set' did nothing to help his case. Gubbins, then Director of Operations, Western and Central Europe, the Foreign Office and SIS all agreed that there should be no response to Trott's memorandum.

Another attempt to contact the Allies was planned for later that year by Count Helmuth von Moltke. The founder of the Kreisau Circle, who after the outbreak of war had maintained contact with friends in England, suggested a meeting with one of those friends in Stockholm in September or October 1942. SOE were prepared to arrange this meeting, but it was vetoed by the Prime Minister himself. Von Moltke kept the rendezvous, but when his friend failed to turn up he wrote criticising the British for failing to use the 'millions of would-be spies on the continent'. He was under arrest before the 20 July attempt on Hitler's life and was not directly implicated in it. Nevertheless he was executed in January 1945. This was as far as SOE went in reacting to any feelers offered from the so-called 'conservative' opposition, much of which could be linked to von Moltke.

The third incident concerns a Dr Söderman, an eminent Swedish criminologist who, in December 1942, approached SOE, with which he was on good terms, in Sweden to say that he was in contact with leading officials of the German Kriminalpolizei who sought some limited assistance by British airborne forces in a revolt against the Nazis and German security forces. The Kriminalpolizei was the former legal police force, which was not on good terms with the Gestapo. They claimed to be ready to take action at the appointed time to arrest or execute all leading Nazis from Hitler downwards, along with all the heads of the security forces. Dr Söderman took this proposal most seriously and wished to pursue it through his friend, Sir Norman Kendall, Assistant Commissioner of the Metropolitan Police.

Understandably, SOE's initial reaction was to regard this proposal as a trap and, in accordance with their policy, to hastily break off contact. But they reckoned without the persistence of Söderman, and it eventually required the personal intervention of Sir Alexander Cadogan of the Foreign Office with Sir Norman Kendall to attempt to terminate the connection in March 1943. Exactly a year later Söderman raised the matter once more when he revealed that his contact in the Kriminalpolizei was none other than Lt Gen Dr Arthur Nebe, its head since 1938. He also claimed that Count von Helldorff, chief of the uniformed police in Berlin, was also associated with the plot. SOE refused to let matters go any further. After the 20 July plot Helldorff was arrested and executed and, with a 50,000 mark price on his head, Dr Nebe was also caught and probably executed by the Gestapo. So in the end this episode showed not only evidence of a real plot, but also of effective Gestapo control. However, no details of this alleged plot have been found in the literature. SOE was doubtless wise in the action it took.

The reasons Britain distanced herself from these, and other, approaches by German opposition factions are complicated. Some maintain Churchill was focusing all his energy on the military effort, leaving no time for intricate political initiatives. There was certainly concern that entering into a dialogue with any Germans would jeopardise the Anglo-Soviet alliance. In addition, London wished to avoid earlier mistakes, when commitments made after the First World War gave rise to the demagogue Hitler.

Outside Germany there had been for years a number of German underground groups in opposition to the Nazi regime. Most had been in exile so long they had little idea of the real conditions within the Fatherland, and by now their contacts with it were rather tenuous. Some groups had associations with others; some competed with fellow groups. Many of their members were Jewish and therefore at a distinct disadvantage where subversive activities against the 'Aryan' regime was concerned. The sum total of the special knowledge within these groups must have been considerable, but with the fragmented nature of the resistance in exile, its use could not be realised.

As far as the insertion of SOE agents into Germany was concerned, they could expect no organisation on the ground or cooperation from groups or individuals. Unlike the situation in the Nazi-occupied countries, they were completely on their own and faced an even more hazardous existence. Whereas in the overrun territories agents could hope at least for a blind eye to be cast on them by a population under strict control by the Gestapo, in the Reich itself every person had to be regarded as an active and mortal enemy. So it is clear to see why up to the time of the Normandy invasion in the summer of 1944 only a handful of attempts had been made to put SOE-trained men into the Nazi heartland.

The first attempt, known as Operation Champagne, was made in 1942, when a 25-year-old member of the anti-Nazi Kittelsbach Piraten (Kittelsbach Pirates) by the name of Richard Kuehnel, who had been captured from a German armed trawler converted to the meteorological ship *Lauenburg* the previous summer, was put ashore in Norway on 20 April.[8]

The capture of the *Lauenburg* was a deliberate operation by the Royal Navy to procure vital code books to assist the cryptographers at the Government Code and Cipher School (GCCS) at Bletchley Park in their efforts to break the German Navy's Enigma code. The ship had been operating west of Jan Mayen Island, north-east of Iceland, sending weather information back to Germany and was selected by Bletchley Park, who knew of such ships from the wireless transmissions they were constantly trying to decipher. They had discovered when the *Lauenburg* had last sailed for its period on station in the North Atlantic and surmised that it must be carrying the vital documents they so desperately needed. But having only recently captured another weathership, the *München*, the code-breakers and the Admiralty were intensely worried that the Germans might put two and two together and realise their losses were not sheer coincidence but a concerted attempt to secure the keys to breaking Enigma. If this happened the enemy would undoubtedly introduce additional security measures to the encryptions which would set back the work of the cryptographers for many months. It was decided nonetheless to take this risk, and four British warships set out from Scapa Flow on 25 June 1941 on Operation EC.

The cruiser *Nigeria* and destroyers *Bedouin, Tartar* and *Jupiter* found the *Lauenburg* and quickly terrified the crew into abandoning the ship by opening fire a little wide of the target. Although the Enigma machine itself was thrown into the sea before they reached the ship, the search by the boarding party found the documents needed so urgently at Bletchley Park. As a precaution, the twenty-two prisoners captured were blindfolded while being transferred to the Allied ships to prevent them observing the removal of the papers. HMS *Tartar* then sank the *Lauenburg* with gunfire.[9]

Without a wireless set, Kuehnel's only means of communication with England was by messages in letters to his PoW friends there. His cover story was that he had been put to work in a shipyard in Aberdeen and had stolen a fishing boat in which to cross the North Sea. The Nazi authorities apparently believed his story. Two messages were received, and then came an obscure report that he had tried to contact the Norwegian resistance in order to escape to Sweden. Since this could have been a trap for the resistance, they were warned. Nothing more was ever heard about Kuehnel, and in June 1945 his name was among eight agents still unaccounted for by the German Section of SOE.

The second SOE man to be infiltrated into the Reich, and the first to be parachuted in, was a young German Army deserter who contacted the British in Spain in the summer of 1942 after, he claimed, carrying out sabotage in the Bremen area in the name of his social democratic ideals. Volkmar Krotsky, alias Kurt Koenig, was subsequently trained by SOE, and on the night of 16 February 1943 in Operation Calvados was dropped just inside the frontier between Germany and Holland under the cover name of Hans Bröcker. He was instructed to contact his friends in the Bremen and Hamburg regions and organise a movement for subversion and sabotage. Luck was not with him: he landed on the thatched roof of a farmhouse where a wedding party was in full swing. One member of the party was a Luftwaffe officer who, in response to Koenig's claim that he was a bailed-out Luftwaffe airman (he was in uniform), phoned the nearest aerodrome to report the matter. He was interviewed by a *Feldwebel* but duped him and asked the way to the nearest station. He went to see a contact named Malinsky in Düsseldorf, who told him he had been warned by the police of his possible arrival. He also went to see another contact by the name of Kalning, who had had a visit from the police. Koenig was convinced this indicated a security leak in England. He went on the run in north-west Germany before deciding to abandon his task and make his escape through Spain. By 26 March 1943 he was back in England. Despite suspicions that Koenig was, in fact, a Gestapo 'plant', his story was thoroughly investigated and accepted.

Koenig was willing to undertake another mission: a single-handed sabotage attack on German railways. He was successfully dropped in the Rhineland on 15 July 1943. Twelve days later he appeared once more in San Sebastián in Spain, claiming to have blown up the railway lines in a tunnel near Oberwesel and to have damaged a locomotive. Although SOE could obtain no independent verification of the statement, they could not fault it under cross-examination.[10]

On 7 January 1944 Koenig set out for a third time. It was intended to drop him in the Freiburg area, but the drop zone could not be identified and so, on his own insistence, he was dropped wide of the pinpoint. There was a general alarm in the district and he was arrested in Baden the next day. Nothing more was heard about him. After the cessation of hostilities attempts were made to trace all the German Section's missing agents. On 6 June 1945 Thornley wrote to ME42, who were organising the searches within Germany, with the suggestion that discreet enquiries should be made of Koenig's uncle in Bremen who, he suspected, had denounced his nephew to the Gestapo. A month later Maj Field-Robinson, X/GER (Head of SOE's German Section), wrote to HQ ME42 with a suggestion that they try seeking further clues to Koenig's whereabouts at an address in the Lilienthal district of Bremen.[11] It was eventually discovered that he had been executed in February 1945.

As the war turned solidly in the Allies' favour, attempts were made to penetrate the Sudetenland, the area on the Polish–Czech border including Bohemia and Moravia that had been assigned to the Nazis in the 1938 Munich Agreement and into which they had begun to resettle German citizens. Two agents were sent from Sweden in March 1944 but were quickly arrested while making the crossing to Denmark. Two more were dropped by parachute in May 1944 and appear to have been free for some time before one was executed and the other committed suicide to avoid interrogation. Some attempts were made to infiltrate agents overland from Turkey, and a few very fragile lines of communication were established. But except for the dissemination of propaganda material, they provided no practical gain.

The effects of these acts of sabotage within Germany was minor; the ongoing acts of subversion, on the other hand, were clearly causing dismay among the authorities and occasionally chaos in specific areas. So Thornley's intelligence on the situation inside the Reich together with the Allies' policy of accepting nothing short of unconditional surrender resulted in SOE distancing itself from the small dissident groups. The fragmented German resistance movement would have to organise itself in a convincing way and demonstrate some pro-Allied sympathies before assistance would be forthcoming.

The other route into the German heartland was through Yugoslavia, which had already been used to gain access to Romania, Bulgaria and Hungary. The proposed infiltration of Austria was to be facilitated by the 'Clowder' mission, an elaborate and somewhat desperate operation mounted amid the political upheaval and inter-partisan feuding of the Balkans. It started when an advance party was flown out to Bosnia on 3 December 1943 to receive Tito's blessing before setting out on a 480km march to the Partisan HQ in Slovenia. From here they went in the depth of winter into northern Italy and the Slovene districts close to the old Austrian border. Early attempts at infiltration failed and the leader, Lt Col P.A. Wilkinson, set off back to Bosnia in late February and then to London in the spring. Here it was agreed he should set up a chain of British despatch posts with Italian and Slovene guerrillas along 190km of mountainous country overlooking the Austrian frontier. It was August before Sq Ldr Count Czernin, who had been reconnoitring the Austrian frontier, was joined by four Austrians, only one of whom could be persuaded to cross the border in civilian clothes. He spent 15–28 August in Austria and entered a second time on 9 September; he was not heard of again. Another party of four Austrians was dropped on 12 October, landing among a German patrol; only one escaped to join the 'Clowder' mission. Attempts to get another Austrian across the border were unsuccessful in the face of intensified German counter-measures, and the whole 'Clowder' mission in north Italy was withdrawn in December 1944.

Meanwhile, in Slovenia Maj A.C.G. Hesketh-Prichard had been reinforced by two Austrian officers in the spring of 1944 and made determined attempts to enter Austria at the end of April, but German activity in the area made this impractical. Examination of many miles of the border found no suitable places through which to introduce agents.

Maj C.H. Villiers, who had been dropped on 14 May on the Italian side of the frontier, and Hesketh-Prichard spent the summer trying to rouse the Korosko partisans into action. It was not easy: the enemy was very active and the population unreliable. Eventually the offer of supplies pushed the partisans into supporting an expedition across the Drava river. Twenty-five tonnes of stores arrived between June and September, and the partisan strength grew from 200 to 2,000 men. In mid-September the plan was agreed but remained conditional on a demand for seventy aircraft-loads of stores, a request that was not granted.

Hesketh-Prichard had to make do with a party of eighty Slovenes who crossed the Drava on 15 October. Five days later they were encamped well within Austrian territory among a friendly but passive population. But with the weather rapidly deteriorating not one supply aircraft could be sent. The party was increasingly harassed by the Germans until messages ceased on 3 December 1944. Some forty partisans survived in the area until the end of hostilities.

In the last months of the war the supply of potential agents from among Austrian PoWs was reasonably promising, and some thirty of them were put through training courses in Italy. There followed six SOE operations in 1945 into Austria:

1. 7 February Lt 'O'Hara' dropped near Graz. Caught and shot 21 March.
2. 16 February Three Austrians dropped near Jedenburg. Party betrayed by one of its members.
3. 23 March Lt 'Kennedy' dropped near Krems. In Vienna he found a nucleus of fighting resistance, mainly deserters from the German Army. Claimed to have commanded 130 armed men harassing the defenders of Vienna until liberation.
4. 24 March Wireless operator dropped near Murzzuschlag in Styria. Survived.
5. 8 April Albrecht Gaiswinkler dropped in Salzkammergut. Raised force of 350 men. Harassed Germans until he had administrative control. Captured eminent Nazis and rescued looted art treasures.
6. 20–24 April Eight men dropped between Graz and Judenburg. Secured Zeltweg aerodrome.

Chapter 9

FOREIGN WORKERS

Germany's original intention was for industry to continue to function in the occupied countries for the benefit of the Reich. But as early as 1941 this strategy was found to be politically dangerous and economically inefficient. So the Nazi regime began a policy of forcing industrial labour in the occupied territories from their homelands and into German factories and mines whose workforces had been seriously depleted by conscription into the armed forces. The first workers to be moved were those in the east: Poles, Czechs and some Russians; but the policy was intensified in the west when the 1941/2 winter campaign in Russia exposed the shortages of German manpower. Huge numbers of workers – in the order of 10 million – from all the overrun countries and from Italy after the fall of Mussolini were deported to Germany.

Foreign workers were in the main housed in hutted camps associated with, though not necessarily close to, the factories and mines in which they worked. If a camp was some distance from the factory, the workers were either marched, transported by coach, or allowed to use bicycles and public transport to get to work. Only western European workers who had proved their reliability over a period had any chance of living in billets. There was usually a guard at the entrance to the workers' camp, but the foreigners were free to come and go outside their hours of work and subject to a curfew that varied according to local regulations but was usually at 2100hr. In earlier years ignoring the curfew had been a risk worth taking, but in the latter stages of the war strict enforcement to prevent the escape of workers was very likely.

Officially, the workers toiled for a maximum of 60 hours a week with one day free, but in practice this figure was more likely to be the average since some men worked as many as 70 hours a week. The pressures on German industry called for maximum effort, and this meant the inevitable continuous working on a shift system. It was therefore assumed that a fair proportion of the foreign workers were engaged on night shifts. If an infiltrated agent could get himself on a night shift he should have an opportunity to transmit on his wireless during the daytime since the cleaning and maintenance of the camps were delegated to the inmates. Any risk from the *Werkschutz* inspection teams could be accommodated, as they were likely to take place at fixed times. If an agent was on a day shift, night-time transmission was the only possibility.[1] This, at any rate, was the conclusion the SOE planners in Baker Street came to. In the event communication was nowhere near so straightforward.

This population of foreign workers would at first seem the obvious basis for a substantial resistance movement within Germany, especially as vast numbers of men speaking the same language were accommodated in nominally guarded camps. But there were serious fundamental obstacles to this: the Gestapo was efficient in the restriction of workers' movement (special permission was needed even for the use of a bicycle) and free in the use of 'stool pigeons' among them; a reliable means of direct contact had not been found; and there was in fact overall, a major language problem. SOE's approach was to attempt contact through governments-in-exile and its clandestine organisations within the occupied countries. But SOE did not get wholesale support from Allied governments for its proposals to encourage their deported nationals to indulge in sabotage while in Germany. These governments-in-exile were far more concerned with keeping their people out of German hands in the first place or at least seeing that their lives under the Nazi yoke were not totally intolerable. The fear was that the effect of sabotage would be further restrictions and possibly reprisals on the families of those accused of perpetrating such acts.

The Political Warfare Executive (PWE) drew up a general directive for those workers in occupied countries who found themselves being forcibly transported to Germany. The intention was for the details of the directive to be explained to the worker by resistance members in his native country or by agents infiltrated in. They were told to spread pacifism, despondency and discontent among the German workers they would be toiling alongside. They should convince them that authority could now be successfully defied on an ever-increasing scale. The foreign workers must not miss opportunities to express surprise at the privileged position of senior Nazi Party members compared with the German common man. These higher-status Nazis were not subject to the same ration restrictions as the ordinary Germans: the so-called 'diplomatic rations' they could obtain were three or four times those of a heavy worker. This 'fact', the ear-marked foreign worker was told, could have been gleaned from fellow worker servants or transport drivers delivering food to the homes of party high-ups. In truth, the order exempting diplomats from rationing could be found on page 367 of a book entitled *Das Bezugscheinwesen der Ernährungswirtschaft* by Dr Dommaschk, available in public libraries.

Foreign workers should also make others aware that Nazi Party functionaries of military age were still largely exempt from front-line service or labour service. In addition, the wives and daughters of senior party officials were given easy office jobs to avoid factory work. A law of 17 February 1943 decreed that party high-ups were also exempt from providing billets in their homes for evacuees, as all other Germans were required to do. Another concession to party officials was that they were able to evacuate their families from war-ravaged cities to special reserved zones or 'focal points of housing shortage' that were not only closed to all other evacuees and refugees but were situated in holiday resorts such as Berchtesgaden, Bischofswiesen, Gern, Koenigssee, Salzburg, Landschellenberg, Martkschellenberg, Scheffau and Schoenau.

Foreign workers were also urged to show a certain reluctant acceptance that German Nazi Party high-ups would, as conquerors, indulge in excesses within occupied territories, but to express surprise, in view of the food rationing, that they should be involved in racketeering, black marketing and gluttonising in Germany itself.

The directive encouraged defiance of the authorities by spreading stories of successful attempts against a background of a breakdown of control. In the occupied countries Germans were successfully deserting because the authorities were unable to determine which soldiers had been killed and which had deserted. Similar opportunities for absence without leave were open to foreign workers during the chaos following the heavy air raids on Germany.

Fellow German workers whose personal businesses had been closed down should be told about those who had found ways of evading the order and continuing in business until now when they had cashed in because the authorities had had to give way to hostile agitation and rescind the order.

Opportunities should be taken, stated the directive, to denigrate the police by commenting on their few numbers and advanced age, both of which were contributing to ineffective tackling of the current crime wave and preventing them even fielding a reasonable sports team!

Foreign workers were encouraged to comment with surprise on the small number of German male workers of military age left in Germany. They were to surmise that these workers must be able to do virtually what they liked because they remained in their jobs owing to their perceived indispensability.

Most of the forced workers from foreign lands were unlikely to have experienced the devastating air raids then being made on Germany. The more they expressed their unholy fear of the bombing and compared the huge Allied aircraft production with the fall in German output of planes from their heavily damaged factories, the lower morale would fall.

They should remind their German colleagues that at the end of the First World War it was the industries of Germany's neighbours, over whose land the war had been fought, that had suffered, not those within the country itself. The longer the bombing of Germany now continued, the more destruction would take place and the greater would be the unemployment after the war when rival foreign firms would take the places of the war-torn German ones. At the same time they should bemoan the hopelessly inadequate protection against air raids, the appalling damage they had heard of in other parts of Germany and the inadequate housing to which refugees from the bombing, which was not likely to diminish, were directed.

Sympathetic questioning of German workers as to the fate and whereabouts of their evacuated or conscripted womenfolk and families was encouraged, as was expressing fear and seeking explanations for the epidemics and diseases (venereal and otherwise) raging over the country.

The workers to be posted unwillingly to work in Germany were also told to complain about the outrageous hours and conditions of work in that country compared with those in others, the lack of nourishment in the food, the huge deductions in tax from their pay and the need to pay a vast amount of 'graft' in order to buy practically anything in the shops.

They should also exaggerate the surprise felt at the dismissal of so many well-known German generals and sympathise with Germans whose soldier-relatives had difficulty obtaining news from home due to the disruption caused by the bombing; but they should add that there was every likelihood of this situation becoming worse.

The slogan '*Schluss!*' (To hell with it all!) could be spread by foreign workers asking for its real meaning and an explanation of its appearance on so many walls, lavatories, etc.

All forms of malingering, going slow and passive resistance were recommended in the directive. These could be encouraged by the workers practising them themselves and telling of successful resistance by others. The lack of doctors to identify self-inflicted symptoms and control sickness absence, together with the desperate need for manpower, allowed workers to get away with such passive resistance.

Foreign workers should seek every opportunity to indulge in 'insaisissable' action (see p. 110) that could be attributed to normal negligence or misunderstanding of instructions. Much time could be wasted by the asking of needless questions of busy officials and the feigned misunderstanding of the German language. Frequent and long visits to the lavatories and spinning out the time taken to obtain tools and materials were other examples. Oil, rags and other consumable materials could all be wasted. Opportunities to start small fires should be grasped and excessive water used to extinguish them, to result in deliberate collateral damage. The workers were exhorted to cause whatever trouble could be made in their own particular trades without arousing suspicion. If they were employed in some other trade, fellow workers should be able to advise on what most frequently caused the usual stoppages.

The directive told the prospective worker to make a point of advising their foreign colleagues to make every effort to return to their own country as soon as they were certain that the Allies had started full-scale action to liberate western Europe. As in pyramid-selling, these workers were asked to instruct reliable friends on the points in the directive and to get them to do the same to their friends.

Unfortunately, little use was made of this enormous potential of forced foreign workers. There was a certain amount of passive resistance and 'insaisissable' acts by them, but any spontaneous organisation among them was in no way directed or controlled by SOE. All it could do was to instruct its agents in the field on the policy regarding deported workers and to encourage known resistance groups to extend their activities over the German border. The French had organisations well placed for such work: the Confédération Générale du Travail (CGT), the General Confederation of Labour, were keen to show their concern for deported workers as a means of enhancing membership when the war was over; they distributed a considerable amount of propaganda, and as early as February 1944 the Mission Varlin was infiltrated into France to organise the work. The communist-inspired Mouvement des

Prisonniers de Guerre et Déportés was another such organisation, although primarily concerned with welfare rather than resistance.

As can be seen, there was in effect deadlock on how to make use of many millions of foreign workers forced against their will to labour for the Nazis in Germany. Part of the difficulty of harnessing this huge potential lay in the Allies' underlying fear of a large-scale massacre of workers if anything went wrong.

On 27 May 1942 the Prime Minister, Winston Churchill, sent a personal minute to SOE's controlling politician, the Minister of Economic Warfare, Lord Selborne, saying:

> I commend to your notice a recent book by John Steinbeck, *The Moon is Down*, published this year by Viking Press of New York. In addition to being a well-written story, it stresses, I think quite rightly, the importance of providing the conquered nations with simple weapons such as sticks of dynamite which could be easily concealed and are easy in operation.[2]

Several copies of the book were purchased and distributed to ministers, and the sentiments within it became the basis for what was initially called the 'Moon' project (but was later renamed Operation Braddock). Ideas crystallised and the plan for the 'Moon' project, which was reduced to two schemes, was submitted to the Chiefs of Staff on 28 September 1942:

- Scheme I was to deliver by parachute 50,000 small packages of arms, explosives and incendiaries broadcast to nationals of whichever country was to be invaded by the Allies, but not until the invasion had occurred.
- Scheme II was to deliver by floating down on instruction cards large quantities of simple incendiary devices to foreign workers and disaffected nationals inside Germany. The deliveries were to start as soon as the devices were ready and aircraft were available.

Sanction for an initial 1 million incendiaries was given and trials of the device were carried out on 9 January 1943. SOE's Station IX (their research and development establishment) produced a device that consisted of a small incendiary filled with petroleum gel and ignited by a time-pencil fuse with a

30-minute delay. It would burn for 4 minutes and reach a temperature of 2,000°C. The instructions were printed in English, German, French, Dutch, Italian, Greek, Russian, Czech, Polish, Serb and Serbo-Croat to reach a wide readership among the many hundreds of thousands of forced labourers in Germany. Trials of the parachute qualities of the instruction cards were carried out from the tower of Birmingham University. Lord Selborne was very keen on the project, and the Prime Minister gave his tentative approval for Scheme II. With half a million incendiaries due to be ready by mid-April and a further half-million by mid-May, an additional 3 million devices were sanctioned on 8 February. An interesting and typically devious proposal was for the dropping of large numbers of the instruction cards rolled into little balls as if thrown away by potential saboteurs who had read the instructions and hidden the incendiaries. The problem of how best to drop the devices was addressed, and it was considered that low-level drops were too dangerous, while high-level drops would result in too great a spread of the devices on the ground. The latter was thought, on balance, to be the more acceptable.

The final form of the incendiary, which was designed by the leader of SOE's Station IX Incendiary Section Maj O.J. Walker and Dr C.H. Bamford, an ex-Cambridge chemist, was 6in long by 1½in by ⅜in and it was estimated that 720 of them would, on average, replace each bomb that would otherwise be dropped. The production rate of incendiaries began to present a problem. The expected rate of 500,000 a month was found to be impossible to achieve, so 300,000 a month had to be accepted. It was proposed to drop 250,000 in the spring over north-west Germany, where there was much forced foreign labour and which was relatively easy to reach, followed by 100,000 in different parts of Germany every fortnight.

By May 1943 the project had been renamed Operation Braddock but there were signs of a diminution in enthusiasm, queries being raised about whether to continue with production of the devices. In September Scheme I was finally abandoned.

At the end of August an impatient Gubbins wrote to Lord Selborne suggesting that Braddock II should be used over Italy as soon as possible after the British invasion, but his proposal was turned down. Italy would get out of the war as soon as it could, came the reply, and the incendiaries should be kept for Germany.[3]

Lord Selborne, still anxious to set Operation Braddock in action, wrote to the Prime Minister on 4 October 1943 arguing that there were an estimated

7.7 million PoWs and forced workers propping up German industry and that among these would be plenty of potentially welcoming recipients of the devices. If only 1 per cent of the 2.5 million incendiaries then available were picked up and used, 25,000 fires would break out in Germany and a high percentage of them would be of some importance. But Churchill had to choose his moment to take the Americans along with him, and he judged that this was not the right time.[4]

In the second quarter of 1944, with almost 4 million incendiaries for Scheme II manufactured, production was stopped. It was calculated that it would require 400 heavy bomber sorties to deliver them, a demand that was sure to meet with resistance from the RAF if it was seen as merely alarming the Germans and perhaps igniting some fires in prominent Nazi establishments. It was decided that Braddock II was to be used only inside Germany and not on enemy-occupied countries. Furthermore, its use should be delayed until conditions had loosened the Gestapo's hold and workers were desperate, owing to the continued and increasingly severe privations as the Allied armies advanced across Europe. The minister did not feel competent to judge when this situation was likely to come about.[5]

With the invasion of Europe imminent, Churchill wrote to Lord Selborne to say that he could not bother Gen Eisenhower with this matter at the present. Selborne tried yet again on 24 July 1944 following news of the 'trouble in Germany', by which he was probably referring to the 20 July assassination attempt on Hitler and to some rioting in various parts of the country, which, although being suppressed by the Nazis, seemed to auger well for a start to the operation. He suggested a preliminary shower of half a million Braddocks (as the incendiaries came to be known) on the Ruhr, which was the centre of German communism and contained many foreign workers. He noted that PWE would need several hours' warning to lay on instructions to finders of Braddocks. Churchill struck through the word 'several' and substituted '7' in his customary red ink.[6]

Churchill's hesitation was in part due to his concern that the enemy would wreak retribution against foreign workers or even PoWs, but the very next day Selborne tried to allay his fears by quoting the Geneva Convention – which seemed a pretty weak argument when one considers the Nazis' record of contraventions of the Convention. Selborne also had intelligence that the Germans were already nervous about the large number of foreign forced workers in their midst.

With almost 4 million incendiaries waiting to be dropped and production of them at a standstill, the frustration of Gen Ismay, the Prime Minister's Chief of Staff, at the lack of action led him to urge Churchill on 28 July to remind Eisenhower of the existence of the weapons and the plan to use them.

Operation Braddock II was started on a very small scale, and the Supreme Headquarters Allied Expeditionary Force (SHAEF) was pleased with the results. Some 250,000 devices were dropped by the US Army Air Force on 25 September 1944 in daylight, despite the Deputy Chief of Air Staff and Gen Spatz claiming night drops would be better. The Nazis were irritated and puzzled, and went to the trouble of distributing warnings throughout Germany. Although there were no reports of actual arson attacks, a modest success was claimed by the disruption caused, and SOE's Head, Gubbins, lent the project some token support, advising Selborne that SHAEF was still considering a large-scale drop. Further efforts by Selborne in November 1944 to inject urgency into the operation met with a 'the present is not the time' reply which exasperated him still further.

Time slipped by until 8 March 1945, when Churchill's friend and scientific adviser, Lord Cherwell, exhorted him to use the weapon. But now Gen Ismay was having second thoughts and expressed his worries that Braddocks might fall near PoWs, prompting reprisals. For the same reason SOE air supply drops near PoW camps were vetoed by SHAEF. Another concern was that they might get into the hands of the German Wehrwolf underground organisation, which was forming groups to infiltrate Allied lines.

Operation Braddock finally ground to a halt on 18 March 1945, when Churchill wrote across the minute in red ink, 'No action'.[7]

The situation in Germany in mid-1944 could thus be summed up as being on the whole steadfast in the face of appalling round-the-clock aerial bombardment, increasing deprivation, mounting casualties and the certainty of defeat. A resistance movement large enough and sufficiently well organised to materially affect the defence of the Reich and its will to resist did not exist. And the long-awaited collapse of the Nazi security apparatus had still not occurred.

By the end of December SOE's German Directorate (as the German Section became from 31 October) was planning to establish two-way communications with foreign worker colonies in the heart of the Reich by the end of the following April. Their primary objective was to be in a position to disseminate the orders of the Supreme Commander Allied Expeditionary Force (SCAEF), Gen Dwight D. Eisenhower, whatever they may be, in the closing stages of the war in Europe. The situation had to be managed very carefully, as several million unwilling deportee workers in the midst of a heavily mauled retreating army desperately defending its homeland was a recipe for a massacre of the innocent.

The German Directorate had no chance of providing sufficient numbers of trained wireless operators in the time available. Their solution was to prepare to send into the foreign worker colonies additional agents equipped with the new miniature wireless sets capable of only receiving messages but small enough to be easily hidden. The thought behind this was to enable the workers to have up-to-date news and to receive instructions. Although it was generally agreed that the war in Europe would end in the summer of 1945, the war in the Far East would certainly continue longer, and therefore technical research into improved wireless transceivers was to continue on the assumption that an armistice was not achieved until late in 1946.

In addition to the planning for lines of communication, it was also proposed to increase sabotage within Germany by means of *coup-de-main* operations close behind the lines undertaken by foreign nationals, including 'Bonzos', or enemy soldiers working for the Allies. These were to be short-term forays of five or six days.

Once again the possibility of worthwhile dissident groups waiting in the wings was considered. If such factions could only be identified and located, the German Directorate would be prepared to place agents in touch with them.

Of the various methods of infiltrating agents into Germany, the through-the-lines route was proving difficult technically and on security grounds, especially after the Germans' Ardennes offensive (the Battle of the Bulge), which started in mid-December. The jumping-off point for such operations was to have been the Special Forces' forward base on mainland Europe known as SPU22, but this had to be hurriedly withdrawn to a safer location that was less convenient for the infiltration operations.

Agents passing through Sweden and Switzerland were to be disguised as neutrals or Germans travelling legitimately with normal personal luggage, merchant seamen plying their normal trade or railwaymen employed on lines crossing the frontier. There were two other methods of debatably greater risk: as a smuggler crossing the frontier illegally or as a stowaway on a ship or in a van.

A further method of getting agents into Germany was by parachuting them. This was possible only in a specified area of the country, since much of the land was mountainous, much was forested and, as will be seen, there was concern about the risks to Allied PoWs and foreign workers of dropping men or supplies too close to the camps holding these groups.

SOE was at this time urgently seeking suitable personnel to send into Germany on this risky, but in some respects humanitarian, task. French, Belgian, Polish and Dutch agents were required to inveigle their way into the camps posing as foreign workers forced there from their home countries. Women were considered to have a greater chance of survival than men. Relatively fewer Germans were being sought, and they were mainly from the prisoners taken by 21 Army Group. Their best chances of success were thought to be by going back into Germany in uniform, but it was known that any soldier found moving away from the front line within a 14km-deep zone behind it was automatically arrested.[8]

In the end the millions of anti-Nazi forced workers in Germany proved to be a liability rather than an asset to be exploited by the German Directorate. The sheer numbers, the diversity of nationalities and languages, the poor fitness and low morale of many, and their desperation to return to their families all presented an insurmountable obstacle.

Chapter 10

THE BIRTH OF A PLAN

The year 1943 marked a turning-point in the Second World War. The Russians had ferociously defended Stalingrad against the German onslaught, killing 146,000 and capturing 90,000, only 6,000 of whom were ever to see their Fatherland again. At the end of the previous year in North Africa Lt Gen Montgomery had defeated Rommel at El Alamein and caused Churchill to announce that 'A bright gleam has caught the helmets of our soldiers and warmed and cheered all our hearts.' But the Prime Minister declared that although this was not the beginning of the end of the war, it was the end of the beginning. As if the British forces had at last caught their breath after the lightning thrusts of the Wehrmacht in the west and the east, the blitz and the U-boat war, it seemed that at last there was some hope.

In January 1943 President Roosevelt and Churchill met at Casablanca in Morocco to discuss future strategies for the conduct of the war. It was here that the Allies' insistence on Germany's unconditional surrender was first announced. From the point of view of those Germans disenchanted with the Nazi regime who could see only defeat in the future, this was to prove an almost insurmountable hurdle. It would be another humiliation, just like the armistice terms after the First World War, without any room for negotiation or an 'honourable defeat'.

Whether the war would have been any shorter without this immovable objective is debatable. While the disillusioned German generals might well have been able to accept terms that fell short of unconditional surrender, there was still the question of their oath to the Führer, which many of them could not bring themselves to break (see p. 67). Unless Hitler led the way in making peace, they felt themselves powerless to move in that direction.

But with the public opinion of Britain and her Allies unwilling to differentiate between good and bad Germans, and governments having knowledge of the atrocities committed in Poland and Russia in the name of

Germany, it is not surprising that the Allies wanted no negotiations with such a barbaric regime. The last year of the war was to reveal many more unspeakable horrors to reinforce their view.

The Casablanca Conference was followed at the end of November by the Teheran Conference, at which Churchill, Roosevelt and, for the first time, Stalin agreed to a Soviet summer offensive in 1944 coordinated with a second front in France. The invasion of Europe had been agreed. Planning for Operation Overlord had already started.

The bombardment of Germany from the air was stepped up during the year as production of heavy bombers like the Avro Lancaster was steadily increased and American forces built or took over airfields in the east of England. The US Army Air Force specialised in daylight bombing; the RAF in night raids. As Air Chief Marshal Sir Arthur 'Bomber' Harris, Head of Bomber Command, said of the Nazis, 'They have sown the wind, and so they shall reap the whirlwind.'

July 1943 saw the Allied invasion of Sicily and the overthrow of Mussolini. Gen Badoglio formed a new government and declared an armistice in September, with the result that most of Italy was then occupied by German forces. The Allies advanced slowly up Italy, meeting stubborn resistance at Monte Cassino and the Gothic Line, while at home preparations for the invasion of the European mainland were gathering momentum. The enemy had to be kept guessing as to where this would take place, so the deception Operation Fortitude was mounted throughout the first half of 1944. Concentrations of troops and equipment were built up in several places on the south and east coasts of England opposite likely landing beaches, with dummy armour included to swell the numbers. And turned German spies who were now working for the Allies through MI5's Double Cross System fed to the Abwehr, the German armed forces' secret service, exactly what their masters wanted them to: some items of truth to maintain their credibility, and some false to deceive the enemy. On 6 June the Allies mounted the largest seaborne invasion the world had seen and secured a foothold on the Nazi-dominated European mainland.

Angus Fyffe was a SOE security officer who had spent two and a half years at Inverlair in the Highlands of Scotland before returning to London in February 1944. After clearing away some outstanding work he was told by Air Cdr A.R. Boyle, Assistant Chief Director of SOE (A/CD), Director of Personnel (D/P) and Head of the Directorate of Counter Intelligence (D/CE), that he was to spend some time interrogating and debriefing returned agents (including some fresh back from Germany) at the Bayswater Special Section. It was during his six weeks with this group, up to the end of September, that Fyffe was told by Cdr John Senter RNVR, deputy to Boyle and Director of Security, of an idea to drop into Germany a German PoW carrying false papers and other documents incriminating high-ranking Nazis as anti-Hitler elements. To ensure the papers reached the Nazi security authorities the German's parachute was to fail to open. Why was the Director of Security involved in a German Section deception plan? According to Fyffe it was normal procedure to pass a project before D/CE for assessment and approval.[1] It is most likely that this idea was one of the steady stream of initiatives emanating from the fertile imaginations of the SOE and Political Warfare Executive (PWE) planners concerned with the subversion of the Nazi regime by any means. Whether it was developed from here or resurrected a few months later, the idea certainly formed part of the original Periwig plan.

The month after D-Day Hitler received his most violent wake-up call yet, when he narrowly survived Stauffenberg's bomb attack at Rastenburg (see Chapter 7). He responded by butchering any officer with the remotest sympathy for the plotters. Regardless of what was happening to his forces, the German population and the country's infrastructure, the Führer was determined to fight to the bitter end. His controversial military decision-making was becoming the stuff of fantasy, but any general who dared point out the error of his ways risked his wild rage. The vision of the Big Three (Churchill, Roosevelt and Stalin) of German unconditional surrender showed no sign of materialising. The Allies' advance through France, the Low Countries and into Germany was to be a hard slog through snow, ice and mud during the severe European winter of 1944/5.

On 19 July 1944, the day before the attempt on Hitler's life, Maj W. Field-Robinson (X/GER), Head of SOE's German Country Section, sent to Maj R.H. Thornley (X), at that time still Head of the German and Austrian Section, the following appreciation of the situation within the Third Reich:

> The position in Germany is likely not to be materially altered (from earlier assessments).
>
> 1. There is no organised resistance in Germany.
> 2. There are disseminated oppositional elements who may be willing to be organised, but that will only happen if we are successful in introducing

organisers to them and that these in turn are able to carry out their mission.

3. Up till now, any local efforts which have been made have been so thoroughly penetrated by the enemy counter-espionage that they have been short-lived. It must therefore be counted upon that any organisational work will have to be done on a local and fractional basis rather than on a widespread basis.
4. There are undoubtedly potential resistance elements waiting to be organised in industrial areas and among transport workers. Whether such elements will cooperate when the time comes with the large number of foreign workers in Germany remains, in my opinion, a moot point. If they do, they could, in certain circumstances, develop suddenly a very big, widespread resistance movement. Otherwise it will remain purely local, I believe.
5. So long as the German Army is not very obviously and substantially beaten, or even driven back onto German territory, it is hardly likely that any German oppositional elements will build themselves into active resistance movements. When, however, such a military disaster happens, then oppositional elements may develop into resistance movements and on a wide scale.
6. What political form such resistance would take is difficult to anticipate, but there are indications that it might tend to Communism.
7. There are as yet no signs of the Army turning against either the Party or the People.[2]

From this situation report several things can be concluded:

- A distinction is made between 'oppositional elements' and 'resistance movements'.
- German Section was aware of scattered groups opposed to the regime and of the need for an effective organiser to draw them together.
- German Section had made earlier attempts to contact the opposition groups but their agents had been discovered.
- SOE had for several years had very worthwhile contacts with transport workers' organisations, particularly in the Swiss–German frontier region. Similar opposition appears to have been found in industrial areas. It is likely that both these factions had left-wing tendencies and support.

But German industry was propped up by millions of foreign workers forced to leave their homelands to release Germans for military service. The relationship between the native German workers and their subjugated 'colleagues' is difficult to determine. If they could be persuaded to cooperate in a common cause, their sheer numbers would make them a serious disrupting force. The difficulty was one of coordinating the dissident factions within a population still largely loyal to the Nazi regime.

- At the time this paper was written the Allies had opened the second front and had begun to liberate France. The Russians were driving the German Army from its land. Field-Robinson (X/GER) did not know of the plot being hatched within the Army that was to fail so miserably the very next day and result in the arrest and execution of so many key figures opposed to Nazism. As has been noted before, the morale of the population at large needed to be severely depressed by undeniably disastrous defeats (*pace* the efforts of Goebbels's Propaganda Ministry) in order to set the stage for a revolution. The day and night bombing offensive was aimed at breaking this morale, but when a country perceives the threat of being overrun by an enemy intent on its destruction and humiliation, complex emotions come into play and this objective is not easily achieved.

Peter Wilkinson and Joan Bright Astley imply that the existence of 'an extensive conspiracy inside Germany' had been revealed by the 20 July plot. Ten days after Stauffenberg's failed attempt to assassinate the Führer, Thornley mentioned to Wilkinson in a letter that the dissidents Baron Adam von Trott and Count Helmuth von Moltke had been travelling relatively freely to neutral countries for three years and making contact with the Americans' Office of Strategic Services (OSS). He claimed that Stauffenberg had been helped by Trott in establishing contacts in Berlin. He also considered that Himmler had known about the movement and had deliberately allowed it 'to come to a nice little head'.[3]

There is some logic in this. If Himmler was ambitious to become Führer, what better way than to succeed Hitler upon his assassination which he had privately known was being planned but chose not to intervene in? In the subsequent purge he could remove any threats to his own position while placating the general population. In the event Himmler did indeed destroy his chief enemy, the traditional officer caste, in the post 20 July purges.

The work of SOE was running down as occupied countries were liberated and the need for a resistance organisation in them disappeared. Head of SOE, Gubbins, was only too aware of SOE's diminishing influence in the military sphere and Germany as the last opportunity to make a contribution to the Allied victory. With this in mind he set up a German Committee to consider means of intensifying SOE's activities against the European enemy. At the first meeting on 2 August he laid down that 'Germany must now be the first priority target for SOE and all our energies and resources must be concentrated on the penetration of the Reich itself . . . and upon building up inside it the organisation necessary to see us through the post-armistice period.'[4]

Documents in the surviving German Section files indicate that there was at this time a frequent, not to say constant, re-evaluation of the resistance situation within Germany. One such paper sent to Supreme Headquarters Allied Expeditionary Force (SHAEF) in September began with the definitive statement that 'There is in Germany no Resistance Movement which can be compared with the organisations in Occupied Europe.'[5] It went on to point out that the subversive elements in Germany were opposed to the Hitler regime and ready to bring about its downfall but were not pro-Allied as had been the case in the occupied territories. For this reason the anonymous approach adopted by Special Forces Headquarters (SFHQ), with whom SOE was now working closely, had been as from an anti-Nazi organisation inside or outside Germany to any groups ready to assist in overthrowing the Nazi regime. Direct appeals by the Allies to these opposition elements were considered to be counter-productive until Germany had suffered a complete collapse, whereupon they would have little choice but to cooperate. Some opposition groups, wary of a repeat of the Weimar government, proposed a legislature very different from a British- or American-style democracy: another reason why cooperation would prove difficult.

The main opposition elements were to be found in left-wing political groups in industrial areas; the Catholic Centre Group in the Rhineland and Bavaria; the German Regular Army; and among foreign workers. There was no indication that the groups were well organised or ready to act, owing in the main to Himmler's security service having tight control of the situation. Special Forces had taken great care not to give the impression of supporting any particular opposition group but instead endeavoured to exploit all forms of discontent in the hope of fostering tension and bringing about a state of chaos that would facilitate the entry of the Allies into Germany and its rapid collapse.

The paper states that in the early autumn of 1944 SFHQ did not have a single wireless telegraphy (W/T) operator within Germany, all agents previously infiltrated having been captured. Since there was no intention of organising, arming and supplying German resistance groups, SFHQ seemed content to forgo this quicker means of communication in favour of a relatively secure but much slower courier service via Sweden, Switzerland and Istanbul. Individual agents for this service were despatched by air to Germany while others in still-occupied countries were briefed on how to be conscripted as a foreign worker and sent to their camps in Germany.

Gubbins wanted his last fling against Nazi Germany to have the best chance of success, so in October 1944 he reorganised the relatively small German Section and upgraded it to the status of Directorate. He immediately set about earmarking additional personnel from the country sections now running down their activities. He established links with Special Forces detachments in the field and organised the supervision of plans for the infiltration of agents direct into Germany. Personnel in missions abroad, particularly in neutral Stockholm, were put under review to decide what help they could be in infiltrating propaganda and people into Germany and as a communications conduit with them.

Gubbins's decision to reorganise the German Section had other important political repercussions. Since June 1942, when Sir Charles Hambro, the Head of SOE before Gubbins, had signed the so-called 'London Agreement' with Col 'Wild Bill' Donovan of the OSS, SOE and its American counterpart had been almost fully integrated within SFHQ. The exception was in Italy, where they had operated separately since September 1941. The arrangement had served British interests well enough, but Donovan, who had plans to set up a postwar strategic intelligence organisation in the United States, found it increasingly limiting. He took the opportunity of the reorganisation to withdraw the OSS liaison officer from the German Section and thereafter conducted his operations into Germany independently and on a large scale. Both SOE and OSS were operating under the general direction of SHAEF and did receive various directives from it, usually in rather vague terms and after an extended period of consideration. In practice a degree of coordination was achieved by Col R.E. Brook, the chief British liaison officer for both SOE and the Secret Intelligent Service (SIS) at SHAEF.

Gen Eisenhower, the Supreme Commander Allied Expeditionary Forces, became increasingly concerned at the stubborn resistance experienced on all fronts. In a telegram dated 20 November 1944 he informed the Combined Chiefs of Staff of his opinion that they should 'redouble our efforts to find a solution to the problem of reducing the German will to resist and then bring every appropriate weapon to bear to achieve this end'.[6]

In SOE Gubbins's German Committee was already addressing the problem. In PWE the German Will to Resist Committee was set up, with Sir Robert Bruce Lockhart in the chair. Sometime in the late summer to autumn period the discussion had centred on what action could be taken and what could be achieved by a German resistance movement of disaffected officers, exhausted anti-Nazi local officials and renegades within government. Now Thornley, the German expert, was once again asked for his assessment of the chances of a resistance movement arising from the rapidly diminishing remains of the Third Reich. Just how accurate his information was is impossible to say now, but he considered there to be no chance. A paper from PWE German and Austrian Intelligence Section dated 19 January 1945 and entitled 'Resistance and Resistance Groups in Germany and Austria' discovered in the National Archives (TNA) gives an analysis of the perceived state of German resistance and concludes with the comment that although it is impressive, one must bear in mind that:

- There is no general 'underground movement' or 'preparation for revolution' in Germany.
- Almost the whole of 'resistance' on the part of the Germans has a personal or anti-Nazi basis rather than being pro-Allied.
- The fear of the Gestapo is still so great that members of 'groups' are more likely than Germans who are not members of groups to be suspicious of strangers and to denounce them to the authorities.
- The spontaneous, individual and totally unorganised evasion of regulations by German and foreign workers is on a considerable scale and seriously injures the war effort, more so than all the other forms of resistance put together.[7]

Postwar revelations included more opposition groups than Thornley appeared to know of: could the SIS have been withholding information from the service it feared might compromise its own agents? What, then, were the chances of SOE contacting dissidents to organise them into some form of cohesive force that could undermine the German will from within? Again, Thornley thought the idea not worth pursuing. It was therefore accepted that SOE was not going to be able to assist military operations in Germany in the same way, and certainly not to the same extent, as they had in the liberation of the occupied countries. The absence of a powerfully organised resistance inside Germany itself precluded this. So it is said that the basic idea of Operation Periwig came to be thought of in much the same way as Voltaire thought of God: if a German resistance movement did not exist, it was necessary to invent one.

Precisely whose thinking was lateral enough to come up with the idea of creating a fictitious resistance movement is not known. It might have been someone with knowledge of the Twenty Committee's (see p. 10) 1941 experimental deception plan which exercised the creativity of members of MI5's Section B1A as well as of the committee. This was Plan Stiff, ultimately to prove impractical but intended to infiltrate by parachute into Germany a wireless set, instructions and codes to persuade the enemy that an agent had been dropped but had abandoned his mission. It was hoped that the Germans would waste time and effort in searching for the missing agent and that, more importantly, they would use the equipment to play back messages to us, enabling British experts to gain a great deal of knowledge about their techniques of deception.[8]

Thornley was lukewarm about the idea for a fictitious resistance movement but Gubbins was enthusiastic and set up the Periwig Planning Section within the German Directorate on 12 November 1944. Periwig as a plan to create an imaginary German resistance force needed to provide convincing evidence of the kind that could well have been discovered by the civilian population, the military and the security authorities had the movement been a genuine one. Thus SOE and PWE were to use all the means at their disposal to supply and back the movement: the despatch of agents and stores, the sending of messages in code, open appeals by wireless and leaflet, planting of rumours and 'sibs', and so forth.

SOE's enthusiasts for the plan were convinced that, given a free hand, they could by these means persuade the German security authorities in particular and the German population in general that there really was some organised resistance in Germany. The spreading of this belief, and the increasingly desperate measures that the Nazi authorities would take in consequence of it, would, when the reactions to the intense Allied bombing then taking place were also taken into account, bring about administrative chaos within the Reich. But it was realised that to produce this effect against what was clearly a very short time-scale would require coordination of all SOE action against Germany with the various other agencies involved – and all under the overall control of SHAEF.

After years of poor relations with the older secret organisation, SIS, consideration was given to their interests. It was thought possible that the chaos it was hoped to achieve by Periwig would provide an excellent cloak for the genuine activity of their agents. It was further hoped that the isolated groups and, indeed, like-minded individuals with an inclination to resist the regime might be encouraged to take positive action by the evidence to be provided of resistance elsewhere. There was always the hope that SOE's intelligence information might not be as discouraging as it appeared and that there might be a genuine embryonic German resistance starting to develop. They therefore adopted two principles: that fiction should, in fact, supplement reality, and that (in business terms) a quick turnover justifies a low rate of interest, i.e. a rapid and widespread dissemination of evidence was worth only meagre results.

The outline plan was submitted by the Periwig Planning Section on 22 November and the idea was considered by Bruce Lockhart's German Will to Resist Committee five days later.

On 10 December the German Directorate was under Gubbins's old friend Maj Gen Gerald Templer, in the final stages of recovery from wounds sustained in Italy and not yet released for 'full' duties by his medical board. He was equally keen on the operation and criticised Thornley's coolness to it. He accepted the outline plan for leaflet drops, propaganda broadcasts, agent infiltration and supply drops, and the following week the Planning Section was ordered to proceed urgently with the complete operational plan. It can well be imagined that those organisations which opposed the scheme were using this period to marshal their arguments, for when the refined plan was put before the Will to Resist Committee on 12 January 1945 it met with stubborn resistance from the SIS. This committee meeting was a turning-point in Periwig's fortunes. It was held in London at Bush House in the Aldwych, with the objective of setting up a formal progress and review procedure for the operation. Present were Bruce Lockhart and Col P.R. Chambers of PWE, Lt Cdr McLachlan of the Psychological Warfare Division (PWD) SHAEF, and Lt Col Sporborg, Gen Templer and Sqn Ldr H.M. Potter from SOE. Also in attendance were Lt Col Ryder of PWE and Lt Col Pearson of SOE. SIS's objections were that the creation of an imaginary resistance in Germany would increase security measures and make the work of their agents more difficult.

Furthermore, they maintained that the aim of overburdening the security organisations until the controls were no longer effective was beyond the power of SOE. They suggested that it was the responsibility of the chiefs of staff to decide whether the value of this scheme would be greater than the results of the SIS work in Germany it was likely to disrupt.

The Foreign Office was greatly concerned that on no account must the Russians get to hear of the plan: they considered the Soviets incapable of understanding this concept of 'German resistance', to which they would attach totally different connotations. Recognising that time was not on their side, SOE, SIS and PWE accepted a compromise plan: for the first two months of the operation the appearance of resistance in Germany should be created, provided no evidence was given that it was connected with or controlled by the Allies. This would reduce the risk of increased security activity directed at identifying SIS agents and provide a second line of defence against the Soviets discovering the true nature of the plan. It should also minimise the risk of carelessly manufactured evidence which might endanger real Allied contacts. After two months it would be reconsidered in the light of progress and the then political situation. In this form it was agreed that the operation could commence under the authority of Bruce Lockhart's Will to Resist Committee.

The modified plan to which they were to work was as follows:

Periwig – Possible Operations

1. AGENTS
   i) Arranging arrest of an agent by neutral police, to make revelations to them which will be passed to German SD [Sicherheitsdienst – security service].
   ii) Briefing genuine agents about Periwig in addition to their real mission so that if they are caught they will impart appropriate information about Periwig which they believe to be true. For example, an agent will be asked to keep his eyes open and to report to us any information he received about German resistance. This briefing will be arranged so that it does not in any way endanger the agent on his primary mission.

2. GENUINE ACTIVITY
   i) Establishing apparent connection with genuine organisations such as Edelweiss Piraten.

ii) Linking successful phoney organisations, such as Red Circle Escape Club, with Periwig.
iii) Inducing neutral firm or military attaché to believe in Periwig and to perform small services for the organisation.
iv) Association of as many failures as permitted of genuine penetration of Germany with Periwig.

3. PLANTS

A. *Neutral and Occupied Country*

i) Attaching significance to meetings between Germans and neutrals, by planting evidence.
ii) Suggesting clandestine communication by planting messages, codes, lists of members, orders, cables and letters, etc. by errors in delivery or blowing boites aux lettres by telephone calls to Germany etc.
iii) Suggesting clandestine organisation by indiscretion, informing, or by allowing penetration by agents provocateurs.
iv) Blackmailing Germans into drastic action such as confession to Gestapo, seeking asylum, suicide; this to be achieved by compromising them with knowledge of the organisation and with documents.
v) Making assassination of Germans by resistance movements in the normal course of their work appear to be Periwig operations.
vi) Suggesting that Germans obtain printing and sabotage materials and weapons, etc. from German sources in neutral countries by planting these materials of German make.

B. *Germany*

i) Genuine warnings to Nazi leaders by neutrals.
ii) Alteration in tone of SHAEF Weekly Intelligence Summary and other official documents; causing forged Allied official documents to fall into German hands.
iii) Infiltration of pamphlets, sabotage materials, etc. through courier lines from neutral states (these materials to appear to be of German make).

4. W/T
   - i) Simulation of traffic from Germany to genuine W/T operator in occupied or neutral territory. The operator is then arrested, or blown and obliged to flee, leaving German authority with evidence that German resistance was communicating with Germany through neutral or occupied territory.
   - ii) Use of a W/T operator known by us to be worked by the Germans (one useful example already exists). The British will show interest in this German resistance and ask for details.

5. POST
   - i) The use of threatening letters.
     - a) To persons 'suspected' of resistance activity.
     - b) To persons urging them to join resistance activity.
   - ii) Anonymous letters.
     - a) To the police in Germany from neutral territory, about members of the German resistance.
     - b) To neutral police about activities of German resistance.
     - c) Warnings to German leaders.
   - iii) Blackmailing letters to 'members' of German resistance by private individuals for money.

6. SUSPICIOUS ACTIVITIES

A. *Neutral and Occupied Territory*
   - i) Arranging a démarche to the Vatican by a section of Periwig resistance.
   - ii) Intensive activity of 'cut-outs' in neutral territory.

B. *In England*
   - i) References to German resistance in the Houses of Parliament, questions, etc.

7. RUMOURS
   - i) Sibs, confidences, verbal indiscretions, in neutral/occupied territory, German and Allied territory, to back up factual operations.

8. PAMPHLETS
   i) Distribution in neutral, occupied and German territory, of pamphlets consisting of:
      a) Instructions.
      b) Hints at the existence of the organisation.
      c) Details of an escape organisation.
      d) Encouragement to malinger, desert, strike, go-slow, etc.

9. BBC
   i) Blackmail messages.
   ii) Allusion messages.
   iii) Orders and encouragement disguised as historical talks, and discussion of contemporary events.
   iv) Black broadcasting, including preparation of German soldiers, etc. for the revolt.

10. PRESS

A. *Neutral Territory*
   i) Publication of German resistance activity inspired by Periwig.
   ii) Playing up of genuine events implying resistance in Germany.

B. *Occupied and German Territory*
   i) Insertion of personal notices and advertisements, to give the impression of clandestine communication.

C. *UK and Allied*
   i) Building up of events in Germany.
   ii) Alternatively by omitting reference to neutral press reports of resistance.
   iii) Articles on 'the attitude of the British Government to German resistance and to a new German Government'.
   iv) Indiscretions.[9]

This plan may be compared with the original, which is shown in Appendix 1. The actions to which the SIS took exception can, in the main, be seen as linking any German resistance to the Allies. It is worth recalling the SIS's strong aversion to this. In the first place a spontaneous uprising would be far more likely to spread. Secondly, it would carry more credibility when the lack of pro-Allied sentiments among Germans was taken into account. Then there was the Foreign Office's fear of an Allied-sponsored resistance movement becoming known to Stalin.

Anything dropped from the air could only have come via either the RAF or the USAAF. Similarly, activity involving German refugees or important PoWs would most probably have come to the attention of the Allied authorities, who could therefore be seen as being implicated in the action. But the objection to arranging for the discovery of dead agents carrying incriminating documents (provided they had not been dropped by parachute) does not fit with the overall objective of distancing the Allies. It might have been seen as too difficult to arrange, or perhaps as plainly unethical. The use of double agents in a deception scheme carries in principle a high risk, which might have been the reason for the vetoing of this part of the proposal.

One additional idea was added: the suggestion that the dissident Germans were obtaining printing and sabotage materials as well as weapons from German sources in neutral countries by planting these German-made items in appropriate places where they would be discovered.

The operation would be controlled by the Periwig Committee which would be composed of F.T. Davies as chairman, and Potter from SOE with SIS and PWE representatives and Capt Dawson acting as secretary. This small committee would meet every Monday and Thursday afternoon, before which the secretary was to receive progress reports from relevant parties.

Three objectives for the committee were agreed:

1. To consider Periwig plans submitted by SOE, PWE and the SIS.
2. To allocate responsibilities for action between the above three organisations on approved plans and ensure that proper coordination was maintained.
3. To progress action decided upon at previous meetings.[10]

Despite the problems with and antipathy of the SIS, the idea of creating an imaginary resistance movement and of 'selling it' to the Germans appealed strongly to some members of Baker Street as an entirely suitable culmination of SOE's endeavours. To many, the genuine reports of Germans in a state of near hysteria as the Soviet Red Army approached the borders of Prussia and Silesia, and the multiplying opportunities for creating confusion and panic throughout the Reich, were signs that this venture showed every promise of being a success.

The details of the plan were tackled under eight broad areas: Wehrmacht, Separatists, Church, Railway workers, Foreign labour, Industrial and mining labour, Party and police, and Industrialists. To each of these areas of interest a framework was constructed on which could be hung key elements of the imaginary resistance organisation. These elements covered control, locations of active units, and means of contact and communication. These details were, of course, confidential to a few key personnel directly involved in Operation Periwig: the copy of document R.3299 in the TNA file FO898/354 carries the prominent stamp TOP SECRET at the head of the first page. The text of this description of the fictitious situation within Germany is given below.

R.3299

WEHRMACHT

1. A committee of senior Wehrmacht officers in England, under our control, are in touch with the HQ of the movement in Berlin.

2. In addition to the HQ at Berlin there are also cells in the following Wehrkreise:

Breslau	Munster
Dresden	Hamburg
Nurnburg	Danzig
Wiesbaden	

These cells are all linked with Berlin HQ through normal army communications and personal contact.

With the cooperation of the London committee two organisers, chosen from Ps/W, have been infiltrated into Germany from England. One is at present at the Berlin HQ and the other is touring the remaining cells.

3. Communications

a) A German signals officer is able to make use of a W/T operator in the Danish resistance to communicate with London. He is linked to Berlin via Hamburg through normal army communications.

b) A commercial traveller maintains contact between the British Legation in Sweden through cut-outs, and a Wehrmacht representative in Hamburg.

c) German officers occasionally take important despatches to England by surrendering at the front line.
d) German officers occasionally take important despatches back to Germany by being taken prisoner for a few hours and 'escaping'.
e) A neutral military attache in Berlin uses the diplomatic bag to his own capital to maintain contact between the British Embassy in that country and the nerve centre of the Wehrmacht in Berlin.

SEPARATISTS

1. Contact has recently been made with a representative of the Bavarian Separatist movement in Switzerland. London HQ is in contact with the legation at Berne who possess the necessary contact for the representative.

2. About 8 small groups of Separatists, mainly professional men, exist in Bavaria, the HQ of the movement being at Munich. There are also two or three safe houses in the Bavarian alps.

3. With encouragement from London and the materials which they are now able to receive the organisation will spread and grow in numbers.

4. Communications:
a) A smuggling line, recently opened across the Swiss–Austrian frontier through Lichstenstam [*sic*], for sabotage and assassination materials.
b) A courier line following the same route.

CHURCH

1. A representative of the RC church visits the London HQ. He is in touch with a sympathiser in the Vatican. London HQ's participation in the direction and help of this organisation is done mainly through Switzerland and British HQ in Italy.

2. About 10 monasteries and other clerical centres contain organisations in Austria and Southern Germany. The 10 monasteries are at:

Mariahilfburg	St Florian
Wilhering	Gÿttweig
Kremsmünster	Klosterneuburg

Beuren	Mariazell
Buxon (Bresanone)	Gurk

Village priests, in touch with those centres, have organised small groups of sympathisers in their parish. Small stores of arms, and sabotage material, etc. have been accumulated. A small quantity of subversive leaflets are printed. There are a few safe houses for couriers and for Allied airmen.

3. Communications
   a) A line across the Austro-Swiss frontier between two monasteries, to an Italian partisan priest, via a partisan radio to British HQ in Italy.
   b) A line via Roman Catholic customs official at Constanz to a church organiser in St Gallen, to a German friar in Milan, to an Italian partisan priest, through a partisan W/T set, to a British HQ in Italy.
   c) A group of pro-German Swiss in Berne are in touch with an ardent Roman Catholic employed in the German Legation and with the church group at St Gallen.
   d) The organisation has recently worked as far north as Würzburg; a representative is at present working in Frankfurt, and a small group in Augsburg has started working through a Separatist line.

RAILWAY WORKERS

1. The railway workers are handled from London in the same way as industrial and mining labour. It is in the Field that they are largely a separate organisation.

2. Cells exist in the undermentioned main railway centres:

Vienna	Hamburg
Innsbruck	Berlin
Nurnburg	Magdeburg
Mannheim	Leipzig
Cologne	Breslau
Hagen	Cracow
Hamm	

Most of these cells developed spontaneously. They are in loose personal contact with each other via the railway system.

3. Visiting organisers have made contact with these cells to brief them in how to follow BBC instructions and prepare for a general strike. Three organisers (drawn from Ps/W) are at present in Germany at:

   Innsbruck Mannheim Cologne

   These three organisers are due to visit the other cells.

4. Communications
   a) Agents, who have been parachuted or infiltrated.
   b) Organisers, who are able to cross the Danish and Swiss frontiers through their railway employment. There is a Danish railway official in Denmark in touch with the Reichsbahn Movement who send messages on his behalf to London. He also assists the infiltration of our agents. In Zurich, a Swiss railway official sends messages to London via the British Legation at Berne and also helps with the infiltration of agents.

FOREIGN LABOUR

1. The attitude of the German labour cells towards foreign workers is one of toleration, but not cooperation. They do not consider them reliable, and they fear penetration by the Gestapo. Foreign workers have formed a few cells, but more for actual protection than for action.

2. The cells exist as follows:

Russians	–	Halle, Hagen
Poles	–	Linz
French	–	Kaiserslaurtern, Wiener-Neustadt
Belgian	–	Magdeburg, Solingen, Lübeck
Dutch	–	Münster
Italian	–	Innsbruck
Danish	–	Altona
Czech	–	Dortmund

In one case only is a cell in contact with a German labour cell, viz. with the Poles at Linz. The Italian cell at Innsbruck is dependent on the church.

INDUSTRIAL AND MINING LABOUR

1. The organisation is controlled in varying degree by HQ in London, with an advisery committee of refugee social democrats, etc. Small cells are in existence in the following industrial centres:

Nr Vienna	Nr Saarbrucken	Bremen
Linz	Dortmund	Hamburg
Regensburg	Essen	Berlin
Nr Villengen	Dusseldorf	Stettin
Mannheim	Chemnitz	Danzig
Darmstadt	Nr Halle	Poznan
Frankfurt	Hanover	Cracow
Mainz		

Some of these cells were started by organisers from England and from Russia. In some cases the organisers have stayed on the spot and have built up a small network with communication to England; in other cases they have stayed only long enough to start the cell and brief the leader on how to take his orders from the BBC.

2. The following organisers who have been infiltrated into Germany are still there:

1. From Russia to the environments of Vienna.
2. " " " " " " Cracow.
3. " " " " " " Poznan.
4. " " " " " " Danzig.
5. Dropped by parachute near Linz.
6. One W/T operator dropped by parachute near Dortmund.
7. Dropped by parachute in S Germany, now near Bremen.
8. One W/T operator dropped by parachute near Hamburg.
9. From Denmark to the environments of Hamburg.

3. Communications
   a) Agents who have been parachuted into the country, infiltrated through the lines, or from occupied territory.
   b) W/T, where a W/T operator has been dropped or infiltrated.
   c) Cells formed by visiting organisers rely upon the BBC to keep them abreast of events.

PARTY AND POLICE

1. A senior P/W SS officer in England directs this movement under our supervision. He communicates with Germany with the assistance of the London HQ as in para 3.

2. The movement is comparatively new and consists at present of only a few scattered members in the following main cities:

Hamburg	Nurnburg
Berlin	Munich

   In principle they are organised on the same lines as the industrialists, i.e. each member carefully lists the followers upon whom he can count, when the time comes. In some cases two or three officers are known to one another, as in one instance, they have between them the control of a Volksturm battalion, a Police HQ and armoury, and a company of Waffen SS. One organiser has been sent to Germany from England and is at present in Munich. He was chosen from SS Ps/W in England.

3. Communications
   a) A Gestapo agent in North Holland who relays W/T messages.
   b) A few agents infiltrated through Switzerland and through the lines, of whom one or two were Gestapo agents working in France, known to this officer, and a few carefully selected and very high quality SS Ps/W.
   c) An SD agent in Sweden is in touch with the sympathisers in Germany and through cut-outs, including a pro-Nazi Swede, with the British Legation in Stockholm.

INDUSTRIALISTS

1. Negotiations between certain German industrialists and London have been completed. Their views are similar to those of the Wehrmacht movement.

2. The industrialists are not organised in cells as it is too dangerous for them to gather at meetings. Each man has the temper of his business associates finely gauged and knows exactly whom to count upon when the time comes. His contacts are only those of a like kind

in other firms in Germany whom he meets on genuine business. Such industrialists are situated as follows:

Berlin	Frankfurt
Stettin	Dusseldorf and Essen area
Breslau	Hanover
Katowice	Hamburg
Munich	Brandenburg
Nurnburg	Fulda
Stuttgart	Chemnitz

This movement is linked up with the Wehrmacht in Berlin where there are one or two leading industrialists in touch with the Wehrmacht conspirators.

3. Contact and communication with industrialists is maintained in neutral countries:
   a) A German industrialist in Hamburg visits Sweden and is in contact with the British Legation through cut-outs. He despatches all negotiations of special importance by a Swedish friend to London.
   b) A Swedish firm, represented in Berlin, maintains an important link between the British Legation in Stockholm and a number of German industrialists in Berlin.
   c) A German–Swiss firm in Switzerland maintains contact between the British Legation at Berne and the industrialists in Berlin.
   d) A German–Swiss firm at Basel maintains contact between German industrialists in the Ruhr and the British Embassy in Madrid.[11]

The creative minds in SOE and PWE were now set to be exercised in one final deception plan – Operation Periwig.

Chapter 11

THE INITIAL PHASE

After over half a century history has allowed us to see what opposition to Hitler's regime really existed in the final year of the war in Europe. It is probably true to say that, as happened in many provinces of the lands occupied by the Nazis, when the Allies were victorious it became advantageous to one's status in society to be shown to have been working tirelessly for the winning side all the time, regardless of whether one was exposed to the danger of arrest, torture and execution or merely expressed dissatisfaction in the privacy of the home to trusted friends and relatives. This 'jumping on the bandwagon' was a cause of confusion among those charged in the immediate postwar period, for either legal or academic reasons, with establishing the true extent of opposition to National Socialism.

What must have been far more difficult was to form an accurate picture of the extent of this opposition in the last months of summer 1944, when the Allies had broken out of the bridgehead following the invasion of the Normandy beaches, and all eyes were set on the advance towards Berlin.

On 19 January 1945, seven days after approval had been given, subject to various limitations, to launch Operation Periwig, a paper was prepared by A.R. Walmsley of the German and Austrian Intelligence Section of the Political Warfare Executive (PWE) on their understanding of resistance and resistance groups in those two countries. Introduced as a 'preliminary note of general conclusions', it was sent to Col P.R. Chambers of the Political Intelligence Department (PID) and set out to attempt to disentangle the various kinds of opposition in Germany whose 'nature, motive and extent of resistance varies widely'.[1] The paper was concerned with answering these questions:

- What is the activity and planned activity of the 'groups' and
- Would the individuals and groups be willing to assist Allied agents before the close of hostilities?

Genuine partisan activity was restricted to a 'well-organised' group of self-styled communists, probably mainly of Slovene descent, on the Yugoslav–Austrian border. Although this group had agents in some parts of Austria and, indeed, may have had links with a group south of Melk on the Danube, it was not thought that they planned any organised resistance actions in Germany and Austria proper: their activities were restricted to the Yugoslav border area. The likelihood of their assisting Allied agents was very uncertain, and a warning was given that these partisans may actually betray them unless reassured by the parent organisation.

An area of concern to the Nazi authorities was the widespread anti-Hitler Youth groups similar to the Edelweiss Piraten. Thought to be purely local in organisation, their members sought adventure by gangster or criminal methods: by petty sabotage and assault on party and State representatives. They were not unlike many teenage boys with hooligan tendencies: they did not wish to conform to the regimentation of the Hitler Youth and preferred their own form of Führer. The authorities were concerned by them because they were undermining the spirit of unquestioning obedience demanded of the young. But these groups were certainly not pro-Allied and could on no account be relied upon to assist agents.

Catholic youth groups, on the other hand, restricted their activities to discussions led by priests. Because these were outwardly pro-Catholic they could not fail to present an anti-Nazi outlook to the youths. But there was no evidence that these groups intended to do anything practical before the collapse of the Nazi regime; and they, too, were not pro-Allied. The best that could be hoped for was an individual member assisting an individual Catholic agent seen to be fleeing from Nazism and endeavouring to bring about its overthrow.

There was another anti-Nazi faction, numbered in tens of thousands, that while a worry to the authorities because of their lawlessness, would provide no help to the Allies. These were the bands of fugitives, foreign workers, PoWs and German deserters who had abandoned their units and were eking out a precarious existence in the ruins of bombed towns and in remote parts of the country. Their aim was their own survival, and they damaged the German war effort only in so far as they had to steal to keep themselves alive. There was no reason to suppose they would assist an Allied agent.

Throughout Germany and Austria there were other groups who for one reason or another did not take active steps to sabotage the war effort except, perhaps, for the scrawling of anti-Nazi slogans on walls. These were the discussion and propaganda groups, whose members tended to know each other personally and who conducted anti-Nazi discussions and even formed listening committees to tune in to foreign radio broadcasts to hear what was often censored out of their home news programmes. One such scattered Austrian group was said to number around a hundred people.

These groups seemed to be made up of the survivors of the old Social-Democratic, Communist and Centre Parties; religious groups; students; and those who now despised the Nazis but had no previous political affiliation. The only groups offering any likelihood of assisting the Allies were those affiliated to the Social-Democratic and Communist Parties, and this was thought to be conditional upon the contacting agent being of the right political complexion and having impeccable bona fides to assure them that he was not an undercover member of the Sicherheitsdienst (SD).

Fear of infiltration by the SD also plagued the potentially very useful population of foreign workers. Although there was little sign of any uprising among them, the Poles at least did make some preparation for such an event if German collapse appeared imminent. Following the liquidation in September 1944 of a Polish organisation in Pomerania which had prepared for a rising when arms were dropped to them, the groups were extremely wary of assisting Allied agents and were only likely to help them on receipt of cast-iron assurances that they were not SD agents.

Some acts of sabotage had taken place in Germany by infiltrated agents, whereas others had probably been by foreign workers, but overall the damage was not significant. Furthermore, there was no evidence to suggest this was organised beyond the small-groups stage. But after August 1944 there was evidence of the increasing strain under which the German population then lived, for, despite the widespread purges following the 20 July attempt on Hitler's life, isolated and spontaneous acts of open defiance by individuals against the authorities had become more frequent. They were by this time not uncommon in cities suffering heavy air raids. But these demonstrations were not politically motivated and were mostly prompted by some sudden reaction to what many considered an injustice.

Escaping prisoners had reported isolated instances of assistance by individual Germans, sometimes out of humanitarian considerations, sometimes out of anti-Nazi feeling and sometimes, in remote parts of the country, in the hope of gaining additional farm labour.

Walmsley's concluding remarks did not augur well for the German Section's agents preparing to infiltrate the Reich. They could not expect to find organised underground movements, only individual anti-Nazis who would not welcome members of the Allies. And denunciation to the feared Gestapo was still a significant risk.

Of all the opposition activities mentioned in Walmsley's paper, the one that was on a considerable scale and was considered to be seriously harming the German war effort was the evasion of regulations by both German and foreign workers. This activity, a sign of widespread dissatisfaction, was individual, spontaneous and totally unorganised, and yet it was estimated in London to be more harmful to the German war effort than all the other forms of resistance put together.[2]

It is interesting to note that there was no mention whatsoever in this paper of any resistance within the military. One can only assume that the far-reaching purges following the failure of the 20 July plot had liquidated almost every semblance of opposition by arrest and terror; the few remaining scattered survivors were then leaderless.

Such was the report that was presented to the Periwig planners.

Since Operation Periwig was an unusual and highly imaginative concept, and since the Secret Intelligence Service (SIS) had already demonstrated its disapproval of the plan, if anything was to be achieved it was essential to set up an adequate control-and-coordination body. A joint committee of SOE, SIS and PWE was formed and first met on 22 January 1945. Col F.T. Davies, a member of the SOE Council, was in the chair. Sqn Ldr Potter was the other SOE representative and Capt Dawson was the secretary.

The SIS, which had never been enthusiastic colleagues of SOE and were at best unwillingly associated with Periwig, announced that they considered themselves mere observers, protecting their own interests but not being required to take any action. Davies, known to be one of SOE's 'hard men', made the point that, as far as he was concerned, there was the possibility of their being asked for assistance. One can sense in these recorded notes an atmosphere at this first meeting, if not of acrimony, then at least of tension. It was immediately clear where the enthusiasm for the project lay and that the initiative would have to come from SOE. The hope that this committee would nurture a genuinely cooperative joint operation was soon frustrated. After several years of irritable relations with the SIS, and with everyone pretty well worn after the strains of five years of war, SOE was seen as trying to use the committee as too much of a means of control. But here was a job to be done and if SOE was not only the originators of the plan but now the only real enthusiast for it, it would have no option but to take the lead.

The initial phase of Operation Periwig can be said to be the period when the SIS managed to impose severe limitations on SOE's proposals. 'C' was understandably intent on maintaining the best conditions for his own agents within Germany. To this end, any increase in security operations by the Gestapo or any other enemy agency would be seen as putting them and their clandestine work under greater risk. Yet increasing security activity to the point of chaos throughout Germany, albeit by means of a hoax, was a stated aim of Gen Gubbins's plan. However, if the Nazi security apparatus could not find any link between dissident factions within the Reich and the Allies, searches for SIS agents should, in theory, be no more intense.

The initial restrictions placed upon Periwig of no air activity or any action that could be associated with the Allies had two objectives: to allow any uprising in Germany to be seen by the generally patriotic population as spontaneously anti-Nazi as distinct from pro-Allied; and to maintain intense secrecy around the operation so that the USSR was denied any knowledge of it, hence avoiding diplomatic complications. This restriction was to last from 13 January to 14 February.

Operation Periwig had not been conceived with the kind of restrictions now imposed by the SIS in mind, and it very soon became apparent that it stood to lose much of its effectiveness. One of the key points of the plan had been to alarm the Germans by the infiltration of scores of agents trained by the Allies, the coordination of various opposition groups by the Allies, the arming of the resistance by the Allies and the undisguised use of the BBC for communications. During this initial period all these connections with the Allies had to be forgone.

There remained only three aspects of the plan that could be pursued: propaganda by means of leaflet drops, radio broadcasts and 'sibs' or rumours spread in neutral countries. These activities had, of course, been under continual review and development for several years and in some respects had become highly refined. But as with so many things in wartime, the demand always exceeded the supply: of paper for printing the leaflets; of aircraft for dropping them; and of air-time for radio broadcasts. But the contacts in such neutral countries as Sweden, Spain and Switzerland readily exploited the receptive ears of pro-Germans with carefully crafted rumours, as they had been doing successfully since 1940.

Among the host of rumours initiated in the early days of PWE were two at opposite ends of the credibility spectrum. One was spread via a station known as Radio Inconnue which started broadcasting in November 1940 and was supposed to be located in the Paris area but in reality was in England. In July 1941 it made its first reference to Les Chevaliers du Coup de Balai, a fictitious resistance organisation which issued instructions for sabotage and the assassination of traitors.

At the other end of the scale was a feeble rumour which was duly attacked in the *Daily Mail* that the British government had imported 200 man-eating sharks from Australia and had let them loose in the Channel as an additional deterrent to an invasion by the Germans.

From the middle of January 1945 SOE missions in neutral countries were drawn into Periwig operations. The idea of giving Periwig a kick-start from neutral countries was pursued vigorously, SOE officers being sent to Sweden and Switzerland to launch it. Here they were in a position to sow many wild rumours that were certain to reach the ears of German sympathisers and be passed back as 'intelligence' to Berlin. The work of these units involved associating notable Germans in these countries with anti-Nazi factions by planting incriminating evidence and spreading discrediting stories about them, all aimed at giving a clear impression to all that German resistance to Hitler was active and growing. The mission personnel were on the look-out for any suitable circumstances by which they could demonstrate a link with various of the fictitious German resistance groups set out in London's instructions to them. The difficulties these SOE members had to overcome were immense. Not only had they to be very well aware of what was happening within the German community in their country of operation, they had also to come up with suitable ideas for exploiting the situation; get approval from SOE's German Directorate in London – which in turn had to clear the proposal through SIS, who were not inclined to afford Periwig the priority its success demanded; make preparations that, in order not to 'blow' the entire scheme, had to be meticulous; and then carry out the operation, provided the circumstances had not changed in the meantime so much as to invalidate it. Not least of the obstacles was that of working largely against a timescale dictated by the Allied advance and the rapidly changing events in Germany itself.

As it turned out, a large number of operations from neutral countries were proposed but, owing to the difficulties mentioned, most of them were either aborted or never grew beyond the ideas stage. Of those that were carried out, an assessment of their value proved impossible to gauge.

One such operation was proposed in January with the collaboration of the mission in Stockholm to indicate imminent activity in industrial and mining labour resistance cells. A message indicating a code for labour resistance was to be planted on a German who might be travelling from Sweden to Germany. It was hoped that the message would be either discovered by German customs officials or at other security controls, or that it would be found by the traveller himself, who might hand it in to the Gestapo for investigation. Either way, suspicion would be aroused and, depending on the dedication of the officer involved, time would be wasted in investigating it and another seed of doubt in the future of the Reich would have been sown. But if the traveller discovered the planted message and, realising the implications of being found with it, out of fear and a sense of self-preservation destroyed it, the whole operation would have failed. A suitable document was prepared and sent to Stockholm at the end of the month, but for undisclosed reasons the operation (listed as L.1) was not completed. The code number allocated to each operation indicated the area of German life against which it was directed: C for Church; I for Industrial; L for Labour; P for Party and Police; R for Railway; S for Separatist; and W for Wehrmacht.

In the same month, an operation with the code number L.2, D/Q.10 (whose identity has not been found) assisted in the spreading of a rumour to the effect that Hitler's scorched-earth policy – the systematic destruction of buildings, industry and crops as the Wehrmacht retreated in the face of the Allied advance – was really being carried out largely to cover up the sabotage work of labour cells of resistance.

The second meeting of the Periwig Committee was held on 25 January. Gen Gerald Templer stood in for Davies; Lt Col Ryder represented PWE and Maj Hadrill of Section V represented the SIS. The SIS's position on the sidelines was again recorded by Templer, reiterating that they could not help, nor would they be asked to unless it was for passing controlled messages through one of their double agents. Rumours were to be handled by SOE but cleared by the Rumour Committee, the details of which have still not come to light. Scurrilous rumours and letters had already been prepared implicating the Wehrmacht, industrial labour, railway workers and the Church but matters concerning the latter had yet to be approved by the Foreign Office, sensitive to the repercussions of offending this international establishment.

D/Q.10 also spread a rumour in early February that resistance cells among German workers had established radio communication with the Russian spearhead groups approaching from the east (Operation L.3). It is interesting to note that this rumour concerned only German workers and Soviet forces. The Foreign Office's great sensitivity to Anglo-Soviet relations had been spared by giving no hint of western Allied involvement.

Operation R.1 was aimed at railway workers' cells, of which it was known some genuine ones existed and had carried out 'insaisissable' sabotage over a period of several years (see p. 110). In January propaganda pamphlets and an associated letter were prepared giving evidence of a railway resistance organisation. These were to be planted in a railway station waiting room or in a truck on the Swiss–German frontier to give the impression they had been abandoned in haste. It was hoped they would be found by German officials or by pro-German travellers who would hand them to the security police. The material was prepared and sent to Berne on 30 January. Just how these delivery operations were carried out quickly is not at all clear; one must assume the regular diplomatic bag exchanges between nations not at war must have carried a great deal of such material for the war effort. Unfortunately, this operation was not completed.

Another operation, code-named R.2, involving D/Q.10 was undertaken at the end of January when a rumour was put about that railway workers had decided not to call a general strike until all civilians had been evacuated from Berlin. Operation R.2 demonstrates the subtlety of some of these schemes. Not only does it imply that secret meetings must have been convened widely to make arrangements for a general strike without the State security apparatus becoming aware of them, but it also fosters defeatism in anticipating the imminent fall of the capital. Furthermore, when civilians were not evacuated from Berlin the railway workers would be disgruntled at the casual attitude shown by the administration, while the citizens of the city would become more fearful of the forthcoming catastrophe about to engulf them and of their government's lack of concern for them.

The Church had always been a source of resistance to Hitler and Nazism, so it was natural to use it in the propaganda war. There was, however, great concern that any operations involving the Roman Catholic Church should not compromise any genuine resistance that remained. Rumour was therefore felt to be the safest way of bringing them into the orbit of Periwig. At the end of January Franz von Papen, Hitler's ambassador to Turkey until the previous year and Germany's leading Catholic, undertook a mission to Madrid. D/Q.10 was able to spread a rumour in Operation C.3 that the real reason for his visit was to persuade Spanish Catholics to act as intermediaries in securing from the Vatican, now within the Allies' zone of influence, testimony to convince the Allies that German Catholics were not implicated with the Nazis.

Col Davies was back in the chair for the next, the third, meeting of the Periwig Committee on 29 January, and Walmsley represented PWE. Davies, whose directorate also controlled SOE's Research and Development Section (concerned with equipping agents and resistance organisations with specialised stores for their operations), undertook to look into what could be done to provide receptacles in which compromising documents could be dropped from the air. He was also to follow up an idea to convert Deutsche Kleinempfänger (DKE) or German 'People's Radios' (a standard wireless receiver of the time) in order to simulate clandestine wireless telegraphy (W/T) traffic of German origin. SOE had somehow purchased sixty of the sets that country sections had been interested in to conceal the new Miniature Communications Receivers or MCRs developed by Brig F.W. Nicholls's Radio Communication Division workshops in Watford.

Within a week or two D/Q.10 had instigated yet another rumour, Operation C.4, this time in Stockholm and concerning a Hungarian Catholic bishop. Hungary, of course, was largely pro-Nazi, having attacked Yugoslavia alongside the Germans on 11 April 1941 and later that year having assisted in the attack on Russia. The rumour was to the effect that the bishop had come to terms with the advancing Russians and had inveigled himself into the position of being appointed administrator of some of the areas being occupied by the Red Army. This was intended to indicate to the Germans, who were still in control of much of the country, that certain of the Hungarian clergy had already started organised collaboration with their new overlords from the east. The rumour also implied that they were possibly in touch with a similar group of anti-Nazi clergy with headquarters in northern Switzerland who were working into southern Germany.

Another idea which it had been intended to foster was that of separatist cells, mainly concerned with an independent Bavaria. The difficulties in this field were considerable, and no operations were actually commenced. A couple were, however, planned: Operation S.1 proposed to use a known Gestapo stool-pigeon as a Periwig plant, but it was vetoed by SIS, and there was insufficient time to revise the scheme to their liking. The second proposal, known as Operation S.2, was a rumour linking up with church schemes and hinting that the anti-Nazi Prince Rupprecht, heir to the throne of Bavaria and First World War field marshal, had instructed a certain well-known Bavarian to contact the Austrian bishop in Austria to coordinate plans with him.

Ten days elapsed between the third and fourth meetings of the Periwig Committee at which Maj Howarth appeared for SOE. Working on the premise that the ban on air drops would be rescinded, the search for a suitable receptacle for dropping compromising documents had continued and borne fruit. Not only was Camouflage Section obtaining German document cases, or making copies indistinguishable from them, but Sefton Delmer of PWE was working on an incriminating document and, importantly, successful trial drops of a briefcase had taken place.

In an important, if unexplained, report Capt Dawson, the committee's secretary, stated that Templer had told him that 'C' and CD, the Head of SOE (Gubbins), had agreed in principle to the original Periwig scheme of unrestricted action. What exactly did this mean? Had the two chiefs agreed to the plan drawn up by SOE? If so, was the ban on associating Periwig operations with the Allies now lifted? And were the items deleted by the SIS from the original plan now reinstated, in particular the use of air drops of personnel and supplies? The degree of reinstatement is not spelt out, but the most likely explanation is that this agreement was a prelude to the period of qualified operational freedom that commenced shortly afterwards, on 15 February.

At this fourth meeting the possibility was discussed of sending recently captured PoWs back into Germany at a time of advance. Their task would be to create widespread disaffection by spreading defeatist propaganda or to form resistance groups within the Wehrmacht. This proposal would have been fraught with difficulties: of preparing the prisoners in the short time available and of risk to the men themselves bearing in mind the severe penalties meted out to any soldier found heading away from the front line without good reason.

Other encouraging matters reported at this meeting included the approval at long last of Operation Braddock to drop hundreds of thousands of small incendiary devices for use by opposition elements. Although this was not part of Periwig it was nevertheless welcomed as being a potential help. Other work included the development of a fake German stamp issue implying an attempted coup by Himmler (much sought after by philatelists after the war) and work by MI19 on an intercepted PoW letter. In addition, a carefully conducted briefing about Periwig for SOE agents destined for Germany was arranged. Everything they said or did, either deliberately or unintentionally, had to promote the idea of the imminent rise of a significant resistance organisation.

A London luncheon of the Foreign Press Association on 15 February was the opportunity for D/Q.10 to attempt to convey a rumour to Dr Egli of the Berne newspaper *Der Bund* about the extent of resistance organisations in Germany. This was done in conjunction with the periodic reconfirmation and re-emphasis of the press censorship stops and conveyed the impression to neutral journalists that the stories about German resistance activity printed in the neutral press, often planted by the SOE missions, were not only true but of considerable interest to the British on security grounds. One such article concerned the parachuting of women's clothing into Germany, although the alleged purpose of such a drop is no longer evident. The use of BBC wireless messages was also cited. The Director of Military Intelligence (DMI) at the War Office was asked whether this organisation would make a démarche, or political explanation, of the issue to the neutral press, but he refused to become involved. Unfortunately, progress of the whole Periwig operation had not been good enough to encourage anyone to challenge the DMI's objection.

When the SIS had imposed their embargo on SOE the Allies on the western front had just repulsed 70-year-old FM von Rundstedt's Ardennes offensive, inflicting 120,000 enemy casualties. They were once again advancing relentlessly towards the frontier of the German Reich. The SIS had agreed to a review of their ban after eight weeks, perhaps hoping that by that time the need for Periwig could no longer be argued. But after six weeks they agreed to lift the ban, SOE and PWE being permitted what was referred to as Qualified Operational Freedom.

In anticipation of this the German Directorate in SOE had taken steps to set up training courses and to start the recruitment of agents. The most likely people to be found working against the regime in Germany would be disaffected German nationals, and the best available source of such men for SOE would be among the hundreds of thousands of PoWs incarcerated in camps throughout the British Isles. Any men recruited had, of course, to be volunteers, and they had to be individually and thoroughly vetted to ensure they would undertake the mission to which they were assigned. In order to protect the real objective of Periwig, the recruits volunteered for what they understood to be genuine anti-Nazi missions to Germany. Even the instructors on their training courses believed they were going to organise real resistance within the Reich. But the results of SOE's trawl through the PoWs, the interrogations to establish genuine suitability and the other tests necessary before letting a man risk his life and perhaps jeopardise the operation, were disappointing. It was in some respects not surprising that men who were being fed the very latest propaganda about how well the war was going for the Allies and how much destruction was being wrought on Germany should not wish to risk their lives further when hostilities would come to an end in the foreseeable future and they could then look forward to repatriation to their homeland. This meant that those prisoners who did volunteer were committed anti-Nazis with an evangelistic zeal, Nazi sympathisers who saw it as their duty to try to return to their Army at the first opportunity or men so desperate to return to their families in the ruined cities that they were prepared to risk everything. The interrogation procedures were able to identify and eliminate the last two categories.

The fifth meeting of the Periwig Committee on 12 February saw an enlarged attendance of nine persons: Davies, Ryder, Walmsley, McLachlan, Hadrill and another SIS representative, Thornley, Potter and Howarth. It was agreed that Operation Braddock, which had been conceived as early as 1942, would assist Periwig's general aims. For practical reasons it was best carried out during the daylight sorties of the US Army Air Force. Details of the successful trial drops of the briefcase now had to be discussed with Bomber Command to reassure them of the technique involved. Consequently a joint SOE/PWE meeting was called two days later. Maj Douglas Everett, as Head of the Air Supply Research Section of SOE, attended, along with Sqn Ldr Potter and representatives of the Air Liaison Section (AL) and PWE. Formal minutes of this meeting were not issued, but Everett took notes from which it is clear that while no mention was made of the use of agents, the feasibility of dropping briefcases was high on the agenda. Bomber Command was unhappy with dropping such items from the jump hole since they might be caught in the aircraft's slipstream and strike the tail, causing serious damage. Consideration was therefore given to releasing such items from the bomb bays. The Air Supply Research Section thereupon took the matter up in detail with Bomber Command; the equipment required for the dropping of dummy stores and the possibility of using Mosquito intruder aircraft were discussed. Among the items it was proposed to drop from these aircraft were empty parachutes, empty containers, empty panniers, small-arms simulators and booby-trapped food tins, all intended to suggest they were being despatched to resistance groups and some had already been retrieved from their containers. But the dropping of empty containers and empty panniers presented a fresh set of technical problems, as they behaved very differently from full ones when they entered the aircraft's slipstream, and that had to be considered by the scientists of the Air Supply Research Section and the aerodynamicists at RAE Farnborough.

At least four operations involving railway workers had been planned by SOE. The first was to be a plant of information giving evidence of a resistance organisation among railway workers, and although the papers were printed and sent to Switzerland, it was not completed. The second was a rumour spread at the end of January. The fifth meeting of the Periwig Committee was told that the third operation, a plan referred to as Operation R.3, which was to plant documents regarding railway sabotage in Germany in such a way that they would be found by enemy patrols on the German side of the frontier with Switzerland, would not be accepted by SIS. Their chief 'C' had told Gubbins not to involve railway workers because such operations would tighten border controls, with a subsequent increase in risk to their operations. This proposal was therefore vetoed, and subsequent plans appear to have been dropped.

Among the ideas submitted was one that transmitters disguised as DKEs (People's Radios) should be designed, and a specification was drawn up. They were to be battery-powered, crystal-controlled and arranged to be switched on by static line as they left the aircraft. After an arming time of 30 minutes, which would ensure any transmission was from ground level, they would transmit for three 7-minute periods each day for seven to ten days, after which they would self-destruct. To prevent close examination by the security authorities they would be fitted with an anti-disturbance switch that would destroy the set if dismantling was attempted. The Radio Communications Division of SOE was asked to produce a prototype within two weeks prior to a production run of thirty sets. How far this technically interesting idea progressed is not recorded.

Another operation (R.5) was planned in March and involved the planting of a faked Reichsbahn (National Railway) circular concerning sabotage. The intention was for this to fall plausibly into the hands of a Swiss railway official. The document was sent to the field on 21 March, but for some unknown reason, possibly SIS objection to operations involving railway workers, the operation was not completed.

A project (C.1) that had to be abandoned for fear from the Swiss and Austrian Sections of SOE of compromising a serious, active Catholic resistance line from Switzerland involved faking a letter to an Austrian bishop demanding his cooperation with the movement. It had been intended to despatch the letter in such a way that it would almost certainly have been intercepted. It should not then have implicated the bishop but merely made him, or the authorities, aware of the resistance movement claiming to have sent it. The letter said:

> Your Grace,
>
> The tragic times in which we live oblige us to write to you in terms of urgent appeal.
>
> Our beloved Church is in danger. Many million pious souls die and suffer, but more tragic still for future unborn generations, their Mother Church is no longer able to call them for her true service.
>
> We look to the future, and watch with fear the identification of our spiritual body with the powers of earthly evil. We respectfully submit to your Grace the plea that the chosen ministers of our Church should lead their flocks away from evil designs, soon to suffer the true judgement of God. The sheep are huddled in small scattered flocks, but the shepherds do not all heed their needs. If the shepherd leaves his flock during the storm, will those sheep ever heed their shepherd again?
>
> We trust most earnestly that your Grace will reflect upon the seriousness of our words, and will be disposed to receive our messenger in due course.
>
> The Council.[3]

The creativity of the Periwig planners cannot be denied, even if many, perhaps most, of their schemes were vetoed, deemed impractical or were never completed owing to difficulties in the field. Two operations against the Wehrmacht are cases in point. A forged letter from a neutral in Sweden was to be written to a German military attaché in that country warning him that his activities were known and that too much was known also of the Wehrmacht cell with which he was concerned. The letter was to have been delivered to another German in a way whereby he was most likely to open and read it, or it was to be handed to him with the claim that it had been found open and dropped somewhere. This operation (W.1) was eventually abandoned as impractical.

The second example proposed to make use of a certain Oscar Jurgens, a person working for PWE who was alleged to have contacts in Germany.

Jurgens was to be given an imposing interview with a senior officer representing one of the British secret services. The officer was to suggest to Jurgens that he might care to make use of his German contacts to help improve communication links with the Wehrmacht and Abwehr resistance movements with which the British were already in touch. This was an operation which, when clearance from SIS was sought at the end of February, met with a refusal. This was probably Operation W.2.

The SIS also vetoed a proposal (Operation I.4) put to them at the same time for Dr Fischer of the German industrial giant I.G. Farben, who was expected to visit Switzerland on business, to be told of the existence of resistance groups within his firm.

Towards the end of February it was proposed to use a German officer refugee named Willi Mattes who had arrived in neutral Sweden on an exit permit allegedly issued by Hermann Goering, the Head of the German Air Force (GAF). The Swedish group who began to 'run' him was regarded by London with some suspicion, but even so it was hoped to use his connections with the German film industry to exploit the arrest of Alfred Hugenberg, director of the UFA film production company and a prominent German Nationalist Party politician. In the event no operation of any value could be designed around these facts.

Another opportunity to use Mattes did arise: a plan (I.5) to send him as a courier to 'negotiate' with Gen der Flieger Koller, Chief of Operations of the GAF. It was proposed that should he be unmasked he would unwittingly implicate the general. What exactly he was intended to negotiate is not divulged. Most probably he was to reveal or hint at a resistance cell in the GAF. A genuine letter of introduction was obtained with the help of a German PoW and a method of contacting the general was devised. Meanwhile, Mattes had been convinced of the genuineness of an Allied-controlled resistance in Germany. But at the last moment, realising the war was virtually over, he changed his mind and refused to undertake any mission to Germany.

Another scheme, typical of those dreamt up by the Periwig planners, involved the sending by Siger Hegner & Co. of Zurich of an invitation to tender for the complicated design of a plant to treat vegetable oils. The invitation was sent to a known anti-Nazi, Adolf Pfaender of the well-known German firm Rheinmetal Borsig, in the hope that he might visit Switzerland, when the opportunity would be taken to make use of him in Periwig schemes. The letter was sent on 22 February after the sender within Siger

Hegner had been given guarantees that if the Allies found the letter it would not be held against the firm for helping the Germans. Care was taken to brief all the relevant departments in order to protect Siger Hegner if necessary. Rheinmetal Borsig replied on 17 March that their Director, Luebke, would be available for a meeting on Lake Constance at the end of the month. Alternatively, someone else could be sent later. The latter arrangement was requested, but subsequent events dictated that this operation (I.6) could not be completed. (This operation was listed as I.7 but is more probably I.6)

German soldiers interned in camps in Switzerland were periodically repatriated, and this was seen by SOE's mission in that country as an opportunity to pass heavy hints of a resistance organisation into the German security police. In Operation P.1 a letter purporting to be from a well-meaning, loyal German soldier described attempts to recruit him as a liaison man for a Goerdeler-type resistance organisation in southern Germany. The original intention was to address the letter to Musgai, Chief of Stuttgart SD, but since his whereabouts at this time were uncertain, it was sent in via the repatriated soldiers at the end of February addressed to Dr Heu. As with so many operations of this kind, whether the letter ever reached the addressee and, if so, what his reaction was can never be known. The potential effectiveness of plans such as these depended on the influence of the German target, the frequency and breadth of targeting and the credibility of the material used.

There were certainly some tenuous contacts at this time between individual Germans and the Allies. SOE was quick to recognise the potential to further the Periwig schemes, although completion of such plans was rare. One such target was SS Gruppenführer Ministerial Director Hans Hinkel, whom it was proposed to implicate through a Swedish cut-out or security intermediary in Berlin in Operation P.2. It transpired that Hinkel was in fact already being used genuinely in connection with an attempt to sell to the Allies a copy of the film ordered by Hitler of FM Witzleben's execution (on 8 August 1944, following the 20 July plot). In view of this the plan was abandoned but Hinkel remained a possible later Periwig target.

Another German making attempts to contact the Allies was Dr Hesse, a senior official in the German Foreign Office. While he was in Stockholm on a peace-feeler mission it was proposed under Operation P.3 to divulge to him the existence of a German resistance movement, suggesting that he might be very valuable to it. His approach to his task was very much one of playing down German atrocities and comparing them to the heavy air raids being targeted on their cities. In accordance with Allied policy the peace feeler was, of course, declined and this operation was not completed. One could well imagine that in a meeting of this nature it would require only a few 'indiscreet' words to such a high-ranking official to sow the seed that would ensure Periwig was taken back to the Nazi government.

Operation P.4 involved the use of a double agent, always a tricky task. Ambuhl lived in the Austrian frontier region and was considered by SOE's Berne mission to be a suitable subject for Periwig plants. It was proposed to reveal to him the 'existence' of a German resistance movement in a town near Memmingen, 72 miles south-east of Stuttgart and 38 miles from the Austrian border. Knowing the revelation would soon be passed to Ambuhl's German controllers, arrangements were made to lay on a parachute drop of stores in the area to confirm the story given to him. Unfortunately this promising operation had to be cancelled when Supreme Headquarters Allied Expeditionary Force (SHAEF) banned all stores drops after 13 March.

Despite resistance from the BBC, which considered its broadcasting services to resistance groups in occupied countries to have been virtually concluded with their liberation, PWE and SOE arranged for a special German programme to include operational messages linked to air operations. Just as the BBC had broadcast daily coded messages to the French resistance when drops of agents or supplies, or delivery by Lysander or Hudson aircraft landing and taking off again from fields in occupied territory were imminent, so similar messages were put out in connection with Periwig air drops. They were made to give the impression that a reception committee was listening out and would later be waiting in some remote field. As was the case with genuine air operations, the location of the drop was, of course, never so much as hinted at.

Apart from the broadcasts by the BBC which were, naturally, verbal, there was considerable W/T traffic to Germany in morse code. This was generally under the cover of the W/T 'umbrella' of dummy transmissions put out by the Signals Section of SOE under Brig F.W. Nicholls (D/SIGS). This had been created in anticipation of some genuine traffic to Allied agents in Germany. The fact that the German wireless detection service, which had developed through the war years to become a fairly formidable operation, could not detect any return radio traffic out of Germany was to have been explained by their discovery of planted 'squirt' transmitters. These were devices by which a morse message could be transmitted in a few seconds instead of the customary 10 to 15 minutes. Unless they were very lucky, the German triangulation methods of detection required at least this duration of transmission to locate a clandestine wireless transmitter. The 'compressed' transmission had to be recorded at the receiving station in England and then played back slowly to allow the operator to write down the coded message in the usual way. The Radio Communications Division of SOE worked alongside and closely with its Research and Development Section and certainly embarked on a project to develop a squirt transmitter. Test transmissions were even carried out between Scotland and SOE's station at Fawley Court in Henley-on-Thames but, according to the records, no squirt transmitters were used 'in anger' in the field. The fact that they were used for deception purposes goes some way towards justifying their partial development.

There were other plans involving suspected or real W/T traffic. It was intended to plant W/T sets on Germans in neutral countries, their discovery presenting them with the risk of falling under suspicion and therefore encouraging them to give the sets up promptly to the German legation authorities who would in turn become concerned at the possibility of resistance groups – exactly as intended by SOE. Where possible, sets would be left for the use of sympathetic individuals so that transmissions could be picked up by the German detection service. However, this is yet another of the plans that time and opportunity prevented from reaching fruition.

A part of the Periwig operation that proved an undoubted success was the superimposing of morse traffic on the broadcast musical programmes of the PWE black propaganda *Soldatensender* stations. These stations claimed to be on the European mainland but in reality transmitted from PWE's country section at Woburn Abbey to German troops on the continent, and were popular among them.

The preparation and transmission of morse recorded on the new medium of magnetic tape involved considerable labour and was often frustrated by the frequent interruption of the process for Air Ministry requirements. Nevertheless, this provided a valuable enhancement to the essential background of the whole deception operation.

An operation (W.8) requiring extremely careful planning and the assistance of the Scandinavian Section of SOE involved the planting of a BBC 'strip' for interpreting coded speech broadcasts on the wireless. The victim of the plant was to be an individual known to be closely associated with a senior

Wehrmacht officer. The strip carrying the message was to be somewhat carelessly cut in half, but in such a way that the piece that, it was anticipated, would soon be passed into the possession of the Wehrmacht gave sufficient clues for the Germans to decode the last few words of the message which would actually be broadcast over the BBC. When they heard this the Germans would start listening out for further messages in the code they had now cracked. But the subsequent broadcasts were to be in a different code, not only disappointing the Germans but making them realise there must be other BBC strips in existence. In order not to jeopardise any members of the Norwegian resistance this operation needed meticulous preparation which, in the event, took more time than was available.

The neutral press was a good medium through which to spread rumours, for one could be sure that German diplomats in the countries concerned would avidly scan the columns of the newspapers to glean any item of 'intelligence' to pass back to their masters in Berlin. Methods were available for convincing the editorial staff of the accuracy of the stories submitted, often by means of a German cut-out. In February SOE Berne succeeded in placing a general Periwig story in the Swiss press, making use of Allied successes in the process. By 26 March reactions were coming in. Further work involved the spreading of indiscretions in a way to ensure they reached German ears.

As has been shown, the planting of incriminating documents and faked letters was a popular feature of Periwig plans. Dr Best, a Gestapo chief in Denmark, was to be the target of such a scheme in Operation P.6. The document to be planted purported to turn down Dr Best's recruitment to a resistance group because of his past record, in spite of his alleged offer to help. A faked letter on these lines was prepared and sent to the SD at the end of March. Like so many of these schemes, the outcome, or even whether the plant was successfully made, was never known.

An opportunity arose in March for the planting of rumours of a German resistance movement in the very heart of the Nazi regime. The SOE officer in Stockholm learned that the local Swedish representative of a Jewish agency, a man named Storch, was going to Berlin to consult with Himmler regarding an offer to release Jews from concentration camps and evacuate them from Germany. Storch was apparently convinced of the genuineness of Himmler's offer and was therefore keen to do what he could to further the idea. SOE saw the possibility of his trying to ingratiate himself with Himmler by revealing anything he knew that could be of interest to the Gestapo chief. In Operation P.7 they therefore proposed to plant with him rumours regarding the existence of a German resistance movement. The details were completed by the end of the month but, sadly, Storch had already left for Berlin before he could be contacted.

The simple threat, apparently from an internal resistance organisation, was not overlooked among these more esoteric plans. In Operation G.7 a number of postcards bearing clear threats were sent to prominent Germans. The postcards, referred to internally as 'horse cards', bore the outline of a prancing horse, an emblem that SOE hoped would become synonymous with a particularly active resistance group. Many other 'black propaganda' operations similar to this were carried out from London with the cooperation of PWE and from some of the neutral missions with the aim of assisting Operation Periwig.

Some far-fetched rumours were circulated in March with the help of D/Q.10. The first, listed as Operation W.3, was to the effect that von Rundstedt's Alsace (*sic*) (perhaps Ardennes?) offensive was a deliberate attempt to tie down troops and so have a convincing reason to prevent them being sent to the dreaded eastern front to confront the mighty Red Army. It was further suggested that von Rundstedt intended to keep his own army for a second Wehrmacht putsch, the first presumably being the failed attempt on Hitler's life on 20 July 1944.

An even more fanciful rumour circulated the same month as Operation W.7 stating that the Royal Navy had landed German and Austrian resistance members at Soroy in Norway disguised as old women. It went on to maintain that some of the old women taken off by the Navy were, in fact, German resistance agents from among the Wehrmacht garrisoning Norway, who were being brought to England for consultation about the state of support for the resistance in the Germany Army.

Despite the severe restrictions placed upon them during this first phase of the operation, SOE continued to make preparations for the full-scale implementation of the plan. It was important in the interests of reality that the build-up of activities be at a measured pace, but at the back of everyone's minds was the realisation that time was running out and if success was to be achieved in assisting in the collapse of the Nazi regime by overloading its security structure, then every opportunity had to be grasped.

Much of this period was spent in working up the plans and ideas to a state where final permission could be sought to implement them. Despite the need for urgent action throughout this process if success was to be achieved, Periwig did not receive the priority necessary. Templer, an enthusiast for Periwig, pressed hard to get sanctions lifted and priorities adjusted in its favour.[4]

Chapter 12

Qualified Operational Freedom

When on 15 February 1945 the Special Intelligence Service (SIS) ban on all but propaganda operations and work from neutral countries had at last been partially lifted, the German Directorate of SOE was fully aware that the end of the war could not be far off. The period of Qualified Operational Freedom which they now entered was to last, although they did not know it at the time, until only 13 March. To recover even something from the plan for Periwig meant a determined effort by all concerned to convey to the German authorities, and no less to the population at large, for they were the people to rise up and create a real resistance organisation, that internal disaffection had been growing within the Reich for the last two or three years. But the SIS ban had not been removed completely, and several individual operations that were regarded by SOE as being of considerable importance were still excluded from the permitted plan. The exploitation of large industrial concerns such as I.G. Farben, activities on the Swiss–German frontier, a high proportion of the eminent German personalities visiting or living in neutral countries, and even the German railway workers who, as we have seen, numbered useful dissident groups in their ranks, were still protected by the SIS from SOE's subversive attentions. One can only speculate as to the reasons behind the SIS's apparent protection of these SOE and Political Warfare Executive (PWE) targets. No doubt the Foreign Office had one eye on the postwar situation in Germany: the colossal amount of reconstruction that would be necessary of dwellings, industry and infrastructure. Furthermore, the political carve-up of the country was set to initiate many – and serious – diplomatic problems. For all these reasons the antagonising of persons in positions of influence required extremely delicately balanced judgements.

No record has been found of the sixth meeting of the Periwig Committee which was held on 19 February. Such a record might have been significant in revealing just how much of the original plan had been reinstated.

During the previous period preparations had been made in anticipation of the lifting of the ban. Operations had been prepared for both the February/March moon and the following inter-moon periods. As no Periwig agents were yet available, these operations were confined to the dropping of materials bearing a suitable relation to the details of the plan. But while there was some relief that the plan could at last be implemented, certain limitations had still to be observed. The Supreme Headquarters Allied Expeditionary Force (SHAEF) had two main concerns: to avoid any impression of a move to arm our PoWs and thus invite reprisals; and to avoid interfering in any way with the flights being carried out in the same moon period by the SIS, Office of Strategic Services (OSS) and SOE for 'genuine' operations. They therefore insisted on the selection of dropping points outside a radius of approximately 50km from pin-points to be used for the 'genuine' operations of the other clandestine forces, and outside a radius of approximately 40km from PoW camps. In practice these were severe restrictions which placed serious administrative problems in the path of Periwig and incurred further disastrous delays.

Six operations had been prepared for the initial phase, in which it was planned to drop wireless telegraphy (W/T) equipment, propaganda and sabotage material, documents, a German uniform and carrier pigeons. Bad weather conditions and a shortage of aircraft meant that only four of these flights could be mounted.

For the sake of realism, the dropping of supplies to the fictitious German resistance movement started in a small way with the intention of a steady build-up as more resistance groups became involved in the 'uprising'. The first of the supply drops was flown on the night of 21/2 February, when a Hudson of 161 Squadron flew a mission embracing Operations Postbox, Carham and Pathino.

The aircrew's report of this operation shows that the Hudson first made a blind drop – that is without having a reception committee on the ground to guide in the aircraft and retrieve the supplies – of two packages as Operation Pathino. One of these packages contained a German sergeant's uniform: the object of this operation was to create the impression that an agent or group of agents was in contact with the Allies and required the cover of a member of the Wehrmacht in order to do some specific task. Between 2100 and 2200hr that night the hazy conditions in the Rhine valley gave way to clear air in the target area. The Hudson's navigator was able to map-read from the aircraft's last turning-point at Hachenburg, 80km north-west of Frankfurt-am-Main, to the dropping point near Friedensdorf where, slowed down to 130 miles per hour and at only 500ft, they flew a circuit and dropped the packages at 2203hr.

The two standard methods of dropping supplies to resistance groups were in cylindrical metal containers 5ft 6in long and 15in diameter or cubic wire-framed panniers measuring up to 29in × 18in × 13in. The cylindrical containers were carried on adapted racks in the bomb bay and released in the normal way, the parachute, which was stowed in one end of the container, being deployed by means of a static line. The panniers, on the other hand, had to be stowed within the cramped fuselage of the aircraft, manoeuvred to a hole in the floor and pushed out at just the right moment, the parachutes again being activated by a static line attached to an anchorage in the plane. The term 'packages' in the operational reports most probably referred to standard panniers, as, in the interests of avoiding damage to the rear section of the aircraft anything non-standard being dropped had to undergo thorough testing. The use of standard items of stores also lent authenticity to the operation. In addition to the German sergeant's uniform, the material dropped on this occasion included appropriate documents, maps, a miniature communications receiver (MCR) and batteries.

Half an hour later the Hudson made a dead-reckoning run from Hersfeld, 66 miles north-east of Frankfurt, identified the village of Gospeuroda and found the exact pin-point for the drop 2 or 3 miles from it. This time one person was dropped blind from 700ft at the slower speed of 120 miles per hour at 2233hr in what was listed as Operation Carham. The identity of this agent, and whether he was part of Periwig or another German Directorate operation, or whether indeed he was an SIS agent, has not been conclusively established, but a factor that indicates this was not a Periwig operation is that both Operation Pathino and Operation Postbox are listed in The National Archives (TNA) file HS7/147, covering Operation Periwig without any reference to Operation Carham; whereas file AIR20/8501, dealing with the operational records of 161 Special Duties Squadron, gives details of all three. But the question of whether Operation Carham was a non-Periwig SOE or an SIS mission has not been resolved. During this flight leaflets were dropped in the 19 miles between Treysa and Lauterbach, 44 miles north-east of Frankfurt, before the aircraft started the final part of the operation.[1]

On the last drop of the flight, another blind drop code-named Operation Postbox, one package was pushed out at a pinpoint found by dead reckoning from Lauterbach to a railway junction 3 miles to the west. Flying again at 130 miles per hour and 500ft the Hudson made one circuit before making its delivery at 2254hr. This drop was intended to create the impression that there was an agent who had been in W/T communication with Britain but who now required spare parts for his set. The contents of this package were W/T material and spare parts, two miniature communications receivers, crystals for wireless sets and a signals plan.[2]

These three drops were made over the low-lying land between Frankfurt and Kassel to its north, an extensive area almost surrounded by heavily wooded, hilly country. Such a large area would be relatively safe for parachute drops, and the wooded regions which show up distinctively in the moonlight must have assisted in the navigation.

Following Pathino and Postbox, the third air operation planned during the period of the SIS ban was code-named Operation Opinion and was carried out on the night of 24 February. This was targeted on an area to the north-east of Coblenz and consisted of a drop of twelve containers of incendiaries, food and ammunition. The object of this operation was to create the impression that the Allies were sending supplies to a fairly strongly organised group but that the operation had miscarried, leaving some of the supplies uncollected at the dropping point. The inclusion of ammunition is at first surprising, because SHAEF did not feel able to sanction the dropping of either English or German weapons. It appears, therefore, that SOE's interpretation of SHAEF's prohibition did not extend to the ammunition for the weapons. It is difficult to see how they could have satisfied the objective of the operation without including the ammunition.[3]

The seventh meeting of the Periwig Committee was held on 26 February, when Col F.T. Davies, the Director of Research, Development and Supply and a council member of SOE, had the usual two SIS men around the table with Walmsley, Potter and Wintle of PWE. PWE were always on the lookout for eminent Nazis who could become targets for Periwig actions. The possibility was discussed of using one or more members of the German Skorzeny group, the special forces unit that had rescued Mussolini from his partisan captors in the mountains of northern Italy. Five air operations into Austria had been planned for the March/April moon period: Prentice, Percher, Perigee, Permagy and Petworth. These were to be mounted from Special Operations

(Mediterranean) or SO(M) who were instructed to clear them with their local SIS representatives.

As Davies had stated at the first meeting, he was prepared to ask the SIS for assistance despite its reluctance to become involved in Periwig. He now needed a senior officer 'from a British secret service' to plant Periwig information on an unnamed man selected by Sefton Delmer of PWE. It was left to Potter to obtain the agreement of 'C', the Head of the SIS.

At this meeting Maj Hadrill revealed that the SIS held a high-quality 'Bonzo' (a former German PoW) under very secure conditions and that he had been given an outline of Operation Periwig. In view of the nature of the deception it seems astonishing that it had been revealed, even in outline, to such a potential agent.

On 5 March the eighth meeting of the Periwig Committee discussed a suggestion to arrange for an apology to be made to the Swiss government following a supposed mishap during a parachute supply drop near the German–Swiss border which resulted in the material inadvertently falling into Swiss territory. The apology was also to request its return without any publicity. In the event, this plan had to be abandoned when SHAEF placed its ban on air operations. Although the drop would have been a fictitious one, in the interests of realism it, too, had to be stopped at the same time as the genuine ones were vetoed.

Another story it was proposed to feed the Germans concerned the considerable RAF supply-dropping operations in connection with ever increasing German commitments. Maj Howarth was asked to proceed with an operation to implicate a high German official with an incriminating letter addressed to a Gestapo official and 'accidentally' delivered by an agent to the wrong person with a similar name.

By early March it was recognised that deception opportunities had been insufficient and unless the number of operations increased it would not be possible to overtax the German security system. So far plans had been restricted to high-grade deception operations, but now it was questioned whether standards should be lowered. It was agreed at this meeting that a pigeon service to Germany should be run as a Periwig operation.

During the inter-moon period a fourth operation, Impinge, was attempted on 9 March, but the aircraft had to turn back owing to bad weather en route and a troublesome engine. The object of this operation had been to create the impression that a group was ready to undertake industrial sabotage on behalf of the Allies. At the second attempt, on 13 March, a container of incendiaries was dropped at a point south of the town of Homberg, 22 miles south of Kassel. Many of these incendiaries were devices designed for ease of use by anyone picking them up. Fire-raising was a very effective means of sabotage when carried out carefully, and pointing the finger of blame for a conflagration was not straightforward. Provided flammable material was arranged around the initiating device and a plentiful source of oxygen was present, a very small incendiary could cause a great deal of damage. By this time in the war a total of almost 4 million small incendiary devices had been produced for Operation Braddock, the plan described in Chapter 9 to entice foreign workers in Germany to commit acts of sabotage. Whether the incendiaries dropped on this occasion were 'Braddocks' or some of the standard SOE stores has not been disclosed.[4]

One of two uncompleted supply operations was Preference, designed to create the impression that London was in contact with a group willing to undertake for them tasks such as the distribution of defeatist propaganda. A package containing black propaganda material, forged ration cards, etc. and a container of food was prepared for delivery.

The other operation was Pettifog, the aim of which was to drop a box of carrier pigeons with instructions in German for their use. It was hoped to persuade the enemy that the British were trying to contact a resistance group which they knew to exist in a certain area, the pinpoint for the drop having been passed to them by a courier.

In addition to these last two stores operations, twelve more were prepared and packed in readiness for the March/April moon period. The stores to be used in these included, in addition to the sabotage material mentioned above, a number of devices and booby-traps such as gunfire simulators, empty containers, empty parachutes both deployed and packed, pintail bombs, explosive coal, explosive logs, explosive rats, tins of German food, explosive Army ration tins with the fuses disconnected, women's clothing and German cigarettes. In different ways these items could all suggest resistance activity, although the dropping of a packed parachute, unless attached to a severely damaged container to indicate its failure to deploy, requires considerable imagination.

Five air operations were also prepared to be carried out by SO(M) during this moon period in an area between Passau in southern Germany and Vienna in eastern Austria.

SOE's search for suitable agents from among the German PoW community had met with very little success. The first two were available for preparation on 1 March: Gerhardt Bienecke, alias Breuer, alias Preacher; and Leonhardt Kick, alias Kauffmann, alias Plaintiff. They were despatched to Station 19 at Gardner's End, Ardeley, near Stevenage in Hertfordshire, on 5 March for a specially shortened version of a normal paramilitary course lasting ten days. This covered weapon training, demolition, physical training, map-reading and movement by night. At the same course these men received instruction in codes, and Kick, who was to take a 'squirt' transmitter with him, was instructed in its use (see p. 173 above). This period was followed by a six-day course at Group B, the finishing schools around Beaulieu in the New Forest and a shortened course at Special Training School 51, the parachute school at Ringway near Manchester, where two jumps were completed. The intense urgency to get something worthwhile out of Periwig dictated that they must be despatched at the earliest possible opportunity, and therefore all the preparatory training courses were cut to the bare minimum.

Bienecke and Kick were provided with both military and civilian cover. They were also given addresses in both Germany and neutral countries with which to communicate if they ran into difficulties. In what seems a somewhat cavalier, if not ruthless, move, the latter addresses were of persons whom it was wished to compromise should the opportunity arise. One can only wonder to whom the addresses in Germany belonged.

Bienecke was ordered to convey codes, crystals for wireless sets and a signals plan to a supposedly important agent working for the Allies in the Berlin area whose W/T communication with the UK had failed. The materials in his care were camouflaged in a packet of coffee. He was supplied with the appropriate documents to permit him to pass the routine checks: a civilian *Kennkarte* and a *Marschbefehl*. Before he was dropped in German uniform he was instructed to commit to memory the name of *Sturmbahnführer* Dr Eggen who, if all else failed and he was unable to contact any of the cut-outs whose names and addresses he had been given, he was to contact direct to hand over the material he carried. In his search for the fictitious contacts Bienecke was certain to spread a few hints about the resistance, and when forced finally to contact Dr Eggen his action was designed to compromise the *Sturmbahnführer*. How he was to carry this out and escape is not recorded in the archives.

Kick's task was to act as a courier to an organisation in Bremen with which London had contact. He was also to provide the organisation with the means of high-speed W/T transmission. For this he was provided with a type B MkII wireless set, a set of 'squirt' equipment and a hand generator to provide power. In addition he had plan codes, crystals and a vocabulary hidden in a packet of coffee. Like his colleague he was dropped with military cover and identity papers together with a *Marschbefehl* and a civilian *Kennkarte*. Were these men being sent in the hope that their enquiries about opposition groups would reach the ears of the security authorities? Or were they genuinely attempting to locate such factions and possibly initiate some organisation into larger, more effective units?

The ninth meeting was the last of the Periwig Committee and coincided with the end of the period of Qualified Operational Freedom and the start of the SHAEF ban. Maj Wall of PWE was the only new face at the table. The chief point made at this meeting was that the restrictions that SOE had been battling against meant that the original concept of Periwig could not now be realised. In future, only small-scale operations through neutral countries would be pursued.

The meeting discussed the case of the recalcitrant agent Mattes, whom it had been proposed the previous month to infiltrate back into Germany in order to compromise a high official in the German Air Force. A senior German Foreign Office official in Stockholm was to be implicated in sending out peace feelers to the Periwig 'resistance movement'. Yet another suggested candidate for 'Periwigging' was a Danish Nazi businessman by the name of Povl Bihesen. Finally, Potter was asked to consult Sefton Delmer and Col 'Bertie' Blount, one of SOE's scientists, about the problems of broadcasting instructions on home-made explosives.

On 12 March, the day of the last Periwig meeting, Col Davies wrote to Templer, 'The original concept of Periwig cannot now be realised as a result of new limitations', and the need was now to confine itself to 'small nuisance operations through neutral countries' which were unlikely to produce any appreciable feeling of apprehension among either the German security organisations or the people. The next day SOE was struck a serious blow when SHAEF, ever more fearful of reprisals against Allied PoWs, imposed a ban on all air supply operations. With no other means of infiltrating supplies into Germany, the future of Operation Periwig looked bleak.

One operation that avoided the SHAEF ban and was carried out successfully was Operation I.2, which involved the dropping of a German briefcase (*Aktentasche*) on a German railway station during a low-level air attack by Mosquito aircraft. The briefcase contained, among normal business documents, an incriminating paper suggesting a clandestine opposition organisation in a large industrial firm. The *Aktentasche* operation had been the subject of scientific work to establish the best method of dropping it from the aircraft to ensure it was not caught in the slipstream to strike, and possibly seriously damage, the tail. Together with its contents the briefcase was sent to No. 3 SF Detachment on 7 March and was dropped on 12/13 March, the last opportunity before the SHAEF ban came into force.[5]

Many of the infiltrations into Germany were made from an advanced base on mainland Europe known as SPU22. This unit was formed following the despatch to Lille in early September 1944 of Lt Col Hazell of SOE's Polish Section with the task of investigating and settling the affairs of the 'Monica' Polish organisation in that area of France. Hazell recommended that a small mission be formed to wind up the Monica organisation and encourage Polish infiltration into Germany. The mission was set up first in the Lille–Roubaix area and then moved with the Allied advance to the Belgian Ardennes, closer to the frontier with Germany and more suitable for infiltration through the front lines. Political difficulties delayed the despatch of the first twelve Poles, but the time was well spent in foraging for German identity documents, ration cards, uniforms, etc. for use by SOE's forgers in London. This activity was so successful that it became an established duty of SPU22. It also proved to be a most suitable centre for infiltration and soon expanded into various houses in the Belgian and French Ardennes, and by mid-December 1944 it was processing Germans and Frenchmen in addition to Poles.

SPU22 had become effectively SOE's advanced headquarters for overland work from the west into Germany. But von Rundstedt's Ardennes offensive forced it to evacuate hastily into northern Belgium, where it eventually re-established itself near Ghent. It also found itself operating in a US area, albeit with the verbal approval of SHAEF but not of the 12th US Army Group and the 1st US Army, who were immediately responsible. This resulted in some administrative difficulties, and Hazell was restricted to carrying out infiltration operations in the constricted areas of the 21st British Army Group and the 3rd US Army rather than the more suitable fronts of the 1st or 9th US Armies.

Although described as a 'vigorous' unit, SPU22 infiltrated for long-term work in civilian clothes only five Poles and one German. By the end of March 1945, with the end of the war in sight, French, Belgian and German agents were used for short-range intelligence- and Commando-type work, often with highly successful results. SPU22 accompanied the 21st Army Group on its advance into Germany and was absorbed into ME42, SOE's mission attached to the British occupying forces.[6]

There is little in the files to indicate what the Head of the German Directorate, Maj Gen Templer, was doing at this time. We know he must still have been recovering from the serious injuries he sustained in Italy the previous August. From his arrival at Baker Street in early November he was involved in the debates surrounding Operation Foxley, the plan to assassinate Hitler. These continued until late March, when it became obvious that the war would soon end and there was no way in which final planning and training of personnel could be achieved in the time available. By this stage Templer was already in his new job at FM Montgomery's headquarters in Germany, and Lt Col Thornley must have had control of the Directorate to himself.

Chapter 13

THE FINAL PHASE

Leonhardt Kick's mission within Periwig was originally located in the Göttingen area, where both he and Gerhardt Bienecke were to have been dropped, but owing to the Allied advance the dropping point was altered to the Bremen region and Kick's task changed accordingly. On the night of 2/3 April 1945 a Halifax took off from Earls Colne airfield near Halstead in Essex to carry Bienecke and Kick on Operation Polacca/Polder to a dropping point near Wildeshausen, 48 miles south-west of Bremen in northern Germany. They dropped successfully, each with a leg-bag containing personal kit. A parachute package of wireless telegraphy (W/T) material was dropped with them. The loss of Kick's Type B Mark II wireless set during the drop meant that his mission to provide the Bremen organisation with the means of high-speed W/T transmissions was effectively over. It is not known if he also lost the cumbersome squirt transmission equipment or whether he attempted to carry it to Bremen. Unbeknown to him the 'squirt' equipment was useless for sending back messages at high speed because SOE did not possess suitable receiving apparatus. Its value on this operation was in being found by the Germans, who would then realise why they had been unable to intercept any radio transmissions from the underground organisation in their midst. As long as it found its way into the hands of the security authorities by capture or any other means, its purpose would have been served.

The final preparations for this flight from Earls Colne were to cause some anxiety. The flight was also to carry another 'Bonzo', or German PoW working for the Allies, Wilhelm Borstelmann, on Operation Chalgrove, a normal SOE German Directorate mission to sabotage U-boat yards and machinery and to assassinate U-boat officers. Among the equipment carried for this task was a Welrod, SOE's silenced assassination pistol, and a supply of battery pills. These had been developed by SOE's scientists from platinum and would ruin a submarine's batteries if introduced into them.

Why the Halifax for this operation was at Earls Colne instead of Tempsford is not clear, but what is evident is that the final arrangements for the boarding of the three men were not so thorough as those at the usual aerodrome. Borstelmann had been warned beforehand that he must on no account discuss his mission, drop zone, etc. with the other agents he would meet at the airfield. It is to be expected that Kick and Bienecke's conducting officer would have issued a similar warning to them. But all three agents with their conducting officers were taken into the Intelligence Room at Earls Colne so that the pilot could discuss the dropping points with them, something that was never done at Tempsford. To the dismay of the SOE officers, the Bonzos could clearly see wall maps marked with the respective dropping points and the track to be taken by the aircraft. Then, in the usual high-security procedure immediately prior to boarding the plane, the Chalgrove and Periwig agents changed their clothing, but at the same time and in the same Nissen hut, and so they could not help seeing each other's operational clothing and even some of their respective equipment.

The defence for this lack of security was that this was the first combined flight of its kind SOE had undertaken (that is, a Periwig operation and a 'normal' one), and it was the first time Bonzos had been sent out from Earls Colne. Furthermore, it was unlikely that the RAF authorities or even the SOE liaison officer knew of the complications or particular security aspects of Periwig as opposed to 'genuine' Bonzo operations.[1]

Bienecke's adventure finished when he was recovered from the Russian zone of Germany in August 1945. No record has been found of his activities in Germany during these four months, or of what transpired between the British and the Russians to secure his repatriation.

Kick gave himself up to the advancing Allies and was returned to England on 30 April. When he landed he noticed Gestapo activity in the vicinity of the drop zone and was unable to recover the package of W/T material that had been dropped with him. He had an uncomfortable time when a Gestapo man questioned the authenticity of his papers and had to be shot by Kick, who then continued on his way to Delmenhorst, south-west of Bremen, where he remained in hiding until the British arrived. In the event he produced no information of any value, but the package of wireless equipment and the killing of the Gestapo agent must have caused concern within the security authorities in the area.[2]

The second two agents to have volunteered from behind the barbed wire of the PoW camps started their training on 2 April. Otto Heinrich (alias Hoffmann, alias Hawker) and Franz Lengnick (alias Lange, alias Lawyer) were trained at Station 19 in fieldcraft, map-reading, movement by night, use of weapons, unarmed combat and a bogus landing ground course. The pressure to get these men into the field was now so intense that the courses at Group B (instruction in the use of codes and W/T), and even the training in parachuting at STS 51 were omitted. In the case of Heinrich and Lengnick this indicates a degree of ruthlessness: if lack of training were to lead to their death or capture, the Germans would discover their task to contact the 'underground organisation' from what they carried. Put bluntly these men might have been more use to the Allies dead than alive.

The two agents were tasked with contacting an organisation in the Bavarian Redoubt area, a region in which rumours suggested the leaders of the Nazi regime planned a last ferocious stand. They were to instruct its members in SOE's latest methods of arranging landing operations in order to exfiltrate important persons back to Allied territory. Addresses of contacts in both Germany and neutral countries were provided, as in the case of the first two agents. This time the men were provided with only German Air Force (GAF) cover, including the necessary military identity papers. On the night of 18/19 April a Hudson flew the men from Tempsford on Operation Periscope (P.10) to drop them with a parachute package of personal kit in an area west of the Chiem See, a large lake between Munich and Salzburg. They attempted to carry out their mission and actually made contact with more than one small subversive group. There is some evidence that they took part in an abortive rising and that only the chaotic conditions prevailing at that time in Munich prevented their activities arousing suspicion among the security authorities. However, they both managed to avoid arrest and gave themselves up to the advancing Allies in May.[3]

An attempt was made to infiltrate an agent from Stockholm into Hamburg on 12 April. The identity of the agent has not been found, but the operation was listed as P.8. His mission was to weaken any desire the German authorities might have had to conduct a 'last stand' type of operation in the north German ports, and in particular in Bremen. Exactly how he was to attempt this is unclear, but one can assume he might have been able to contact opposition groups and through them spread defeatist propaganda. Unfortunately a failure on the part of one of his contacts resulted in his being unable to cross the Danish frontier into Germany, and so he returned to Copenhagen, where he tried to make himself useful to the Allies.[4]

Even the most mundane of events were examined by the SOE planners to see if there was some way in which it could incorporate some Periwig-type action. Such was the case when an agent was due to leave SOE Tangier in March to carry out work in Barcelona and Madrid. Tangier saw this man as a suitable target for a Periwig brief. This was agreed on 27 March as Operation I.3, but the details of his task have not been found, nor is it known whether it was put into effect.

In one of the rare recorded instances of cooperation by the Secret Intelligence Service (SIS), its Section V agreed in Operation W.9 at the end of March to transmit over one of their controlled W/T sets a rumour to the effect that the saving of the Remagen Bridge over the Rhine was the result of sabotage by a British agent within the Wehrmacht.

The Wehrmacht continued to be targeted in Operation W.5 when advantage was taken of the genuine mis-sorting of German PoW letters that sometimes occurred. A prisoner in the United Kingdom writing to another in, for example, a camp in Canada would have addressed the letter to PWIB. When re-addressed, these letters occasionally found their way into the bag for Germany. Several forged letters purporting to come from German prisoners in England and hinting at the existence of a resistance movement within the Wehrmacht were despatched at the end of March with the help of MI19, the branch of the Intelligence Service dealing with PoWs. (See also p. 176.)

Operation W.6 was a proposal to plant a letter on a ship sailing from Spain to supply the German garrison at Bordeaux which, cut off from land contact, maintained W/T communication with Germany. The letter was to purport to have come from a German in Spain and was to be addressed to an officer in the Bordeaux garrison, both parties being referred to by code names. The letter was to state that the reorganised party of the executed resistance organiser Erwin von Witzleben (see p. 69), who had been ready to assume command of the Wehrmacht had the 20 July 1944 coup succeeded, would soon be ready to seize power and that sympathisers in Bordeaux should await further communications. It was suggested that the sender should claim to be a German by the name of Goeritz who had refused orders to return to Germany, but this was not adopted. Material incorporating code names was sent to Madrid on 26 March, but too late for the operation to be completed.

A similar proposal had been made by SOE's Sqn Ldr Potter to Sefton Delmer of the Political Warfare Executive (PWE) on 17 March with respect to the commander of the German garrison at La Rochelle on the Bay of Biscay, Rear Adm Ernst Schirlitz. This garrison was being supplied by aircraft from Zellhausen that landed at Stuttgart and then flew across France. The commanding officer of the Stuttgart base was Col Paul Ludwig. Potter's plan was to implicate both Schirlitz and Ludwig in a letter being prepared for despatch to the La Rochelle garrison. The form of the smear is not described in the records. In a letter to Delmer the previous day Potter had referred to an intriguing 'brothel operation' and the ordering of lipsticks and powder puffs in Brussels. But again, details have not survived in the files.[5]

Planted material did not always consist of letters or documents. One such plan (Operation W.4) involved the issue of forged charity stamps which were to be smuggled across the Swiss frontier disguised as routine goods and discovered near a railway station not too far into Germany, when they would be burst open to reveal the true contents. This proposal was intended to give evidence of a Wehrmacht resistance movement operating from Switzerland with good contacts for the distribution of its material. This operation needed time to finish the preparations – time that, in the event, it did not have.

Another subversive operation, known as C.2, involved the printing of a quantity of leaflets giving action signals disguised among biblical texts. The material was sent to Berne at the end of March for planting in such a way that it stood a good chance of falling into the hands of the German authorities. The instructions for this operation were as follows:

1. This operation requires a small quantity of prayer book leaflets which can be produced locally (in Switzerland).
2. The text should include:
   i) A typical front page.
   ii) The following message:
   Devout Catholics should keep these texts. They should have a meaning for all true sons of the Church.
   iii) Five numbered scriptural texts which are short and unmistakable, which might well be quoted from the pulpit, but which are not too common. They may if possible be not too unlike their operational meaning.
   iv) A slip to go inside the pamphlet giving the following key to the texts:

1. Spread the word diligently, our life is short.
2. Hold yourself ready for the word.
3. Declare yourself for the righteous.
4. We are persecuted, be patient.
5. Do not heed the false prophets, await the true message.[6]

This was another of those actions aimed at persuading the enemy of the presence of opposition cells within the Church. Unfortunately this one was not completed.

Operation L.6 concerned an agent working on the Austria–Swiss frontier in the Bregenz/Dornbirn region at the south-eastern end of the Boden See or Lake Constance. In April it was decided to give him a Periwig briefing to convince him that a resistance movement among the industrial and mining labour faction was in existence. Special Operations (Mediterranean) (SO(M)) claimed that the operation was being carried out by an agent known as Vorprlberi, but in the rush to get it started while there was still a little time, the exact nature of the briefing was not made known to London. In view of the lateness of the date it is most unlikely that the operation can have borne any fruit.

Work aimed at subverting the Nazi Party included one operation (P.5) whereby a clown by the name of Sambalo, who had arrived in the Swedish capital at the end of March, was to take a supposed message from Stockholm to a German security official in Oslo. The contents of the message and the results of the operation have not been traced.

In April a last-minute operation (P.9) was planned, following information from Madrid that one of their contacts had been approached concerning possible employment by Marous von Spee, the former chief Spanish–German agent in Andorra. By the end of April it was planned to 'Periwig' him by asking his views on the organisation of a courier line into the so-called Bavarian Redoubt. It was, however, too late to complete this operation.

The Allies were concerned that the Germans might decide to attempt to hold out in the northern ports, and particularly in Bremen. SOE wanted to carry out an operation known as Porkpie (P.8) to weaken any faith the German authorities might have had in such a venture. The air operation Polacca/Polder had successfully dropped Bienecke and Kick in the area with this objective in mind. A further air drop involving the agent Tietiz was also proposed. In addition it was hoped to make use of a W/T operator with the code name Teapot, then being used by the SIS. Teapot was a triple agent who had landed in

England, been captured and turned to work for MI5, and who was apparently suspected of passing information to his former masters. The minutes of the 218th meeting on 15 March of the Twenty Committee, the 'Double Cross' Committee of MI5 that so successfully ran 'turned' German agents for much of the war, record that it had been suggested that Teapot might be used for Periwig and that the committee saw no objection to this.[7] He was to be told on 31 March to move to Bremen for an important new task, and later to be told of plans for an Allied-sponsored rising. This latter revelation would, if the suspicions of Teapot's changing loyalties were true, be quickly passed to the Germans and directly into the hands of the Periwig targets. In the event the war progressed too quickly for the plan and so it proved unnecessary.

Operations aimed at industrialists could threaten, incriminate or personally harm individuals who were sympathetic to the Nazi cause or place pro-German firms under suspicion of housing resistance groups. I.8 was an operation aimed at revealing the existence of opposition to the regime among industrialists. SOE wanted to create yet another disparate source of information to be fed back to the Germans from persons with ostensibly impeccable credentials. They had in mind a Japanese diplomat in Lisbon by the name of Inoue who was known to have close relations with the Germans. It was proposed to ply him (through a cut-out) with rumours concerning the presence of resistance groups within Germany and the inevitability of the collapse of the Reich. This scheme was proposed towards the end of March but had insufficient time to be completed.

Another suggestion for an operation using a foreign person was I.7. This proposal originated from SOE Berne and involved sending a compromising letter to a German member, Dr Bernard Malblanc, of a Swiss firm blacklisted by the Allies for carrying out war work for the enemy. The operation was approved at the end of March, again too late for completion.

Operation I.9 was an elaborate plan to be implemented in Morocco through SOE Tangier. In its initial form a clerk by the name of Gumpert, who worked in the German consulate in Tetuan, was to become the unwitting carrier of information regarding a British-controlled German resistance movement among German U-boat crews. Gumpert was to be told through a cut-out that a German agent under the control of the British was shortly to be landed in Tangier from a U-boat. It was to be impressed on the clerk that this agent must at all costs preserve his status and cover, and that Gumpert should try to assist him in contacting the British authorities without in any way compromising him.

But Gumpert was found to be unreliable, so this plan was dropped in favour of a modified one. This time the cut-out would tell him a story of a fisherman, close to whose boat a German submarine had surfaced. The commander of the U-boat had interrogated the fisherman about his political views and asked him if he was in contact with any Allied or anti-Nazi factions. The fisherman was convinced by the commander that there was a move by an Allied-supported resistance, or anti-Nazi group in the submarine service, to gain outside assistance for infiltrated agents. It was mid-April before the final details of this operation were agreed, much too late to carry it out.

An aspect of the Periwig plan that received considerable attention was the use of carrier pigeons to augment PWE broadcasts in deceiving any German people who might pick up the birds, and the German authorities to which the birds might be taken, that pigeons were being successfully used by the Allies to obtain information from inside Germany.

The Army Pigeon Service, then at Wing House in London's Piccadilly, provided the necessary equipment in the form of parachutes, containers, etc. and experienced men to look after the birds that were housed in lofts at RAF Tempsford, the airfield in Bedfordshire from which most SOE air operations were flown. For despatch the birds were placed in specially developed containers with a small parachute attached. Also fixed to the containers was everything to make it easy for the finder to cooperate and return the bird with a message: message forms, small message containers for attachment to the bird's leg, pencils, food and instructions in German to the finders encouraging them by means of a reward (although how this worked has not been discovered) to send back information by the pigeon. Illustrations were provided of the correct method of fixing the message in its container to the bird's leg and of how one should launch it on its return journey.

At first, concern that the distances involved would over-tax the pigeons caused the first hundred to be obtained from No. 3 Field Force Pigeon Service at Eindhoven in Holland on 15 March, just two days after the Supreme Headquarters Allied Expeditionary Force (SHAEF) ban had come into effect (see p. 173). The intention was to house the birds in the RAF Tempsford lofts and drop a number each night when other operations were being flown. Provided they were not kept there too long, when they were launched back by their German finders they would home to their familiar lofts at Eindhoven. However, it was later realised that this concern for the homing distance to be flown was unfounded.

Sender of message from ______	Forwarding carrier pigeon post at ______ from ______	Pigeon reception point at ______ from ______	Person receiving message at ______
Pigeon message number at ______	Confirmation of arrival at ______ in ______	In the case of message in transit at ______ in ______ from ______ to ______	Useful additions (sketch maps, etc)

Absender des Spruches: ab:	Befördernde Brieftaubenstelle: an: ...... ab:	Empfangende Brieftaubenstelle: an: ...... ab:	Empfänger des Spruches: an: ......
Taubenspruch Nr. ...... an:	Ankunftbestätigung am: ...... in:	Bei Durchgangssprüchen an: ...... in: ...... ab: ...... nach:	Dienstliche Zusätze (Anlagen usw.)

Hier abtrennen!

Eingetroffen ist dort. Spruch Nr.	Es fehlt noch dort. Spruch Nr.	Empfangsbestätigung fehlt über hiesigen Spruch Nr.	Zahl und Fußringnummern der aufgelassenen Tauben: ......

S & Z 42

Detach here

Following message arrived No. ______	Following message still missing No. ______	Confirmation of receipt lacking for message No. ______	Quantity and footring numbers of pigeons released

Pigeon-post message form used in Operation Periwig. The translation of this form was kindly made by Lady Cicely Mayhew, who translated intercepted German wireless transmissions at Bletchley Park during the war. *(Author's collection)*

It was originally intended to start pigeon drops during the 19 March moon period, but unsuitable weather conditions delayed the despatch of these birds. On the night of 4/5 April twenty pigeons were dropped during a German Directorate operation code-named Curland, despite many of them being stale – that is, no longer capable of homing to Eindhoven. It had also been decided to make deliberate use of some 'dud' birds which were known not to be able to home, by attaching faked messages to their legs in the expectation that they would find their way into German Army lofts or be handed over to the German authorities after landing at the homes of other European pigeon fanciers. The impression to be created from the messages they carried was that disaffected German elements were making use of the birds as a means of communication. As genuine 'dud' birds had not at this stage been procured, six of the stale pigeons with appropriate messages composed by PWE were dropped on that April night from a sand-weighted release sack.

The Army Pigeon Service, at this stage of the war no longer stretched, now offered to cooperate further by providing a regular supply of pigeons, and an arrangement was made whereby 150 fresh birds a week were supplied, and any stale birds not required by SOE were returned.

As the general situation in Germany moved inexorably towards Allied victory and the cessation of hostilities, covert operations into the enemy heartland began to be curtailed, and the possibility of frequent dropping operations from Tempsford or the 38 Group airfields became significantly less. It was therefore arranged through PWE that No. 406 Leaflet Squadron, which operated alongside the Office of Strategic Services (OSS) Carpetbagger operation from RAF Harrington (Pinetree) in Northamptonshire and flew, weather permitting, every night over Germany, would undertake to drop the pigeons also. This arrangement proved very satisfactory.

On the night of 11/12 April a batch of birds was dropped in the Ludenscheid, Iserlohn and Magdeburg areas. On 13 April a returned message was received. The unsigned message was dated 12 April 1945 and said:

> The pigeon was found at 4 o'clock in the morning in our village. There are no German military personnel in our village. The name of the village is Hellensen. As far as I know Ludenscheid will not be defended because there are many hospitals in the town. The Party swine have all cleared out. Kreisleiter Jost [?Post] was seen in the town yesterday in civilian clothes. I am also a pigeon fancier and send my greetings. Good flight!

At least this demonstrated that the system worked. Between the nights of 11/12 April and 26/7 April a total of 304 pigeons were dropped.

Drops continued, usually with ten birds at each location, throughout April over a wide area embracing Hagen, Hamburg, Lüneberg, Quedlinburg, Remscheir, Bremerhaven, Reisach, Dresden, Rathenow, Döbeln, Treuenbrietzsen, Brandenburg, Kiel, Kyritz, Regensburg, Schwerin, Augsburg, Landshut, Wilhelmshaven, Glückstadt, Lübeck, Wuppertal, Erlangen and (by mistake) Amsterdam.

One bird that was picked up in Rouen, France, carried a cryptic message in German dated 14 April: 'Contrary to misleading reports English wireless KK with company is not repeat not yet on way to Hamburg.' Who knows whether this was genuine or a hoax and what it implied.[8]

Details of the design of both the special containers for the pigeons and the weighted sacks for the 'duds' have not been discovered. The use of the latter caused the only problem for the 406 Squadron aircrews, as they were heavily weighted with sand to ensure their opening and required static line equipment which the Pinetree aircraft did not possess. This led to some development work that had its roots some years earlier in a totally different place.

While serving on the north-west frontier of India a Sq Ldr Ken Callow was faced with a telegraphed request from an isolated outpost asking that a supply of eggs be dropped to them. It might have been a joke request, but Callow took it seriously. His solution was to put a chicken in a brown paper bag and drop it from a low- and slow-flying aircraft. The paper protected the struggling chicken from the effects of the aircraft's slipstream just long enough for it to break out of the bag and flutter to the ground. The same technique was used in 1945 to deliver pigeons to Belgian resistance groups after a large number of birds had been killed or incapacitated in mishaps using the standard pigeon dropping containers. SOE's Research and Development Section, in which Callow served, devoted considerable effort along with the parachute experts at RAF Henlow to designing a container incorporating a parachute-opening delay device, and this was tested successfully from the practice bomb racks of a Mosquito intruder aircraft. Then someone remembered Callow's technique.

In the case of the Periwig pigeons, further work with paper bags was carried out and was on the point of being tried out by 406 Squadron when operations came to an end.

A total of 330 pigeons were dropped during the month of April; 9 birds homed to the UK and 2 were discovered in France, while 5 of the pigeons brought back messages written by Germans, but there was no information of value in them. It is claimed that one of the messages thanked the British senders, reporting that the pigeon's brother had been tasty and asking for more! More seriously, there were reports of the Periwig pigeon campaign in the neutral press, so its objective had been achieved at least in part.

On 18 April SHAEF lifted its ban on all SOE air supply drops into Germany. By this time it was clear that their objections to Periwig were groundless and, furthermore, the dropping of essential (non-Periwig) stores was likely to become vital in certain areas. Three days after the lifting of the ban and at the start of the tumultuous three-week period culminating in the total collapse of Germany, a fifth agent, Kurt Tietiz (alias Fatkow, alias Tinker), started training at Station 19. It soon became clear that events in Germany were progressing so rapidly that the infiltration of more agents was pointless. Tietiz's training was abandoned, and he was returned to his PoW camp on 4 May.

It is interesting to note that security at this time was such that throughout the training courses attended by these agents none of the instructors was let into the Periwig secret. Of those in direct contact with the agents, only the conducting officer was aware of the nature of the operation.

The military chaos now prevailing in Germany made it both increasingly difficult to initiate any operation of even nuisance value and, since the rush to victory now had a gathering momentum of its own, somewhat irrelevant. PWE's enthusiasm for the exercise ensured that birds continued to be delivered until 27 April. Three days later the pigeon operations were officially cancelled, and with them ended the last vestige of Operation Periwig.

What of the Periwig operations whose details cannot now be found? Assuming the last-known number to be the end of the series and the numbering to be continuous, the missing operations are:

Foreign labour	G.1–G.6
Industrial and mining labour	L.4, L.5
Industrialists	I.1, I.6
Railways	R.4

Had any of these operations been successful it is likely they would have been mentioned somewhere in the records. Those with late numbers were probably not completed in the time available. This still leaves a few, the details of which could prove interesting.

Chapter 14

FINAL ASSESSMENT

Any assessment of the success or otherwise of Operation Periwig needs to take into account these important factors:

- The chaotic state of affairs in Germany in the first months of 1945, leading up to its total collapse
- The concern felt for the well-being of Allied PoWs and foreign nationals forced to work in Germany
- The general war-weariness of all parties
- The late timing of the scheme
- The resistance to the plan by the Secret Intelligence Service (SIS)
- The overall organisation and responsibility for the scheme

Once the Allies broke out of the Normandy beachhead established in the weeks immediately following the D-Day landings of June 1944, their progress eastwards was virtually assured. Every mile of occupied countryside they liberated, the firmer became their grip on Europe. They were among ecstatically welcoming friends, more than willing to help them. Soon the greater picture of the Allied strategy became clear: advance from the west through France and the Low Countries; advance from the south through France and through northern Italy; while in the east Stalin's huge Red Army was ferociously pushing the invader from Russia, with no intention of stopping at its frontier with Poland or at that country's border with Germany.

The German people, despite the severely censored information available to them from official sources, could not help but take some notice of the grim news revealed in the widely distributed leaflets that fluttered from the skies along with the relentless rain of high-explosive and incendiary bombs. Perhaps they were persuaded that their own border defences would hold; that when the Wehrmacht had withdrawn to within the Fatherland there would be no need for the Allies to continue waging war. An honourable peace could be negotiated.

Having seen the setbacks on the battlefields, the population was also faced with their leader announcing to all how providence had saved him from a treacherous assassination attempt (the 20 July plot). Thereafter the State terror apparatus swung into action and reported on the mass arrests, show trials, convictions and executions of those even remotely connected with the attempt on Hitler's life.

The infrastructure of Germany, particularly in the major cities, was beginning to collapse. Transport and communications had been severely disrupted by bombing. Supplies of fuel and food were becoming scarcer. Hospitals, the fire service and the police were under increasing strain from the day-in, day-out aerial bombardment. The basic necessities of life – shelter, food and water – were becoming progressively difficult to maintain. Destruction of towns and cities grew daily but when conditions allowed the incendiary bombs to initiate huge, raging, unstoppable fire storms such as occurred in Hamburg, the effect on those who got to know of them must have been traumatic.

In these circumstances spirits must have been raised to learn, no doubt suitably exaggerated by Dr Goebbels, of the December 1944 offensive, when German forces in the Ardennes pushed back the Allies in what became known as the Battle of the Bulge. But this proved to be a short-lived success. The land was recaptured, and the inexorable advance into Germany resumed.

As the shortages became more acute, the severest rationing was imposed on the millions of foreign workers forced to prop up the Nazi war effort. These slaves lacked the strength to work any harder; this in turn reduced the production of armaments and other vital supplies. Jews, gypsies, political antagonists and other 'undesirables' cramming the yet-to-be-discovered concentration camps succumbed in their hundreds of thousands to disease and starvation.

And yet, in spite of all this terrible hardship, fear and hopelessness for the future, there was no general uprising against the Nazi government that had inflicted this catastrophe upon its people. The men who could have precipitated such a revolution had failed on 20 July, and the leadership was more determined than ever to suppress any further dissent. With the opposition movements decimated by the subsequent purge, this was not a difficult task.

So this state of affairs in the Third Reich raises two questions: why was the will to resist of the German people so strong? And what were they holding out for?

In the first place Hitler had come to power with promises to replace the democratic Weimar Republic with a system that would expand Germany's influence in Europe, if not the world, and to expunge the humiliation of the Treaty of Versailles that had been impossible to live with. Initially he had met with remarkable success, much to the satisfaction of the population at large. They fell under his spell and began to excuse his excesses as being necessary for the greater good of the nation. As the military successes in North Africa and Russia were at first stopped by the Allies and then the slow, grinding reversals started, the situation on the home front was one of loyal support for the troops in the front line. After the Allied invasion of Normandy and the realisation that there was a distinct possibility that their advance would eventually overrun Germany, fear began to bolster their wills: fear that once again the nation would be forced into a humiliating unconditional surrender and that the equivalent of the hated Treaty of Versailles would be imposed upon them. But for the individuals, particularly those living in the east of the country, the great fear was the prospect of being taken over by the Russians, the nation that had suffered so terribly from the atrocities perpetrated in the name of Germany by Hitler's death squads.

Overriding the increasing disillusionment with Hitler's leadership was another factor of great importance: however anti-Nazi the population as a whole was growing, it was still German and definitely not pro-Allied. And that gave a significant boost to their will to resist.

What did they hope to gain by holding out? First one has to ask how much the general population and, indeed, the ordinary troops knew of the military and political situation surrounding Germany. Newspapers and radio broadcasts were heavily censored, listening to the foreign service of the BBC was an offence and, according to the authorities, the leaflets dropped during air raids could not be believed. On the other hand, people travelling on their normal work or to visit relatives, and soldiers coming home on leave could not fail to see the extent of the destruction in the major centres of industry and population. There could be no denying the frequency of air raids and the increasingly rare sightings of the Luftwaffe.

With a lack of up-to-date information it is likely that the general feeling was one of supporting all moves towards a measured withdrawal from the occupied countries in order to concentrate troops in the defence of the borders of the Fatherland. This would raise further problems: Germany would be surrounded by enemies and effectively blockaded. The country had millions of forced workers to feed. Its administrative system was on the brink of a descent into chaos. How could they support more men fighting for their very existence?

In the event, the will to resist became within a short timespan the will not to cooperate, followed quickly by the will of the individual to survive. This was total defeat, from which the only direction was upwards in a postwar rehabilitation and reconstruction process.

Of primary concern to the Allied Chiefs of Staff in the last months of the conflict was the well-being of their own PoWs incarcerated in many camps throughout Germany. It was plain to see that Hitler himself was becoming increasingly unpredictable. If his henchmen's stability was also suspect, and the Führer, in one last dramatic but terrible act of vengeance gave the order, who knows how many Allied prisoners might be massacred. The chiefs therefore decided to tread carefully and do their utmost not to cause any event that could be construed as a reason to take reprisals against the prisoners. They forbade the infiltration of arms into the camps and to ensure, as far as they could, that nothing of a subversive nature would be found within the wire, they vetoed any air drops of supplies or leaflets within 25 miles of all known camps.

As far as Operation Periwig was concerned, this was a severe limitation. Added to the SIS's ban on any drops near their own agents' areas of operation, this effectively 'sterilised' large parts of Germany.

Similar sentiments prevented the large-scale use of the incendiary devices known as Braddocks, which were intended to be picked up and used in acts of sabotage by foreign forced labour workers. Here again, the fear of precipitating a massacre resulted in their full-scale use being delayed and eventually abandoned.

All parties, including SOE, must have been suffering from some degree of war-weariness. Col Gubbins, Head of SOE, had himself lost a beloved son and had had to come to terms with the terrible consequences of the *Englandspiel* ('England Game') fiasco when, due to mistakes in London, attempts by agents captured in Nazi-occupied Europe to let SOE know of their plight were ignored, with the result that more and more men and supplies were dropped directly into the waiting hands of the Abwehr. The Head of SOE's German

Section, Lt Col Thornley had worked hard throughout the war in what must have been frustrating times. His section had no resistance movement to support and the number of agents passing through his hands was considerably fewer than that for other sections. With the knowledge he had built up of Germany and the Germans he must have had serious doubts about mounting Operation Periwig. The Allies were advancing at a very satisfactory pace, and if it could be maintained, and as long as the enemy did not have a 'wonder weapon' to launch against the Allied troops or Britain, the war must surely be over in a few months. (It is doubtful whether Thornley would have been privy to any hint as to the Allies' development of the atomic bomb, but it was still not absolutely certain how far the German scientists had progressed with their own project.) And with the end in sight it must have been natural to be reluctant to expose either agents already in the field or men under training to further risk.

Operation Periwig was conceived when the Supreme Commander, Gen Eisenhower, recognised the need to shorten what remained of the war as quickly as possible by any means, including by breaking the enemy's will to resist. Gubbins, anxious as usual to do his utmost, sought to do what his organisation was good at: supporting resistance groups. The trouble was, there were none. What else could he do? In a flash of brilliance, he – or someone, we are not sure who actually came up with the idea – announced that since they could not deal with the real thing they would do the next best thing: they would create an imaginary organisation. The operation would be turned into one of the most imaginative deception plans of the war. But such plans need careful developing, and that takes time. Time was something they had very little of.

SOE's old antagonist, SIS, had never more than tolerated it, and that on condition the younger organisation's activities did not impinge on the areas the older one regarded as its own. The SIS was particularly concerned that Periwig should not in any way increase the difficulties under which its own agents in Germany operated, or, indeed, put them at risk. They argued that any additional activity was bound to raise security levels, leading to increased surveillance and investigations by the German security service. The internal conflict was eventually settled by a compromise, but not before valuable time and opportunities had been lost.

The date 11 September 1944 marked a milestone in the Allied invasion of occupied Europe, for it was on this day that American troops crossed the

German frontier to bring the ground fighting to the soil of the Fatherland. On 23 October Soviet troops entered East Prussia. The writing was on the wall for Hitler. At the end of the year the German Ardennes offensive, the Battle of the Bulge, held up the Allied advance in this region, but as spring bloomed the list of German cities captured grew ever longer: Bonn, Brandenburg, Worms and Saarbrücken in March; Göttingen, Hanover, Weimar and Essen in early April; Nuremburg and Stuttgart in the middle of the month. On 18 April 1945 the Ruhr pocket which had been forlornly holding out finally collapsed, and 325,000 German troops trudged into captivity. And all the time, day and night whenever the weather permitted, bombs rained down on the remains of the country's industry and on the hapless civilians in the large centres. Power, water and transport were severely disrupted. Food became scarce. Two deep anxieties spread like an incoming tide into the population: that an outbreak of disease might spread like the plague, and, much worse, that reprisals might be wrought by the relentlessly advancing Red Army, the memories of the atrocities perpetrated during the Germans' rape of their homeland still fresh in their minds.

At the beginning of March it had already become clear to SOE that virtually no chance remained of even a partial execution of the original plan. By the beginning of April Periwig could make no further contribution to the war against Germany, for the military chaos within the country rendered it increasingly difficult to mount any operations that would cause even a moderate nuisance. After all, who would want to divert attention to relatively minor disturbances when there were daily life-and-death decisions to be faced, and where self-preservation was becoming of paramount importance?

But the enthusiasm of PWE for the pigeon operation in connection with Periwig ensured that they continued to be delivered until 27 April, when the realisation dawned that it was no longer worth risking the aircrews in this final gesture.

Had the original plan been implemented fully and immediately in December 1944, according to the officer writing the history of Operation Periwig on 17 August 1945, a contribution would have been made to the Allied victory, even though our armies enjoyed overwhelming success.[1]

How did Operation Periwig, unusual as it was, conform to the principles of deception set out by Lt Col Dudley Clarke, Head of Gen Wavell's specialist unit in the Middle East known as 'A' Force?

The first principle was that a deception must be focused at the mind of the enemy commander – the decision-maker. In the case of Periwig this was the home heads of the German security services: the Schutzstaffel (SS), the Reichssicherheitzhauptamt (RSHA), the Sicherheitsdienst (SD) and the Geheime Staatspolizei or Gestapo. After over five years of war there is little doubt that SOE had a good appreciation of the mindset of these men. The purpose of the deception was to so overload the German security services that effective chaos would result and provide an opportunity to initiate a revolution to terminate the war.

Clarke considered that control of deception operations should rest with operations staff – those who decide on the object, tempo and time of replacement of the plan. The deceivers should be in close and constant touch with the commander's ideas and wishes, and the head of the deception unit should have direct access to the commander. There must be proper coordination throughout, with command placed at the highest level and centrally controlled.

In the case of Periwig, SOE's German Country Section within the Directorate, who were the operations staff, had to defer to Supreme Headquarters Allied Expeditionary Force (SHAEF). Gubbins and Templer were hardly in 'close and constant touch' with Eisenhower's thoughts, and certainly did not have 'direct access' to him. Furthermore, proper co-ordination of all the agencies concerned – SOE, PWE, SIS, OSS and even SAS – was a very difficult task in a rapidly changing scene.

Clarke understood the crucial importance of preparation in a deception operation. The timing of its launch needed to be logical and, having been initiated, it had to be given time to work. In respect of these prerequisites, Periwig was on a hiding to nothing. The German Section had very little time to prepare, the timing of the launch was late, even before the delays incurred by the SIS's intransigence, and the rate of the Allied advance did not allow time for the plan to work.

Security surrounding the operation was generally good. Clarke advocated divulgence of information on a 'need to know and when needed to be known' basis and recommended never explaining why a person was engaged on a particular, and perhaps peculiar, task. 'Windfall' inputs of false information were to be avoided unless cleverly disguised: the dead-agent idea would have been convincing if the parachute problem had been solved (see Appendix 1); and the *Aktentasche* briefcase would have been difficult to fault (see pp. 185–6).

If the genuine deception plan were to be discovered it was recommended that its design and timing be such that several interpretations could be placed upon it. In the event none of the four agents despatched in Periwig was captured, and it is possible that in any case the general disruption of life at that time would have provided at least half-plausible interpretations.

The enemy must believe the source of the deception or cover plan, said Clarke. Double agents must appear reliable, and false radio traffic must conform to normal patterns. Periwig did not make use of double agents, although the triple agent Teapot was about to be released by the SIS for work on the plan (see pp. 193–4).

That the deceiver must be capable of doing what the lie suggests he will do is a precept that could not be satisfied by SOE: they could not raise a resistance organisation in Germany, and after the post-20 July purges and enquiries the Nazi regime must have been fairly confident such an event was most unlikely.

For credibility it is necessary to confirm the cover story from a variety of sources, the enemy discovering this 'evidence' by his own efforts or by accident. This is where the parachuted supplies, leaflets, radio traffic, rumours and minor acts of sabotage were to prove useful.

Clarke's final rule was that as real conditions change, so the lie and the feedback from reactions to it could reveal useful, if fleeting, opportunities. Conditions within Germany were changing too rapidly to allow changes to keep up with events, and there was certainly no time to obtain and assess any feedback from Germany.

No one can assert that Operation Periwig was a success. In terms of its original objectives the only people who appear to have been genuinely deceived were: five German PoWs who volunteered to become SOE agents; their instructors; the aircrews; and no doubt many broadcasters and leaflet writers – all on our own side. The extent to which the dropping of 'evidence' of a resistance movement caused annoyance to the Gestapo, let alone widespread alarm, cannot be judged. In the chaos that reigned in Germany by the time SOE was allowed to carry out the drops, the hunting-down of an elusive group of dissidents who had not caused any trouble must have carried a very low priority.

The plans described in this account are only those that were fully prepared, even if the vast majority of them were not actually initiated. Very many others that came within the scope of the original plan were abandoned without ever being committed to paper because of the wide variety of obstacles put in their way during the short life of the operation. This fuelled a critique of Operation Periwig dated 17 August 1945, in which the writer concluded: 'The operation was generally thwarted in its purpose by a lack of coordination between departments, and by the absence of support which it was essential for it to have.'[2]

The German Directorate had been working on the assumption that the war in Europe would continue to the end of 1945.[3] Had Operation Periwig been conceived much earlier, and preparations for its launch been pursued vigorously at not only the tactical but also the strategic level, there might have been a chance to win over the doubters and, in particular, to have won support from other departments, notably the SIS. As it was, the original plan was not drawn up until 22 November 1944, and it took a whole two months at a critical time in the war before the debilitating limitations were accepted, the necessary agreements secured and operations began. By this time Germany's defeat was certain and, although the ideas were flowing from SOE and PWE, there was simply insufficient time to produce the intended degree of chaos before the unconditional surrender in May 1945.

Another criticism of the way Periwig was run concerns the perceived inadequate liaison with Supreme Headquarters Allied Expeditionary Force. The operation was planned for mutual contribution from SOE, SIS, PWE and other agencies according to their abilities, and all as an integral part of the military operations aimed at the destruction of Germany. Periwig had been planned as one of SHAEF's many operational commitments, but some reviewers considered the chief reason for Periwig's failure to achieve what was hoped for was that it was not sufficiently in detail a SHAEF responsibility. Experience showed that once a body such as SHAEF came into existence and exercised real authority, SOE units involved in action against the enemy on land with which SHAEF was concerned should have been a fully integrated part of SHAEF. But in the event, while SOE continued to plan and attempt to put into effect Periwig schemes, it found itself functioning largely on its own with assistance from the other organisations only in individual cases and by request. Moreover, there was little opportunity for direct contact between Periwig officers and the military headquarters that should have controlled it. The outcome was a continual series of requests by SOE for permission to carry out certain operations, SHAEF considering each on its merits and eventually giving its decision to go ahead or not, as the case might be.

An element of lack of internal coordination undoubtedly hindered the more effective prosecution of the operation. It was a plan that was the responsibility of the German Country Section within one country directorate, namely the German Directorate. This directorate had no control over other country sections or directorates, and therefore the SOE officers running the operation came from those concerned with Germany, whether in London, in neutral countries or at forward bases. And yet, SOE's experience showed that in a country as large and as powerful as Germany, which had occupied a great deal of other territory, a subversive organisation with the objective of combating it could not operate successfully on a single-country basis. Since the belligerent country's influence had spread across other states, the SOE sections dealing with it needed to be closely integrated into the operation. The sort of opportunities the Periwig officers sought for providing evidence of German resistance existed in several countries still overrun by Germany, for example Norway, Denmark, Holland and parts of the Mediterranean theatre of war. Schemes similar to Periwig were launched in some of these areas, but the opportunity to put Periwig itself into operation in these parts appears to have been missed. All this drew those officers to the conclusion that a Periwig-type plan needed to be controlled by a General Staff with equal authority over all the regional sections. Had it been a SHAEF responsibility, the chance of success would have been much higher.

The original plan had been drawn up in anticipation that at least a dozen agents would be despatched to Germany each month. This proved to be far too optimistic, as the availability of volunteers from German PoWs resulted in only five men being trained in a specially shortened course, and only four of these actually being dropped into Germany. The obvious impending defeat of Germany cannot have been conducive to persuading prisoners to accept the very real risks involved.

One of the conclusions reached by those reviewing the performance of Operation Periwig was that it was impractical to run a large-scale deception exercise concurrently with genuine, though ineffective, resistance groups. It is easy to understand the confusion that would arise. The deception plan should be all-embracing, while the genuine activity should have specific tasks within it.

This account of a highly imaginative plan to assist in the Allied victory over Germany shows Operation Periwig as anything but a success. By their very nature, most of the operations conducted as part of Periwig were such as to be impossible to monitor with any degree of accuracy. The fact that they were aiming to convince the enemy of the reality of an imaginary situation could only compound the difficulties of judging just how much false information reached the enemy and how much of it was believed.

One of the key factors in the failure of Operation Periwig to achieve even worthwhile success is cited by commentators as its late start. As already mentioned, the original Periwig plan was drawn up in late November 1944 and operations commenced two months later. The Allied advance had been so successful that Germany was by this time assured of defeat, and even with SOE's German Directorate receiving the lion's share of its resources, there was insufficient time to develop the plans to the point where the intended really widespread chaos was produced in Germany. Why did it start so late in the war?

It seems to have been prompted by Eisenhower's appeal to all the Allies to redouble their efforts to break the German will to resist. There seems little point in exhorting armies to such lengths unless the strength of the will to resist has been established first by the campaigns, battles and defeats of normal warfare and then by the effects of the deprivations brought upon the civilian population by the systematic destruction of the enemy's industry and infrastructure. This being so, it is inevitable that such an operation would be countenanced only when victory was within sight. At such a stage an estimate of the time required to properly mount the operation would be needed; and against that would have to be set the likely time to victory. Was there time to mount the deception? If the Allied policy towards Germany had been anything less than unconditional surrender there might have been a faint hope of a negotiated armistice. The disaffected members of the German officer class saw this route as retaining some honour, and they could have argued that a repeat of the post-1918 humiliation and subsequent rise of National Socialism could be avoided only by a radical change in the politics of Germany.

Had there not been an appeal to break the German will to resist, would an operation like Periwig have materialised? The intelligence information available to Thornley as SOE's expert on German matters would have been exactly the same. There were two fundamental factors that militated against the possibility of a spontaneous genuine resistance movement in Germany capable of initiating a revolution: there was no coordination of the small anti-Nazi factions; and while there was some anti-Nazi feeling, there was negligible pro-Allied sentiment. Without the Supreme Commander's exhortation it is doubtful whether there would have been another catalyst for the wide-ranging discussion that gave birth to the Periwig deception plan.

One of the most persistent obstacles to advancing Periwig plans was the lack of coordination between departments, particularly between SOE and the SIS. Every operation had to be cleared to ensure it would not compromise the activities of the SIS, the Office of Strategic Services (OSS) or any other Allied force. This all took time that SOE did not have, and many fleeting opportunities were lost.

The Allies appear to have discounted any assistance in the overthrow of Hitler and his Nazi Party from the opposition within the Army, the civil service and the civil intelligensia. But did the Allies have the full picture? Were their judgements based on sound and adequate intelligence? Would they have acted differently had more knowledge of the 20 July plot been available in advance and those subsequently arrested and executed been available to assist the Allies? Their reaction to the failed coup implied that the Allies had no interest in an alternative regime being established by disaffected Army officers. Total defeat and the expunging of all traces of Nazism was their sole objective. A Western-style democracy would be built in due course, at least in half the conquered Germany.

The Allies had swept across Europe, but the closer to the German frontier the fighting came, the stiffer was the resistance offered. Fighting in one's own country is inevitably charged with additional intensity. What is more, defending troops will have the overall support of the civilian population and can therefore discount the harassing operations and acts of sabotage experienced as they retreat from the occupied countries. Such a climate is far from conducive to the setting-up of a real resistance organisation, let alone a fictitious one.

SHAEF would dearly have liked internal assistance on the scale they had received after the invasion of France. Were they aware of the state of opposition in Germany? The SIS's relations with SOE were very poor, and it is doubtful whether it will ever be known whether they deliberately withheld information on their perception of the state of the resistance in Germany. In any case, the degree of resistance was very seriously reduced after the 20 July plot arrests, and those members who were still free were in no position to continue with subversive action while the manhunt by the SS and Gestapo were at their most intensive. So in autumn 1944 Thornley was right in his assessment that there was no organised resistance to Hitler within Germany.

Another factor that is difficult from this distance to understand is the Allies' attitude to factions in opposition to the Nazi regime. Even before 1939 when desperately concerned anti-Nazis arranged for emissaries to meet senior British government officials to discuss the crisis, they were fobbed off and ignored, sometimes without even the courtesy of an explanatory reply. Historians claim the suspicious establishment officials were puzzled and could not make out what lay behind the approaches, so they played safe and did nothing. Except that 'doing nothing' was just about the most dangerous response they could have made.

There was, of course, a cost factor attached to SOE's work, as there was to every part of the war effort against Germany. In mid-1944 SOE Financial Director Gp Capt J.F. Venner could not have been aware that his eventual balance sheet was to show an astounding £23 million profit, made possible by some extremely dubious currency transactions in the Far East, with the full approval of the Treasury, by a man who lived on the margin between merchanting and smuggling – Walter Fletcher. For the initiators of Periwig starting up, establishing and maintaining as a matter of urgency an entirely new resistance organisation in a country whose population in general may well have been far from supportive could have been seen as costly. But creating and maintaining for a short time a make-believe organisation was, in financial terms, an attractive proposition.

There was also a political factor, acknowledgement of which dictated that not a word about Periwig was to leak out to our Russian allies. The Foreign Office was terrified that if they learned the British were assisting German resistance, it would be impossible to adequately explain the concept to Stalin's men. To them 'German resistance' had an entirely dissimilar significance.

There is yet another aspect of the final months of the Third Reich that might have influenced the Allies in their apparent decision to ignore the resistance elements as the latter plotted to assassinate Hitler, take over control and negotiate an honourable peace. At around this time SOE had dusted off and were updating long-standing plans for the assassination of the Führer in case they were given the go-ahead and could find someone prepared to undertake the task. This was Operation Foxley, which is described in Denis Rigden's book *Kill the Führer*. In the end it was realised that the increasingly incompetent Hitler was actually of more use to the Allies alive than dead, and if a more astute Nazi were to take the reins, the defeat of Germany could take longer and be more difficult. This being the case, they could not support a resistance group whose aim was to kill Hitler, for nobody could forecast for sure the outcome of such an attempt or who would take the place of the Führer should the assassination succeed but the coup fail and the perpetrators be arrested.

SOE's German Section had started with little to do and with proportionate resources. It ended with a great deal to achieve and with all the resources concentrated on the penetration of the Reich itself. But in the time available even the resources of the entire organisation were insufficient to set up a fictitious underground on a scale large enough to be of practical value in the final push into the German heartland. Nine months proved to be too short a period, even though by April 1945 there were a few agents firmly established in both Germany and Austria, and short-term missions were being carried out in relative safety. But there was no standing organisation in these countries; no wireless communications; no reception committees; and there was only slight contact with the native population. Although the nature of warfare has changed dramatically in the sixty years since the closing stages of the war in Europe, if the same circumstances were to prevail today it would still require a year of skilled work at top pressure and on high priority to achieve anything substantial.[4]

In the autumn of 1944, with the outcome of the war beyond doubt, even if the timing of the end was still subject to considerable speculation, the SOE Council met to consider its future. The Director of Organisation and Staff Duties, M.P. Murray, who was also Deputy Chief of SOE and a member of its council, was charged with preparing a paper for submission by SO, as Lord Selborne was known in the symbols, to the Prime Minister. The third draft of this document survives in the archives,[5] albeit with two whole paragraphs deleted under Section 3(4) of the Public Records Act 1958: that is to say their contents might have jeopardised national security or caused other difficulties had they been revealed.

Lord Selborne, the Minister of Economic Warfare, was to recommend the early dissolution of his ministry upon the defeat of Germany. The Japanese situation could be resolved with a blockade by the Allied navies 'without the assistance of politicians'. One can with hindsight speculate whether the fire- and atomic-bombing of Japanese targets inflicted less suffering than would have occurred by a blockade of the islands and the subsequent widespread starvation of the population. While such a blockade was being enforced SOE had important targets to attack in Japanese-held territories in the Far East, but the council were also convinced there was necessary and long-term work to perform in Europe and elsewhere.

There was, the paper said, clear evidence that Himmler was preparing a German Maquis (resistance movement) and a secret organisation to initiate a Third World War. In September 1944 the Joint Intelligence Sub-Committee estimate on the conditions in Germany following the collapse had noted good evidence that Himmler was already preparing an underground Nazi organisation. They considered it unlikely that this organisation would reveal itself in the early period of Allied occupation. The subcommittee also considered it probable that Himmler would arrange for the sabotage of aircraft equipment and a secret association of aircraft personnel as a nucleus for a new German Air Force (GAF).[6] Furthermore, in Part 1 of the *German Directorate History*[7] it is pointed out on p. 15 that Thornley had intentionally included in a draft paper to Col R.H. Barry on 31 October the sentence, 'Use any SOE channels or organisation to investigate the Nazi underground movement and possible methods of combating it.' So there was a real fear of a Nazi resistance movement, and therefore, argued the draft paper to Selborne, it would be 'madness' to scrap SOE so long as such a threat existed – a threat that would in all likelihood be pursued with typical Teutonic patience, thoroughness and duplicity, both within Germany and outside it. How better to counter such an organisation than by making SOE ex-poachers into very good gamekeepers?

SOE had learned the art of underground warfare the hard way, and it was highly probable that similar methods would be called for in a future war. Therefore it made sense for military staff colleges to be able to call upon SOE instructors. Another pool of human resource lay in the 'hundreds of thousands' of men who had risked their lives to work with the British in Europe and who hated Germany and feared another war. Their goodwill should not be squandered but harnessed to keep Germany in a position of powerlessness, weakened by self-interest, apathy and 'fifth column' activities. The leaders of these men were in prominent positions in the governments of the liberated countries: it was essential to maintain contact with them.

SOE's clandestine contacts in the distribution of foreign currency were seen in the paper as a means of monitoring the financial underworld to watch for signs of the Gestapo or fifth columnists attempting to 'spread their tentacles again throughout the world'.

The council felt SOE had a part to play in peacetime, albeit in the years of unrest they thought likely to follow the war. They therefore advocated a nucleus organisation for postwar work, primarily in Europe. They saw this organisation comprising a small inter-service staff to study and develop subversive activities, complete with training facilities, a small technical research station and a communications development branch. It should also include an organisation to control small out-stations in the more important capitals of Europe, initially for clandestine work into Germany for the Allied Military and Control Commission but also to monitor German activity in the countries where they were located. Other work was very possible, subject to Foreign Office policy decisions.

The paper then touched briefly on the thorny problem of control of a postwar SOE organisation. Somewhat surprisingly, considering the problems that had existed between SOE and the SIS throughout the former's existence, it was suggested for the sake of efficiency that it be placed under the same control as, although not amalgamated with, the SIS. The council favoured answering to the Minister of Defence or, failing that, the Foreign Secretary.

Whether this draft was the final one and whether it was placed before the Prime Minister in the last winter of the war has not been determined. Winston Churchill had been enthusiastic about SOE; the Deputy Prime Minister, Clement Attlee, was not. It was Attlee who was to become Prime Minister after the 1945 general election. SOE's fate was sealed, and it was formally disbanded in 1946.

From PWE's viewpoint, David Garnett concludes in *The Secret History of PWE* that Operation Periwig, like many other plans, was carried out too late in the day and on too inconsiderable a scale to have any real effect. It is, however, a plan of abiding interest, since it is an example of political warfare carried to its furthest possible point.[8]

Appendix 1

THE ORIGINAL PLAN

Periwig – Possible Operations[1]

1. AGENTS
   - i) Introduction of agents with genuine mission and genuine belief in existence of Periwig (this in case of capture).
     - a) Infiltrated through the lines, neutral or occupied territory.
     - b) Parachuted.
   - ii) Arranging discovery of dead agents carrying documents.
     - a) Shot while attempting to infiltrate across the lines.
     - b) Killed by parachute failure.
   - iii) Arranging arrest of an agent by neutral police, to make revelations to them which will be passed to German SD.
   - iv) Deliberate use of agents provocateurs and double agents.

2. GENUINE ACTIVITY
   - i) Establishing apparent connection with genuine organisations such as Edelweiss Piraten.
   - ii) Linking successful phoney organisations, such as Red Circle Escape Club, with Periwig.
   - iii) Inducing neutral firm or military attaché to believe in Periwig and to perform small services for the organisation.
   - iv) Association of as many failures as permitted of genuine penetration of Germany with Periwig.

3. PLANTS
   - A. *Neutral and Occupied Country*
     - i) Attaching significance to meetings between Germans and neutrals, by planting evidence.
     - ii) Suggesting clandestine communication by planting messages, codes, lists of members, orders, cables and letters, etc. by errors in delivery or blowing boites aux lettres by telephone calls to Germany etc.
     - iii) Suggesting clandestine organisation by indiscretion, informing, or by allowing penetration by agents provocateurs.
     - iv) Blackmailing Germans into drastic action such as confession to Gestapo, seeking asylum, suicide; this to be achieved by compromising them with knowledge of the organisation and with documents.

v) Making assassination of Germans by resistance movements in the normal course of their work appear to be Periwig operations.

B. *Germany*

i) Genuine warnings to Nazi leaders by neutrals.

ii) Alteration in tone of SHAEF Weekly Intelligence Summary and other official documents; causing forged Allied official documents to fall into German hands.

iii) Infiltration of pamphlets, etc. through courier lines.

4. AIR

i) Dropping containers and packages containing instructions, pamphlets, arms, sabotage material, poisons, etc. with suitable evidence of the organisation and references to BBC phrases and briefing.

ii) Dropping of pamphlets.

iii) Use of Braddock combined with suitable instructions.

iv) Suspicious flying including circling, signals to the ground, etc.

v) Dropping of personal equipment with suitable references.

vi) Use of aircraft W/T to simulate agents' traffic.

5. W/T

i) Simulation of W/T traffic to Germany.

ii) Simulation of traffic from Germany to a genuine W/T operator in occupied or neutral territory. The operator is then arrested, or blown and obliged to flee.

iii) Use of a W/T operator known by us to be worked by the Germans (one useful example already exists).

iv) Dropping of automatic self-operating and self-destructive transmitters.

v) Dropping of W/T material including remote control devices etc., both in Germany and neutral territory so that it will be discovered and become linked up with the organisation.

vi) Dropping of transmitters disguised as 'people's receivers'.

6. POST

i) Use of threatening letters.

a) To persons 'suspected' of resistance activity.

b) To persons urging them to join resistance activity.

ii) Anonymous letters.

a) To the police in Germany from neutral territory, about members of the German resistance.

b) To neutral police about activities of German resistance.

c) Warnings to German leaders.

iii) Blackmailing letters to 'members' of German resistance by private individuals for money.

7. SUSPICIOUS ACTIVITIES

A. *Neutral and Occupied Territory*

i) Arranging a démarche to the Vatican by a section of Periwig resistance.

ii) Intensive activity of 'cut-outs' in neutral territory.

B. *In England*

i) Activity on the part of German refugees.

ii) Activity round important German P's/W.

iii) References to German resistance in the Houses of Parliament, questions, etc.

8. RUMOURS

i) Sibs, confidences, verbal indiscretions, in neutral/occupied territory, German and Allied territory, to back up factual operations.

9. PAMPHLETS

i) Distribution in neutral, occupied and German territory. (The last two by air) of pamphlets consisting of:

a) Instructions.

b) Hints at the existence of the organisation.

c) Details of an escape organisation.

d) Encouragement to malinger, desert, strike, go-slow, etc.

10. BBC

i) Operational phrases (dropping instructions to agents, etc.).

ii) Blackmail messages.

iii) Allusion messages.

iv) Orders and encouragement disguised as historical talks, and discussions of contemporary events.

v) Black broadcasting, including preparation of German soldiers, etc., for the revolt.

11. PRESS

A. *Neutral Territory*

i) Publication of German resistance activity inspired by Periwig.

ii) Playing up of genuine events implying resistance in Germany.

B. *Occupied and German Territory*

i) Insertion of personal notices and advertisements, to give the impression of clandestine communication.

C. *UK and Allied*

i) Building up of events in Germany.

ii) Alternatively by omitting reference to neutral press reports of resistance.

iii) Articles on 'the attitude of the British Government to German resistance and to a new German Government'.

iv) Indiscretions.

Appendix 2

LEO MARKS, SCHILLER AND THE FAULTY PARACHUTE

The intriguing case recounted in Leo Marks's book *Between Silk and Cyanide* of a German PoW who was persuaded to work for the Allies in Operation Periwig has been the source of much speculation. Marks gave the man the name Schiller, and his book implies that he met his death in a contrived parachuting failure over Germany.

Leopold Samuel Marks was born in 1920, the son of an antiquarian bookseller in London's Charing Cross Road. His German and French language skills were 'fair' and he was recruited by SOE, who sent him on a cryptology course from November 1941 to February 1942 and allocated him the symbol D/YC.M. According to his book, Marks worked untiringly to ensure that the communication between agents in the field and London was clear and secure. The book also describes how his suspicions that communications with Dutch agents had been compromised were confirmed by the Abwehr's notorious admission of the *Englandspiel* or 'England game' that cost the lives of so many SOE agents.

There is no doubt that the original Periwig plan called for agents carrying information that SOE wanted to fall into the hands of German security to be killed either by being shot while crossing through the lines or by the failure of their parachutes. This plan was set out by Maj Gen Templer, Head of the German Directorate, in a letter to Sir Robert Bruce Lockhart dated 19 January 1945 which is in The National Archives (TNA – the former Public Record Office or PRO).[1]

There were, however, objections to this plan and a number of proposals within it were struck out, including those above. This is clear from a later, revised document in the same file. But the record of the fourth meeting of the Periwig Committee on 8 February 1945 states that Templer had told Capt Dawson, the committee secretary, that 'C' and CD, the respective heads of the Secret Intelligence Service (SIS) and SOE, had agreed in principle to the original Periwig scheme of unrestricted action.[2]

The idea of killing someone by means of a faulty parachute was certainly being entertained by SOE: during the period from mid-August to about the end of September 1944 Angus Fyffe, who had spent much of his time on security duties and was at that time interrogating and debriefing returned agents, was asked by Cdr John Senter, RNVR, Assistant Director of Personnel, to find a way to make a parachute fail without leaving any trace that it had been tampered with. Despite two weeks of trials at RAF Tempsford under the pretext that intelligence sources had learned of a German plan to use faulty parachutes to drop agents carrying false information that they wished to fall into Allied hands, the parachute packers could not find a way of guaranteeing such a failure.

The German Section was duly advised in early October that their proposal to drop a volunteer German PoW with papers incriminating highly placed Nazis by means of a fatally flawed parachute was not a practical one.

For some reason which is not clear, in November Maj Gen Templer instructed the Head of the Air Supply Research Section in SOE's Research and Development Section, Dr Douglas Everett, to investigate the identical problem. Everett travelled to the parachute school at Ringway, Manchester, where tests were carried out, this time ostensibly in connection with failures experienced in the field. The results reached the same conclusion as the Tempsford tests.[3]

Everett had, of course, to know the reason behind the trials he had been ordered to conduct, and the fact that he was being implicated in a possible murder was not lost on him. While he and F. Boyce were writing *SOE The Scientific Secrets* he recalled to the author a conversation he had had with an historian who had been acquainted with Maj James Joll. Joll's linguistic abilities had brought him to the attention of SOE, to which he was posted in September 1943. It was intended to send him as the Austrian Section's representative on the SOE mission to Hungary the following March, but events in that country caused SOE to abandon its plans for him and he was placed instead on the staff of, first, its Austrian and, later, its German Section, where he was allotted the symbol X/AUS.4.

Joll's personal SOE file[4] reveals that he attended all the usual training courses for prospective agents, and also one on home-made devices, at the Czech Research Group in December 1943 and January 1944. The initial report on Joll soon after his appearance in SOE was somewhat critical, but by the end of 1944 the opinions of Joll's assessors had changed markedly. Now his all-round knowledge of German affairs was of great assistance, he had a clear brain and submitted all plans to sound, constructive criticism. The following March Templer wrote of him: 'A very good young officer indeed.' It appears from Everett's recalled (and purely anecdotal) evidence that Joll had somehow got to know about the plan to drop an agent on a faulty parachute and had pleaded with Templer to abandon the idea. Whether his approaches bore any fruit is not known.

There are two points in Marks's account that cast doubt on its accuracy:

- He describes being driven to a PoW camp near Basingstoke in order to brief Schiller on the use of SOE codes. No record of a camp in this area has been found.
- His book gives the impression that he had an easy-going relationship with Gen Gubbins and Brig Nicholls, the Head of Signals. This is most unlikely as he was, although good at his job, still only a young and possibly pretentious civilian. What is more, Nicholls has been described as a 'real martinet'. Had Marks spoken to either of them in the manner he claims to have done, he would probably have been in serious trouble.

Examination of the records of the Special Duties Squadrons for the early months of 1945 give no clues as to whether anyone likely to have been Schiller was dropped just before Templer left SOE shortly after 13 March.

If there was a Schiller this name cannot be found in any records. If it was the *nom de guerre* of a double agent who, as Templer is claimed to have told Marks, was responsible for the deaths of as many Germans as Allied people, a candidate could be the agent code-named Teapot. This German was in fact a triple-cross, and the Twenty Committee was asked at its meeting on 15 March 1945[5] if he could be used for Operation Periwig. They had no objection, but the SOE *History of the German Directorate* dated 17 August 1945[6] dealing with Operation Periwig shows (on page 11, section vii) that Teapot was already in Germany as a wireless operator.

In 2000 Carlton TV broadcast a series of programmes about SOE entitled *Churchill's Secret Army*. Leo Marks appeared in this, with Douglas Everett, and confirmed the story of Schiller and the faulty parachute. He also commented that 'an agent was undoubtedly murdered'. Shortly before Marks's death at the age of 81 the author met him and raised the same question about Schiller and his alleged fatal parachute jump into Germany. Marks again confirmed it was true, adding that Templer was ruthless and would have covered his tracks well after such a controversial episode. This opinion is at odds with Templer's reaction to the report just before Christmas 1944 that the Norwegian resistance had prepared a bomb disguised as a large traditional Christmas wreath which they intended to deliver to Schutzstaffel (SS) headquarters in Oslo, ostensibly from Quisling's organisation, the Hird (equivalent to Germany's SA). Templer, as Head of the German Directorate, did not support this action and vetoed it as being 'contrary to the Christmas spirit'.

Three other persons in positions of knowledge were asked about the story of Schiller: a well-known writer on SOE and intelligence matters; a leading SOE historian; and a senior civil servant with access to SOE files who had been asked to read the typescript of *Between Silk and Cyanide* and found nothing he could object to on grounds of security. All three cautioned against accepting the work too literally. In the interests of producing a readable account, which it certainly is, Marks's strong passion for a good story might have occasionally caused him to move off the tramlines of strict truth. Marks's personal SOE file[7] contains very little information but does include a note of the award of the MBE and a Danish decoration.

On balance, it seems unlikely that a German PoW was killed in order to ensure that vital papers reached the hands of the German security forces. *SOE The Scientific Secrets* by Boyce and Everett reached the same conclusion, subject to Operations I.5, P.3, W.3 and W.6 being identified. This has now been possible, and they have no connection with the alleged incident. But there are at least thirteen operations of various kinds, assuming the numbering to be continuous, about which the scantiest details cannot be found in the archives.

Appendix 3

AGENT DROPS INTO GERMANY[1]

Between 1 September 1944 and 24 April 1945, that is the period when it became clear that clandestine operations into Germany carried a greater chance of success than hitherto, the operational records of 161 Squadron based notionally at RAF Tempsford show that fifty-three men were parachuted into Germany. This number includes only the successful drops and not those operations that failed owing to the aircraft having to turn back because of bad weather, enemy action, mechanical trouble or even in one case the two parachutists refusing to jump at the last moment. This number is considerably higher than the twenty-eight former members of the German armed forces who went on such missions in this period as revealed in *Gubbins and SOE* by Peter Wilkinson and Joan Bright Astley. The records do not reveal any details of the men despatched on these missions, but the implication is that at least twenty-three were Allied and it is reasonable to assume many were of eastern European extraction. All the operations listed below were 'blind drops' without a reception committee and carried out at night. All but two of them used Hudson aircraft, the exceptions being Operations Downend 2 and Polacca/Polder which used Halifaxes, the latter flown from Earls Colne airfield. The fact that this flight was from the airfield near Halstead in Essex and not from Tempsford probably accounts for the absence of this operation from some 161 Squadron records.

Date	*Operation*	*Agents dropped*	*Approx. area of drop*
1/2 Sept 44	Downend 2	1	Haren
2/5 Oct	Birch	2	Vachingen
26/7 Nov	Ash	2	Marxheim on Danube
26/7 Nov	Vivacious 2	1	Berkc
26/7 Nov	Frilford	2	Lake
31 Jan/1 Feb 45	Alder	2	?
31 Jan/1 Feb	Juniper	2	Goesfeld
21/2 Feb	Carham	1	Gospeuroda
21/2 Feb	Colan	3	Pforzheim
21/2/Feb	Mulberry	2	Opperman
22/3 Feb	Imola Bolingbroke	2	Miltenburg, Bingen
25/6 Feb	Montford/Everybody's Vasco/Telegraph	2	Velden
28 Feb/1 Mar	Colburn	3	Jossa, Neustadt
28 Feb/1 Mar	Neron	2	Lauterbach
28 Feb/1 Mar	Vasco/Telegraph	2	Hochstadt, Lamerstaut

Date	*Operation*	*Agents dropped*	*Approx. area of drop*
2/3 Mar	Tarbes	2	Hienheim
2/3 Mar	Negus	2	52 38N 09 32E
20/23 Mar	Colehill	1	Bergenbruck
2/3 Apr	Polacca/Polder	2	Wildeshausen near Bremen
4/5 Apr	Curland	2	51 20N 11 30E
18/19 Apr	Periscope (Flap)	2	47 53N 12 24E
18/19 Apr	Catmore	1	48 22N 10 31E
19/20 Apr	Mystère (Nabel)	1	54 05N 10 31E
19/20 Apr	Nabel (Mystère)	1	53 54N 10 08E
21/2 Apr	Nachtigal	2	54 16N 12 52E
23/4 Apr	Nase	2	48 44N 13 08E
23/4 Apr	Bruno/Times/Ironsides/Solon	4	48 27N 11 11E
24/5 Apr	Jaeger/Aidan	2	47 59N 10 23E

Appendix 4

AIDE-MÉMOIRE FOR MOUNTING OF AIR OPERATIONS

(X/GER Section)[1]

1. On receipt of Target Intelligence file from X/TGT, decision is taken on its priority, technical and tactical possibility.
2. Discuss with OC Group C personnel available, state of training and individual ability.
3. Discuss the task with operators selected and ascertain their willingness to volunteer.
4. Proposal form PPA to be lodged in triplicate with AD/X. D/CE to allocate a code name to the operation.
5. Discuss with X/AIR the area in which the 'drop' is desired – procure pinpoints acceptable to the Air Ministry and Bomber Command, also photographic air cover and interpretations.
6. Discussion with operators re cover identity, documents and personal equipment. *Note*: Give to X/Q a list of the personal requirements, including rations of each individual, using forms Q/MIL/2, Q/CIV/2 and XF/1. (10 days' notice to be given if possible.)
7. X/S to be informed in writing as soon as possible of numerical priority in relation to other operations. See also Office Instruction No. 2 for details required by X/S.
8. Attend meeting at Station IX to form Technical Plan and decide on stores to be taken. (D/B.1 convenes this meeting.) OC Group C also attends. *Note*: Give to X/Q the list of technical stores to be requisitioned as decided upon at this meeting (Copy to OC Group C), using form X/F1.
9. Arrange conference with OC Group C and the operators concerned, to discuss and formulate the complete tactical and technical plans, including the method and route of withdrawal, also communications (if any). *Note*: Steps to be taken to lay on escape arrangements and communication facilities (where required) with the appropriate mission in country of exfiltration.
10. Discuss with OC Group C what specialised preparatory training is desirable, and establish a timetable for the operation.
11. Form ATF.1 to be lodged with AL Section (subsequent alterations to be on form ATF.1a) not later than three days before op is due. Use form ATF.12 if a landing operation.
12. Application to be made by letter to AD/E copy to AL.X/AIR for allocation of star priority.
13. Lodge with D/FIN.X form F/1 in respect of funds required for the operation. NB F/1 to be initialled by C/S officer as well as by AD/X.1, covering note to state 'funds not recoverable but chargeable to the organisation's expenses'.

14. Lodge with AL form ATF.3 – 'Request for packing of stores otherwise than in containers'. Alternatively if stores being packed in containers use form ATF.4.
15. Lodge with AL form ATF.7 – 'Equipment for personnel being despatched by air'. Include request for extra ration of chocolate and boiled sweets.
16. Offer the operation to AL Section and Conference Room, giving the date from which it will be ready to emplane.
17. Prepare Briefing Instructions under the following headings:
    1. Object
    2. Arrival in enemy territory
    3. Movement after landing
    4. Plan of attack
    5. Withdrawal
    6. Cover identity and documents
    7. Stores – a) Personal
       b) Operational
       c) Maps
    8. Finance
    9. Communications
    10. Special instructions
18. Send copy of briefing instructions to AD/X (1 copy) and OC Group C (2 copies).
19. Briefing of operators and final checking of all stores, equipment, documents, etc. (at least one day before the first day of the flying period).
20. Phone Conference Room at 1100hr on day of emplanement to enquire whether operation is on. If so, arrange with CR transport and facilities for men to have a final hot meal at aerodrome. Ask CR whether or not operators can be accommodated at Stn 61 in the event of cancellation after 1800hr or abortive flight.
21. Conduct party to airport, carry out last general check-over and security search immediately prior to emplaning. Remain at airport until after take-off. Remain at Stn 61 until confirmation has been received that operation was successful. If not successful either stay at Stn 61 or return to holding school.
22. If operation is 'off' on the first day, put it up again to Conference Room for the following day.
23. When operation has been completed
    a) advise Switzerland if operators were to be exfiltrated by Swiss route.
    b) advise Switzerland and/or Sweden if postboxes were allotted.
    c) send details of operators with photographs to X/B for transmission through X/S to SF detachments and for their records. See pink forms.
    d) advise X/S if operators likely to be overrun soon on American front.
    e) send one copy of financial agreement to D/FIN.
24. When news is received from the field send in ATF.15.

Note: Stn 61 refers to the Special Training School at Gaynes Hall near St Neots in Huntingdonshire, the nearest accommodation to Tempsford Airfield.

Appendix 5

PWE Black Propaganda

The range of black propaganda disseminated by the Political Warfare Executive or PWE was vast and can be judged by this selection of the subjects covered:[1]

Swedish and Swiss Christmas cards; French postcards; 1916 postcards *England uns aushungern* ('England is starving us out'); Go-slow; Two coloured stickers; *Der Soldat* ('The Soldier'); propaganda on cigarette paper; Moelder's letter; *Scheisse* ('shot'); Admiralty leaflet; Hess's flight; Ruhr material; Yellow peril; Catholic sermons; *Rundschreiben* ('circular letter') 5; Ley and parole stickers; Sex leaflet; Song postcard; Three leaflets from Sweden; *Bomben fördern* ('call for bombs'); Lantern sticker; Water closet sticker; Bavarian separatist; *An alt-deutschen Soeleute*; *Donkt bei jeder Bombe dran*; Toilet paper propaganda; Delmer's leaflet; Goebbels's speech; *Deutschland ist zu klein für mich* ('Germany is too small for me'); *SS Booklet;* Höfliche verse ('Polite verses'); *Drückeberger an die Front!* ('Draft-dodgers to the Front!'); *Stereos; SS songs; Feindpropaganda* ('Enemy propaganda'); *Nur für Nazis!* ('Only for Nazis!'); 6 Pfennig Hitler head; Accident circular; Sexologist's stories; Astrology booklet; Dorpmueller letter; Bread booklet; *Langsam arbeiten* ('Go-slow'); *Merkblatt* ('Leaflet'); *Schluss!* ('To hell with it!'); *Wir wollen ein freies und unabhängiges Öesterreich* ('We want a free and independent Austria'); *Führer Befehl* ('Fuehrer's order'); *Schlag auf Schlag* ('Blow upon blow'); *Frühlings-Schlacht* ('Springbattle') postcard; *Leibeigene* ('Serf') leaflet; Red Circle Letter; *Winterhilfswerk* ('Winter relief work') stickers; Malingerer's booklet; Ballistics booklet; Sauckel leaflet; Naples letters; Sermons; Genesis, Exodus and St Matthew; *Der Zenit* ('The Zenith'); December 1942; *Macht Hitler Kalt* ('Assassinate Hitler'); *Wer Isst* ('Who's eating?'); Corpse photo 2; NSV booklet; Passive resistance stickers; Plague booklet (Pest); Rose (Advent) sermon; Health chart; Home Front folded leaflet; *Winterhilfsbriefmarken* ('Winter aid stamps'); *Die Front will Frieden* ('The Front wants peace'); False pregnancy; Pornography; *Wenn der Arbeiter Wüsste* ('If the worker knew'); *Berchtesgaden Parole* ('Berchtesgaden watchword'); *Fragebogen* ('Questionnaire'); Miscellaneous Posting; Left-wing leaflet for factory workers; VD leaflet; Brandt-Rasputin booklet; *Nachrichtenhelferin* ('Signal-communication woman auxiliary'); Nostradamus; Luftfeldpost stamp; *10 Pflichten* leaflet; Malingerer diary; *Wie lange noch* ('How much longer?').

NOTES AND SOURCES

Introduction

1. Marks, *Between Silk and Cyanide.*

Chapter 1

1. Latimer, *Deception in War.*
2. Luvaas, *Frederick the Great on the Art of War*, pp. 122–3.
3. Latimer, *Deception in War*, p. 78.
4. Latimer, *Deception in War*, p. 78.
5. Pakenham, *The Boer War*, p. 398.
6. Gardner, *Mafeking*, p. 65.
7. Baden-Powell, *Lessons from the 'Varsity of Life*, p. 206.
8. Montagu, *The Man Who Never Was.*
9. Cruickshank, *Deception in World War II.*
10. TNA (PRO) file FO898/373.
11. TNA (PRO) file FO898/398.

Chapter 2

1. TNA (PRO) file HS7/27.
2. Richards, *Secret Flotillas.*
3. Macrae, *Winston Churchill's Toyshop.*
4. Foot, *SOE: The Special Operations Executive 1940–46.*
5. Garnett, *The Secret History of PWE.*
6. Garnett, *The Secret History of PWE*, p. 4.
7. Garnett, *The Secret History of PWE.*

Chapter 3

1. TNA (PRO) file HS6/642.
2. TNA (PRO) file HS7/145.
3. TNA (PRO) file HS7/145 German Directorate History Part 1 Germany, p. 8.
4. TNA (PRO) file HS7/145 German Directorate History Part 1 Germany, p. 13, para. 12.
5. TNA (PRO) file HS6/635.
6. TNA (PRO) file HS7/148 SOE Handbook German Directorate, Chapter IV.
7. TNA (PRO) file HS7/147 German Directorate History Part II 1(a), p. 1.

8. Boyce and Everett, *SOE: The Scientific Secrets.*
9. Rigden, *Kill the Führer.*
10. Garnett, *The Secret History of PWE*, pp. 435–6.
11. TNA (PRO) file HS6/687.
12. Freedom Stations were PWE broadcasting installations purporting to be secret stations operating in an enemy-occupied or satellite country.
13. Mackenzie, *The Secret History of SOE*, p. 712.
14. Correspondence with Angus Fyffe, May 2003.

Chapter 4

1. Wilkinson and Bright Astley, *Gubbins and SOE.*
2. The Bilderberg Group emerged from a small discussion group formed by Prince Bernhard of the Netherlands in 1952. It eventually came to include politicians, industrialists, bankers, writers, trades unionists, scholars and other leading personalities and became an influential forum for informal exchanges of views.
3. Bruce Lockhart, *Memoirs of a British Secret Agent.*
4. Rigden, *Kill the Führer.*
5. Cloake, *Templer – Tiger of Malaya.*

Chapter 5

1. Hoffmann, *German Resistance to Hitler*, p. 13.
2. Reynolds, *Treason Was No Crime*, p. 44.
3. Snyder, *Hitler's German Enemies*, p. 27.
4. Reynolds, *Treason Was No Crime*, p. 117.
5. Snyder, *Hitler's German Enemies*, pp. 176–83.
6. John, *Twice Through the Lines*, p. 33.
7. Tarrant, *The Red Orchestra*, pp. 62–9.
8. Reynolds, *Treason Was No Crime*, p. 182.

Chapter 6

1. The Fourteen Points legend refers to US President Wilson's peace programme, much resented by the Germans. The continuing blockade legend referred to an alleged continuation of the Royal Navy's wartime blockade of German ports which denied them essential supplies. Postwar shortages were blamed on this allegation.
2. Fraser, *Germany between Two Wars*. This book was written by an academic and former BBC German News commentator in the spring of 1944, i.e. even before the Allied invasion of Europe had started. It was aimed at persons concerned with the occupation and administration of Germany after the end of the war. It was also intended to show Germans how they had been misled by their propagandists before and during the Nazi regime.

On p. 15 Fraser gives an interesting explanation of the so-called 'stab-in-the-back' legend. In order that the German Army in 1918 should appear not to have been defeated, all final negotiations for the armistice were carried out by civilian authorities. The Army manoeuvred itself into a position where they were apparently advocating a continuation of the war in the face of demands for peace from groups of defeatist civilians. Gen Ludendorff succeeded in 'saving his Army' from the humiliation of final capitulation.

Shortly after the armistice Gen Neill Malcolm was dining in Berlin with Ludendorff who was seeking words to explain his Army's defeat. Malcolm sought to crystallise the verbose Ludendorff's meaning in a sentence. 'You mean, General Ludendorff, that you were stabbed in the back?' Ludendorff's eyes lit up. 'That's it exactly. We were stabbed in the back!'

Sir Frederick Maurice later issued a formal denial of the rumour to the German press, adding, 'There is no doubt that the German armies were thoroughly and decisively beaten in the field.'

3. John, *Twice Through the Lines*, p. 52.
4. Fest, *Plotting Hitler's Death*, p. 126.
5. John, *Twice Through the Lines*, p. 53.
6. The Decree on Military Law transferred responsibility for punishing crimes against enemy civilians from military courts to individual division commanders.

   The Commissar Order was for Red Army political commissars to be segregated upon capture and 'as a rule immediately shot for instituting barbaric Asian methods of warfare'.
7. Reynolds, *Treason Was No Crime*, p. 22.
8. Fest, *Plotting Hitler's Death*, p. 201.

Chapter 7

1. Fest, *Plotting Hitler's Death*, p. 230.
2. Tarrant, *The Red Orchestra*, p. 94.
3. Tarrant, *The Red Orchestra*, p. 199.
4. Fest, *Plotting Hitler's Death*, p. 236.
5. Fest, *Plotting Hitler's Death*, p. 232.
6. Fest, *Plotting Hitler's Death*, p. 231.
7. Rigden, *Kill the Führer*, pp. 50–9.
8. Fest, *Plotting Hitler's Death*, p. 337.

Chapter 8

1. TNA (PRO) file HS6/692.
2. TNA (PRO) file HS6/692.
3. TNA (PRO) file PREM3/409/5.
4. Boyce and Everett, *SOE: The Scientific Secrets*, pp. 67–9.
5. TNA (PRO) file HS6/695.

6. Rigden, *Kill the Führer*, pp. 125–6.
7. TNA (PRO) file HS6/639.
8. Mackenzie, *The Secret History of SOE*, p. 692.
9. Sebag-Montefiore, *Enigma – The Battles for the Codes*, p. 145.
10. TNA (PRO) file HS6/652.
11. TNA (PRO) file HS6/689.

Chapter 9

1. TNA (PRO) file HS6/637.
2. TNA (PRO) file PREM3/408/5.
3. TNA (PRO) file HS8/199.
4. TNA (PRO) file PREM3/408/5.
5. TNA (PRO) file HS7/287.
6. TNA (PRO) file PREM3/408/5.
7. TNA (PRO) file PREM3/408/5.
8. TNA (PRO) file HS6/637.

Chapter 10

1. Correspondence with Angus Fyffe, 2003. See also Appendix 2.
2. TNA (PRO) file HS6/639.
3. Wilkinson and Bright Astley, *Gubbins and SOE*, p. 208.
4. TNA (PRO) file HS7/147.
5. TNA (PRO) file HS6/635.
6. TNA (PRO) file FO898/354.
7. TNA (PRO) file FO898/354.
8. Masterman, *The Double Cross System, 1939–1945*, p. 83.
9. TNA (PRO) file HS7/147 Section f.
10. TNA (PRO) file FO898/354.
11. TNA (PRO) file FO898/354.

Chapter 11

1. TNA (PRO) file FO898/354.
2. TNA (PRO) file FO898/354.
3. TNA (PRO) file FO898/354.
4. Much of the detailed information for this chapter is drawn from TNA (PRO) file HS7/147 SOE History German Directorate Part II Section 1 (g) Deception Scheme in Neutral Countries and Germany – Operation Periwig.

Chapter 12

1. TNA (PRO) file AIR20/8501.
2. TNA (PRO) file AIR20/8501.
3. TNA (PRO) file HS7/147 SOE History German Directorate Part II Section 1 (g).
4. Seaman, *Secret Agent's Handbook of Special Devices.*
5. TNA (PRO) file FO898/354.
6. Mackenzie, *The Secret History of SOE*, pp. 710–11.

Chapter 13

1. TNA (PRO) file HS6/674.
2. TNA (PRO) file HS7/147.
3. TNA (PRO) file HS7/147.
4. TNA (PRO) file HS7/147.
5. TNA (PRO) file FO898/356.
6. TNA (PRO) file FO898/354.
7. TNA (PRO) file KV4/69.
8. TNA (PRO) file FO898/356.

Chapter 14

1. TNA (PRO) file HS7/147.
2. TNA (PRO)file HS7/147 SOE History German Directorate Part II Section 1 (g), p. 13.
3. TNA (PRO) file HS7/147 SOE History Germany Part I (a), p. 10.
4. Mackenzie, *The Secret History of SOE*, p. 713.
5. TNA (PRO) file HS6/635.
6. TNA (PRO) file HS6/635.
7. TNA (PRO) file HS7/145.
8. Garnett, *The Secret History of PWE*, p. 435.

Appendix 1

1. TNA (PRO) file FO898/357.

Appendix 2

1. TNA (PRO) file 898/354.
2. TNA (PRO) file 898/354.
3. Conversations with Prof Everett 2001.
4. TNA (PRO) file HS9/806/2.
5. TNA (PRO) file KV4/69.
6. TNA (PRO) file HS7/147.
7. TNA (PRO) file HS9/991/2.

Appendix 3

1. TNA (PRO) files AIR20/8499 and AIR20/8501.

Appendix 4

1. TNA (PRO) file HS6/687.

Appendix 5

1. TNA (PRO) file HS6/694.

Bibliography

Army, General Staff, *Design for Military Operations: The British Military Doctrine*, London, HMSO 1989

Baden-Powell, R.S.S., *Lessons from the 'Varsity of Life*, London, Pearson, 1933

Boyce, F. and Everett, D.H., *SOE: The Scientific Secrets*, Stroud, Sutton, 2003

Bright Astley, J., *The Inner Circle: A View of War at the Top*, London, Hutchinson, 1971

Bruce Lockhart, R.H., *Memoirs of a British Secret Agent*, London, Putnam, 1932

Cruickshank, C., *Deception in World War II*, Oxford, Oxford University Press, 1979

Fest, J., *Plotting Hitler's Death*, London, Weidenfeld & Nicolson, 1996

Foot, M.R.D., *SOE in the Low Countries*, London, St Ermin's Press, 2001

Fraser, Lindley M., *Germany Between the Wars: A Study of Propaganda and War Guilt*, London, Oxford University Press, 1944

Gardner, B., *Mafeking: A Victorian Legend*, London, Cassell, 1966

Garnett, D., *The Secret History of PWE*, London, St Ermin's Press, 2002

Haswell, J., *The Tangled Web – The Art of Tactical and Strategic Deception*, Wendover, John Goodchild Publishers, 1985

Hesketh, R., *Fortitude*, London, Little, Brown, 1999

Hoffmann, P., *German Resistance to Hitler*, Cambridge, Massachusetts, Harvard University Press, 1988

John, O., *Twice Through the Lines*, London, Macmillan, 1972

Latimer, J., *Deception in War*, London, John Murray, 2001

Luvaas, J., *Frederick the Great on the Art of War*, New York, Free Press, 1966

Mackenzie, W., *The Secret History of SOE*, London, St Ermin's Press, 2000

Marks, L., *Between Silk and Cyanide*, London, HarperCollins, 1998

Masterman, J.C., *The Double Cross System, 1939–1945* London, Pimlico, 1995

Montagu, E., *The Man Who Never Was*, London, Evans Brothers, 1953

Mure, D., *Practise to Deceive*, London, William Kimber, 1977

Pakenham, T., *The Boer War*, London, Weidenfeld & Nicolson, 1979

Reynolds, N., *Treason Was No Crime*, London, William Kimber, 1976

Rigden, D., *Kill the Führer*, Stroud, Sutton, 1999

Seaman, M., (Introduction) *Secret Agent's Handbook of Special Devices*, London, PRO, 2000

Sebag-Montefiore, H., *Enigma – The Battle for the Codes*, London, Weidenfeld & Nicolson, 2000

Snyder, L.L., *Hitler's German Enemies*, London, Robert Hale, 1991

Speer, A., *Inside the Third Reich*, New York, Macmillan, 1970

Tarrant, V.E., *The Red Orchestra*, London, Cassell Military Classics, 1998

Wilkinson, P. and Bright Astley, J., *Gubbins and SOE*, London, Leo Cooper, 1993

INDEX